Wetland Diaries

RANGER LIFE AND REWILDING ON WICKEN FEN

AJAY TEGALA

Cover photograph © Mike Selby

First published 2024
Reprinted 2024

The History Press
97 St George's Place, Cheltenham,
Gloucestershire, GL50 3QB
www.thehistorypress.co.uk

British Library Cataloguing in Publication Data.
A catalogue record for this book is available from the British Library.

ISBN 978 1 80399 348 5

Typesetting and origination by The History Press.
Printed and bound in Great Britain by TJ Books Limited, Padstow, Cornwall.

Trees for LYfe

Dedicated to

All of my family,
Carol Laidlaw and the
Wicken Fen staff and volunteers
I have worked with over the years.
And young naturalists everywhere.

Charles Lucas (1853–1938)
Eric Ennion (1900–1981)
Alan Bloom MBE (1906–2005)
Ralph Sargeant (1942–2016)

Short-eared owl.
(Joss Goodchild)

Map of the Fens. (Ajay Tegala)

Contents

Praise for
Wetland Diaries

'Ajay's passion for conservation oozes out of every single page.'
— *Iolo Williams*, wildlife TV presenter.

'A wonderful celebration of fenland history and wildlife by an inspiring ranger working at the forefront of wetland conservation.'
— *Nick Davies*, field naturalist and zoologist.

'Ajay's vivid words and illustrations capture life as a ranger in one of Europe's most important nature reserves. *Wetland Diaries* has the pace and energy of a thriller, as it reveals the evolving relationships of wetland plants, birds and grazing animals in an age of potentially disastrous climate change.'
— *Francis Pryor*, archaeologist, author and TV presenter.

'Aloe vera for the soul. I fell willingly headfirst into this glorious volume about the beauties of nature, written with all the respect and sensitivity one expects from Ajay.'
— *Milly Johnson*, bestselling romantic fiction author.

'Ajay's deep connection to Wicken Fen and its wildlife shines through in this gentle deep-dive into the soggy, boggy, reed-rustling world of the Fens. *Wetland Diaries* offers a unique and highly knowledgeable insight into a life dedicated to protecting nature.'
— *Leif Bersweden*, botanist and author of *Where the Wild Flowers Grow*.

'A wonderfully evocative account of life as a ranger on one of Britain's oldest and best-loved nature reserves, packed with delightful stories of the people and wildlife, and written by one of our brightest young naturalists.'

— *Stephen Moss*, naturalist, author and TV producer.

'Ajay's evocative, measured tone holds you as he guides you through tasks both great and small. You are by his side as he cares for livestock, jumps for joy at rare birds, grubs out scrub or says goodbye to old friends as a vet sees them through their final hours.

This is a truly lovely read, non-sensational and deeply loving; it comes from a heart that is utterly in tune with the wildlife of the fen and what it takes to protect it. A book to hold close, a soft down-duvet of a book that will stay by you whenever you need a nature-loving friend.'

— *Mary Colwell*, environmentalist, author and campaigner.

'A wonderfully deep dive into a fascinating and important part of the country. The book is full of practical insights and a pleasure to read.'

— *Tristan Gooley*, award-winning author and natural navigation expert.

'Ajay's intimate knowledge and experience of the place makes this a 'must have' book on this outstanding wetland. From the original 2-acre purchase, Wicken grew to retain existing habitat and, more recently, the previously drained fen used as farmland has been reclaimed for rewilding. Ajay reveals that management by grazing of semi-wild horses and cattle is moving wetland restoration forward dramatically.'

— *Roger Tabor*, biologist, naturalist, author and broadcaster.

'In a dizzying, disquieting world, Ajay has the rare gift of remaining quietly steadfast and true to his mission and passion. A wonderful book, and the next best thing to being there oneself.'

— *Gillian Burke*, wildlife TV presenter.

About the Author

AS A WILDLIFE PRESENTER, Ajay Tegala loves sharing his passion for the natural world. His BBC television credits include *Springwatch, Winterwatch, Wild Isles, Inside the Bat Cave, Coast, Countryfile, Celebrity Eggheads, Curious Creatures* and *Teeny Tiny Creatures*. Ajay's notable radio appearances include BBC Four's *Living World* and *Ramblings*.

As a countryside ranger, he is grounded in the world of nature conservation. A week's work experience with the National Trust on Wicken Fen inspired a 15-year-old Ajay to become a ranger.

Ajay grew up in the South Lincolnshire Fens. He completed a degree in Environmental Conservation and Countryside Management at Nottingham Trent University. After graduating, he became Blakeney Point ranger for the National Trust on the Norfolk coast. His first book, *The Unique Life of a Ranger*, shares his coastal experiences.

In 2018, Ajay moved back to the Fens, returning to where he began his conservation journey. As part of the Wicken Fen ranger team, he protects important habitats and species, watches over herds of semi-wild grazing herbivores and inspires visitors.

Other projects include his imaginative theatre shows *A Year of Birdsong and Bird Songs* and *Witching the Wild Year*, multiple appearances on the award-winning *Get Birding* podcast and writing for *BBC Countryfile* and *Wildlife* magazines. You can follow @AjayTegala on social media.

www.ajaytegala.co.uk

Foreword

BY DAME FIONA REYNOLDS

WICKEN FEN MUST BE one of the most written about and researched nature reserves in the country. From the Victorian Cambridge University academics to use it as a study base, through Nick Davies' wonderful cuckoo research alongside many others, the Fen has revealed its secrets many times and in many ways.

But never like this. Ajay Tegala's frank, on-the-ground, sometimes wide-eyed and always passionate revelations bring something new, and invaluable, to the debate about how to restore Wicken Fen's decimated wildlife, and how to fulfil the National Trust's commitment to this, its first ever nature reserve.

Acquired in 1899, at the very beginning of the Trust's life, it's only in the last twenty years or so that the Trust has been proactive in seeking positive nature recovery as opposed to hanging on grimly to the remnants of a richer (wildlife) past.

So, the story Ajay tells, of the Trust getting to grips with management regimes that will deliver nature recovery, is a new one. And he tells it well, generous in his admiration for his ranger and other colleagues, and excited by the results as they explore new ideas and bring in a key ingredient – grazing animals.

It's not glamorous being a ranger, and Ajay's descriptions of what's involved are moving, sometimes funny, and often down to earth (who knew, for example, how to castrate a calf, or that poo monitoring was an important part of a ranger's role?). But above all, it's a totally authentic account of how someone who longed to be a ranger has become one, and a brilliant one at that.

Ajay reminds us eloquently of the crucial importance of nature recovery and of how the lessons learned at Wicken will help nature in wetlands everywhere. But Ajay's own story, as one of a handful of ethnically diverse rangers in the Trust, is just as fascinating. As we follow his journey, accompanied by his loyal Labrador Oakley, we just want to hear more.

Dame Fiona Reynolds,
Director-General, National Trust (2001–12)

Acknowledgements

FOR THEIR SUPPORT AND company on Wicken Fen over the years, in alphabetical order: Nick Acklam, Lois Baker, Ann Beeby, the late Tim Bennett, Kayley Bentley, Steve Boreham, John Bragg, Judy Brown, Josh and Julia Burling, Mel and Maggie Carvalho, Rose Chalker, Andrew Chamberlain, Peter Charrot, Howard Cooper, Jason Cooper, Hugh Corr and Carole Hornett, Dan and Steve Courten, Paula Curtis, Lizzie Dale, Alan Darby, Nick Davies, Matt Deacon, Maddie Downes, Colin Dunling, Anita Escott, Jemma Finch, Sally Fisher, Tim Fisher, Amanda and Paul Forecast, David Fotherby, Laurie Friday, Joss and Martin Goodchild, Peter Green, Kerry Griggs, Julia Hammond, Alexa Hardy, Beck Hawketts, the late Michael Holdsworth, Joe Holt, Keith Honnor, Leanna Howlett, Matthew Hudson, Francine Hughes, John and Gemma Hughes, Jenny Hupe, Kevin James, Lesley Jenkins, Alan Kell, Phil Kelly, Jonathan Kirkpatrick, Julie Kowalczyk, Carol Laidlaw and Gez Smallwood, Neil Larner, Martin Lester, the late John Loveluck, Alex Margiotta, Tony Martin, Harry Mitchell, Anita Molloy, Richard Nicoll, David Nye, Emma Ormond-Bones, John Pace, Martin Parsons, Josh Pearce, Mark Peck, Wayne Plumridge, Katie Reader, Sally Redman-Davies, Trina Roberts, the late Alan Rodger, Mike Rogers, Chloe Rothwell-Green, the late Ralph Sargeant, Derah Saward Arav, Isabel Sedgwick, James and Mike Selby, Ellis Selway, Norman Sills and Linda Gascoigne, Sarah Smith, Chris Soans, Karen Staines, Dave Stanforth, Pete Stevens and Bruna Remesso, Jackie Stone, Fiona Symonds, Rachel Tarkenter, Chris Thorne, Christine

Tonkins, Luke Underwood, Toby Walker, Stephen and Ulrike Walton, Stuart Warrington, Jack Watson, Chris White, Tony Winchester, Andy Wood, Louise Young, Julie Zac, Christoph Zockler and many other volunteers, colleagues and conservationists who I have had the pleasure of working with and learning from.

Huge thanks, of course, to my family for their support and encouragement, too.

Special thanks to the National Trust – who have cared for Wicken Fen since 1899 and employed me in various roles since 2010 – for their enthusiasm towards this book. Thanks also to Jill Peak, Mike Petty, Cambridge Central Library, the University of Cambridge, Anglia Ruskin University, Burwell Museum of Fen-Edge Village Life, Vet 3 Equine Care, Isle Veterinary Group, Liz Bicknell and Bob Walthew.

I am especially grateful to Dame Fiona Reynolds for kindly writing the foreword and supporting the Wicken Fen Vision project during her time as Director-General for the National Trust. A massive thank you to my colleague Carol Laidlaw for her inspiration, encouragement, suggestions and for generously sharing her wealth of knowledge on Wicken, Koniks and Highland cattle.

Thanks also to Carol for kind permission to use her photographs, alongside those of Mike Selby (including the front-cover image), Richard Nicoll (www.richardnicollphotography.co.uk), Simon Stirrup, Kenny Brooks, Kate Amann, National Trust Images, the Cambridgeshire Collection and everyone else whose photographs appear in the book. Very special thanks to local artists Joss Goodchild and Di Cope, and wildlife artist James McCallum (www.jamesmccallum.co.uk), for kind permission to feature their beautiful artwork, and to Victoria Ennion for the privilege of featuring historical paintings by her grandfather.

For assistance with the editing and publishing process, I am grateful to David Foster and Gerry Granshaw at DFM, Claire Masset and Jeannette Heard at National Trust head office, Jemma Finch at National Trust regional office, Wicken Fen's General Manager Emma Ormond-Bones, Stuart Warrington for kindly sharing his historical Wicken wildlife knowledge and collating the total species count (see Appendix 1), Carol Laidlaw for her diligent proofreading, John Hughes and Isabel Sedgwick for sharing their memories and wealth of Fen knowledge and to Nicola Guy, Elizabeth Shaw, Lauren Kent and all of The History Press team for their support and enthusiasm.

Lastly, sincere thanks to the following positive people along the way: Harry and the hound, Mum and Dad (Bev and TT), Grandma Reen and my late Grandad, Zinzi and Stephen, Ronan and Sarah, all my other Haywood and Tegala family, Di, Hannah, the Mitchells, Zoë and Dylan, the Deeping Lakes gang (Dave, Norah and Brian in particular), my A-Level geography teacher Heather Blades, my lecturers at Nottingham Trent University (including Julia Davies and Louise Gentle), the Norfolk coast crew, Nikki, the Abbey Girls (Gemma, Anwen and Emily) and Quizzy Rascals.

Introduction:
As Far As the
Eye Can See

• **Brief geography and history of the Fens** •
Peat • Growing up in the Fens •
Ranger life on Wicken Fen •

WHEN I LOOK AT a map of England and Wales, I see the face of Old Father Time in profile. Pembrokeshire is his pointy nose, the Bristol Channel forms his open mouth and the West Country is his elongated, bearded chin. On the other side, north-east of London, the ear-shaped bulge of East Anglia protrudes from beneath England's biggest bay, the Wash. Spreading inland from this estuary – into the counties of Lincolnshire, Cambridgeshire and western parts of Norfolk and Suffolk – are 2,500 square miles of low-lying former marshland. The Fens.[*]

---

[*]   A fen is defined as a low area of marshy or frequently flooded land.
      Fens are fed by alkaline groundwater, whereas bogs are rainwater-fed and acidic.

Location of the Fens. (Ajay Tegala)

Southern Britain: the smiling face of Old Father Time. (Ajay Tegala)

The Fens

In ancient times, these flat lands were forested with alder, birch, oak, pine and yew. Known as bog oaks, some of the trees fell into the damp, peaty soil, lying preserved for around 5,000 years. Peat is formed when waterlogged soil conditions prevent dead vegetation from decaying completely. Once drained, this black soil is ideal for agriculture. With such a high water content, peaty soil shrinks considerably when it is dried out. Since the seventeenth century, more than 99 per cent of the Fens have been drained. It is only in the twenty-first century that the environmental importance of peat has been appreciated. Although peatlands cover only around 3 per cent of the world's land surface, they store up to a third of the planet's soil carbon, twice as much as Earth's forests.[*]

For the first eighteen years of my life, home was Market Deeping in the South Lincolnshire Fens, described by Francis Pryor as a 'charming town, just sufficiently distant from Peterborough to retain its local character'. The name Deeping means 'deep place' in Anglo-Saxon language. As a youngster, I was captivated by wildfowl on the River Welland (an ancient tributary of the Rhine) and occasional sightings of lapwing flocks on farmland. Beyond the edge of town, the flat land seemed to stretch as far as the eye can see. All 47 square miles of Deeping Fen have been drained. It had once been a haven for the now rare wetland birds I lovingly looked at in my parents' copy of the *Field Guide to the Birds of Britain and Ireland*, dreaming of one day beholding a bittern. At primary school we learned about how wild the Fens once were and how threatened nature had become. Annual slideshows by local bird photographer Nick Williams were a highlight of my school year.

From the age of 30, I have lived and worked in the fenland within Cambridgeshire's north-eastern quarter. Ranger life on the National Trust's Wicken Fen National Nature Reserve involves protecting a precious remnant of largely undrained and uncultivated fen[**] and

[*]   Source: Global Peatlands Initiative (2022).

[**]   Wicken is one of just four remaining fens in East Anglia, all in Cambridgeshire. The other three are Chippenham Fen, Holme Fen and Woodwalton Fen.

creating more wetland habitat to benefit the birds I have loved all my life. The protection of peat has risen in importance just as the practice of conservation grazing with large herbivores has grown in popularity. At the very beginning of the twenty-first century, herds of free-roaming horses and cattle were introduced to Wicken Fen in order to manage the habitat in a semi-wild manner. Managing both the sacred fragment of virgin fen and this adjoining landscape restoration project brings with it joy and challenge in equal measure.

I have been fascinated by animals and inspired by colleagues. I have seen all weathers, from drought to flood, snow to strong winds. I have watched misty sunrises and fiery sunsets. I have listened to beautiful dawn choruses and been bitten by mosquitoes at dusk. There are flashes of bleakness, moments of sheer solitude and delightful delves into a lost landscape. Maybe flat, never boring.

These are my tales from the flat lands, a wild life on Wicken Fen – including Burwell Fen – with glimpses of times past and Fenland folklore. Join me, my faithful Labrador, the charismatic livestock and a dedicated team of staff and volunteers who protect this very special, often overlooked piece of rural Britain for future generations.

Ajay Tegala, Cambridgeshire
January 2024

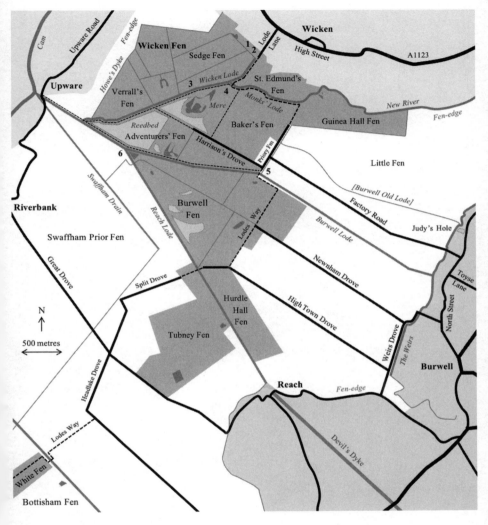

Map of Wicken Fen and Burwell Fen with selected place names. (Ajay Tegala)

1. Norman's Mill
2. Visitor Centre
3. Old Tower Hide

4. Norman's Bridge
5. 'Cock-Up' Bridge
6. Pout Hall Corner

A colour version of this map appears at the end of the central plates section.

The Mists of Time: My Long Road to Wicken

• A foggy fenland walk •
A mysterious fen-edge ride • Fen folk •
A humid evening on Harrison's Farm •
Drainage of the Fens • History of Wicken Fen •
'Cock-Up' Bridge • My family moves to East Anglia •

Ouse Valley: Monday, 14 November 2022 (Part One)

Oakley bounds along the farm track a few yards ahead of me. He heads straight to the apple trees, seeking fallen fruit. Next, he forages along the woodland edge for a good stick. We have both come to know this place well over the last few years. I watch the wildlife while he sniffs the scents.

Autumn is a favourite season in the Fens. This one has been particularly mild. Dusk is twenty minutes away, but the temperature is 12°C. I unzip my jacket, feeling warmer than I have all day, sat at my desk, barely moving anything but my fingertips, occasionally lifting an arm to take a sip of tea. Now, blood is circulating as fresh air fills my lungs.

The fog has not lifted all day. Beads of water cling to every blade of grass, transferring to my wellies as I walk briskly behind Oakley. His black, furry legs are wet and shiny from trotting through the taller grass beside the ditch. It doesn't take him very long to find himself a stick. Looking longingly up at me, I know what he wants me to do. I pick up the brittle branch and throw it along the track ahead. He races after it, overshoots, skids and backtracks to pick up what is now two smaller sticks. I choose the slightly longer of the two and launch it a little further this time. Oakley still overshoots in his enthusiasm, racing off before the stick has even become airborne.

My hands are wet from picking up the dog-stick. And so is my right foot, thanks to a recent split in my boot. Little over a minute later, my left foot also feels soggy. Why does every pair of wellies I own seem to split so quickly? Oakley's stick is falling apart too, now barely 3in long. But he is still more than happy to play fetch with it.

My attention diverts from Labrador to wildfowl as four grey birds fly overhead. They are in fact white. I heard their honking calls before I saw them, whooper swans (pronounced 'hooper'). A family group fly in front of us, two adults with two young hatched in Iceland six months ago. The swan calls are both softened and magnified by the damp air. There is hardly a breath of wind. Such silent stillness is rare in the exposed fenland of East Anglia. I treasure days like this. With visibility reduced, your eyes focus on what is near while your ears can tune in to what is further away. I am literally a mile from the nearest person, a farm worker sat inside a tractor, its lights only just visible in the distance. A freight train speeds across the railway bridge, crossing the Ouse Washes towards Ely Cathedral.

The sound of the train fades. My ears tune in to greylag geese on the other side of the riverbank. Their cackles linger in the air, like the water droplets sitting on my waterproof jacket. Not rain, but fog. Even the moisture soaking my socks feels like a friendly extra layer of warmth. I am genuinely happy. And relaxed. At last. No longer thinking about my to-do list, but free in the Fens. Wet feet seem to bind me to my surroundings, the landscape and its history, too.

Before this corner of north-east Cambridgeshire was drained, wet feet would have been a familiar part of life for the Fen folk. Or cleverly avoided by wearing stilts. There are tales of formidable Fen Tigers fighting against drainage and people putting grass in their boots to keep feet cool in summer, especially 12 miles south-east in the Fen-edge villages of Burwell and Wicken. I think about the lives of these stoic Fen people of old and remember how I came to learn about them 20 years ago.

Judy's Hole: Saturday, 27 April 2002

I hurtle down Toyse Lane on an old blue bicycle, air rushing past as I race along. Barely needing to pedal, I veer right, onto North Street. The ground levels out as the Newmarket chalk hills sink beneath peat and clay. This is the Fen-edge and once upon a prehistoric time would have been the coast. History and geography merge in my 12¾-year-old mind, pondering which way to steer the handlebars. I am free to navigate a village I have visited regularly throughout my childhood, now exploring it solo for the first time.

Do I turn left along towards Factory Road and the river? Or do I continue north? I feel drawn towards the river. But an early memory becomes clear in my mind. The only time I have been this way before was on a family walk one sunny day when I was small. On that riverside ramble, I had developed an intense headache, prompting an abrupt return to Fenview 11, where I lay on the sofa in pain. This memory influences my decision. Today, I will follow North Street, staying in the safety of the village. However, the road soon leads beyond Burwell. Venturing onward, I see a finger-post marking a public footpath to the left.

On this mild and pleasant spring afternoon, the verges are verdant with cow parsley on the cusp of bursting into flower. I follow the track along the edge of a thicket, about an acre in size. Although the ash trees are not yet fully in leaf, their density is enough to reduce the sunlight. Ahead, the trees thin. A battered old caravan stands half in a hedge, it must be some years since its wheels touched the road. Beyond, a narrow footbridge, with yellow handrails, crosses the river to a bungalow. In my childish mind, I decide this is a witch's house, acknowledging the air of spookiness this remote place evokes.

Enamel flour tin, Judy's Hole, 27 April 2002. (Ajay Tegala)

At the same time, there is a feeling of calmness. It is peaceful and pretty. Intrigue takes over as I spy a trail leading into the trees. The ground drops 2ft, carpeted in a mat of clinging ivy. On the edge, a thin elder trunk has been sawn off at waist height. Hanging on it, there is a 1930s enamel flour tin with a stick poking out. Creating a story in my mind, I decide this must be a witches' brew, concocted by the owner of the waterside dwelling. But it merely contains a handful of soil and some dry grass.

I cycle back to Fenview 11 to fetch my sister so I can show her the intriguing, secluded spot I have discovered. Next morning, I feel compelled to visit again, this time with my brother. Neither of my siblings quite share my intense fascination with the place.

The last time I felt such a combination of intense curiosity and subtle unease was at Eden Camp Second World War Museum in North Yorkshire, on a school residential two years before. There, one of the immersive displays recreated the terror of a night-time air raid. Around the corner, a female mannequin, in a green boiler suit, was serving soup.

I found her vacant expression as haunting as the Blitz scene. Behind this frightening figure was a 1930s enamel flour tin, identical to the one in the thicket.

Every time we visited my grandparents in Burwell, I would feel lured to the waterside, always checking to see whether the flour tin was still there. It always was. Eventually, the elder trunk was removed, the tin left lying on the ground, becoming increasingly worn and weathered.

A decade passes. I return to the area and wonder whether the old tin could possibly still be there. Heading to the spot to scan the ivy-clad ground, a flash of white catches my eye. There it is. Bent out of shape with one of its handles missing. I feel a rush of nostalgia and a sudden, uncontrollable urge to rescue it, take it home with me. I pick the tin up and carry it to my car, certain that nobody else could possibly have more of a connection to it than I do.

From my first visit, I knew there was something special about this place. It was wild, wonderful and witchy. So intriguing, idyllic and intoxicating. I felt a sense of solace, sanctuary and escapism. There had to be something more to it. And indeed there was. The area is known to locals as Judy's Hole, named after a long-since infilled pit owned by a wise woman, no less.[*]

---

[*]   Judy's Hole is also a dark winter beer made by the Burwell Brewery, named after this riverside spot.

Squatters' cottages opposite Judy's Hole, c.1920. (Cambridgeshire Collection)

The Fen People

One of the oldest works on my shelf is a charming and very rare book printed in 1930. The title is embossed on its faded red cover, *The Fenman's World*, by Charles Lucas, Burwell doctor and former Fen drainage commissioner. Having lived in the village his whole life, some of his friends thought 'it would be both interesting and useful' to document his knowledge and memories of the Fen areas at Burwell and its neighbouring villages of Reach and Wicken. The book includes an account of Judy's Hole and the Fen people who inhabited six wattle-and-daub squatters' cottages on the opposite side of the river during the nineteenth century.

The men were 'rather tall and big, with very black hair, sallow and swarthy complexions, rough in their manners, gruff in speech, tenacious and cunning, independent and lawless'. Their secrecy and self-reliance earned them the nickname Fen Tigers. These were people who lived off the land, catching fish and hunting wildfowl for food as well as keeping livestock. In summer, they would help with the harvest, dig turf and cut sedge. The turf they dug was peat, cut into rectangular blocks, dried and burned as fuel. Sedge could be burned too or used to stuff mattresses, but was mostly cut for thatching. Like reed, it is a grass-like plant that grows in wet ground. Reed has hollow, round stems whereas sedge has a triangular stem. 'Sedges have edges, rushes are round.'

The characteristic species in this part of the Fens is *Cladium mariscus*, known as saw-sedge because its edges are toothed. Run your fingers upwards along the leaves and the razor-sharp serrations can cut to the bone, each tiny tooth a natural blade. For this reason, harvesting sedge was listed as one of the most horrible rural practices in a television documentary titled *The Worst Jobs in History*. Arms would be bound with hessian and twine for protection, while sedge was cut manually using a scythe. It would then be tied into bundles, stacked and dried.

Life was hard for the Fen people. In the mid-nineteenth century, ague (a malarial fever) was a problem in the Fens, spread by Anopheline mosquitoes. Most Fen gardens contained a patch of white poppies, used as a remedy for ague. Opium chewing and brandy drinking were ways of relieving fever and easing pain.

On Adventurers' Fen, a couple of miles east of Burwell, lived Old Tom Harrison, the last Fen 'slodger'.* He would gather paigles (cowslips and primroses) from the meadows to make wine for relieving the symptoms of ague. Old Tom lived as a hermit in a hut made of turf blocks plastered with clay to make them waterproof. Allegedly, he only ever washed if he fell into a ditch. Payment for the ducks, geese, eels and tench he sold would be made partly in opium.

Following the death of her husband Joseph Finch, Judy also lived alone, in her riverside hut. The 1841 census lists her age as 50, and farmer as her occupation. Lucas describes Judy as 'a very bad character' with a 'vile reputation for dark deeds'. He states 'if there were any devilry going on in the parish, Judy Finch was sure to be in it'. She was the wise woman of the district and in earlier times would have been considered a witch.

I can't help but wonder whether her reputation was unfair. Life must have been hard. Maybe her grief was misinterpreted as evil rather than a sign of inward suffering. Perhaps, like the fictional character Elphaba Thropp (the Wicked Witch of the West in the musical *Wicked*), she was not mean but misunderstood. Judy did, however, contribute something to the village. She sold her 1-acre pit to the Drainage and Navigation Board. It was used to extract thick clay, known as gault, for repairing riverbanks, an ongoing task in the Fens. Judy's Hole held around 2ft of water, which would freeze in winter, making skating possible.

Fen skating had become very popular by the nineteenth century. Many agricultural labourers would compete in races for prizes of money, food and clothing. Cambridgeshire-born horticulturalist and author Alan Bloom describes the fun of speed skating:

When some of us got together in a string, heads down, arms on backs, watching the ice flash beneath us to the rhythm of long, ringing strides, there was no thought of work or worries for hours on end. Men and youths out of work through the frost would get together and play bandy** on their fen runners.

---

*   Fen term for wildfowler, someone who hunts wild ducks and geese.

** A game played on the ice with bent sticks and a puck, which became ice hockey.

The Cambridgeshire Fens produced numerous top skaters. But being champion sportsmen did not rid the Fen Tigers from prejudice. Even at the start of the twenty-first century, at The Deepings School, I remember students from Spalding getting teased unkindly for being inbred and supposedly having webbed feet.

Adventurers' Fen: Wednesday, 3 August 2011

I lock my Volkswagen Fox and head out into the damp, humid evening wearing a crumpled, black waterproof jacket. The buckled concrete of Harrison's Drove peters out into a grassy track, eventually leading me to the reedbed. Here, I join the Wicken Fen bird ringing group for their dusk mist netting session, fitting birds' legs with tiny metal rings as part of a long-term scientific study to learn more about their migrations. An otherwise low-key 22nd birthday had been transformed by a chance meeting with one of the bird ringers, Neil, earlier in the day, as recorded in my diary:

> It was quite wet when I arrived. Neil was stood in the shed entrance with a hat that made him look like Charlie Gearheart.* The swallows and sand martins dropped into the reeds to roost for the night. An incredible 88 were caught. The clouds of birds made for an atmospheric and timeless evening. It was not without its mosquitoes however, and I was bitten no less than 14 times whilst we were taking the birds out of the mist nets.

This was a little taste of the muggy summer nights that Old Tom Harrison would have known, having lived mere metres from where we were working. Thankfully, these modern mosquitoes did not contain malaria. Surrounded only by reeds and roosting hirundines,** it really did feel timeless, as if the reedbed had been there for centuries. However, just two decades earlier, it did not exist at all. Instead,

---

*   Frontman of American country-rock band Goose Creek Symphony.
**   Songbirds of the swallow family, which include house and sand martins.

Adventurers' Fen contained fields of potatoes, sugar beet and wheat, having been drained for agriculture during the Second World War – following in the footsteps of the Adventurers who had dug the Old Bedford River and drained vast amounts of Cambridgeshire in the mid-seventeenth century.

Ouse Valley: Monday, 14 November 2022 (Part Two)

The sun sinks beneath the horizon, not that it had been visible through the fog. I am wrapped up in my thoughts, enveloped in the strangely comforting fogginess, absorbed in the slow rhythm of my feet, which are now completely wet. Oakley is a few feet ahead, leading the way along the Old Bedford Low Bank in his luminous green collar. Visibility stretches little further than the track on the other side of the river, which has been closed for two years while the Environment Agency raise the height of the bank in defence against flooding. This project involves importing thousands of tonnes of material to protect my home village – and numerous others – from potential flooding predicted as a consequence of climate change.

Oakley on the Old Bedford Low Bank, 14 November 2022. (Ajay Tegala)

The Old and New Bedford Rivers are an impressive feat of engineering by Cornelius Vermuyden of the Netherlands and the fifth Earl of Bedford. The mammoth task of manually canalising a 21-mile stretch of river – and digging a second channel of the same length – was undertaken by the Gentleman Adventurers. These English engineers and landowners funded and undertook the drainage of the Fens. In return, they retained rights to some of the land they reclaimed. But a few of the staunch Fen people were fiercely opposed to the drainage of their prosperous fishing and hunting grounds, especially at Wicken. They did not want to be tamed or controlled. The Adventurers were forced to employ armed guards for safety from the sometimes rough and rowdy Fen Tigers.

King Charles I envisaged building a new city, to be named Charlemont, on the Isle of Manea, a mile west of the Old Bedford River. The foundations of a summer palace were constructed, but the king's imprisonment, in 1646, halted any further progress. The New Bedford River (also known as the Hundred Foot Drain) was completed in 1651, when a sluice was built at Denver, in west Norfolk, to control flow of water into the Wash and out to sea. Between the Old and New Bedford Rivers, floodwater is diverted into a large washland, half a mile wide. In winter, the Ouse Washes take on water carried by the River Great Ouse from the counties of Bedfordshire, Buckinghamshire and Northamptonshire, creating an important 6,000-acre roosting area for wetland birds including thousands of ducks and whooper swans.

During the construction of the Bedford Rivers, two attempts were also made to drain the fens of Burwell and Wicken. This caused inhabitants of the latter village to riot, determined to protect their fen's bountiful fish, fowl, fuel, grazing and thatch. The villagers of Wicken made petitions to the Adventurers. As a result, part of Wicken parish, recorded as Sedge Fen since at least 1419, was divided into strips and shared between the commoners. A 10-acre triangle of the adjacent St Edmund's Fen was made available for the poor of the village.

By sheer coincidence, rather than design, rotational cutting of sedge created an ideal habitat for a diversity of plants and associated insects, preventing the fen from becoming overgrown with bushes and drying out. The East Cambridgeshire Fens had become a prime collecting site for nineteenth-century entomologists. A young Charles Darwin was said to have collected beetles in the east Cambridgeshire Fens* in the 1820s.

Much of Burwell Fen was eventually drained in 1840. But the people of Wicken held firm, continuing to fight against drainage. Their fen had become the sole source of sedge in the county and the only area of semi-natural fenland accessible from Cambridge. In 1894, entomologist James W. Tutt wrote a wonderful account of a visit he made to Wicken Fen:

> Attempting to cross a level-looking piece of ground covered with sedge, [I] found myself precipitated at the first step up to my waist in water, and discovered that the smooth-looking ground was a dyke, on which the sedge rested so alluringly.

The Nation's First Nature Reserve

On Monday, 1 May 1899, The National Trust for Places of Historic Interest or Natural Beauty (as it was then called), in its fifth year, purchases 2 acres of land on Wicken's Sedge Fen. It is sold by entomologist J.C. Moberley for the sum of £10. This goes on to become the Trust's first nature reserve, with banker and early nature conservationist Charles Rothschild donating parts of St Edmund's and Adventurers' Fens in 1901. The reserve grows considerably in 1911 when Newmarket-based scientist and politician George Henry Verrall bequests 239 acres to the National Trust. A keen botanist, Verrall had rediscovered multiple plants declared extinct sixty years earlier by the University of Cambridge's Professor of Botany, Cardale Babington.

---

*   Surviving specimens often have rather vague dates and locations, making it hard to prove precisely which fens Darwin visited, many names and boundaries having altered over the subsequent years. Thus, we do not know for certain whether it was Wicken Darwin visited or nearby fens such as those at Burwell or Swaffham Prior. There is even a theory that he merely foraged for beetles in boats of sedge brought from the Fens into Cambridge.

In 1914, Wicken man G.W. Barnes is employed as the fen's first watcher.* His role involves harvesting sedge and the first remedial bush clearance, conserving important invertebrate habitat by preventing the open fen becoming overgrown and drying out (this has been an on going battle ever since). A system of permits is implemented to avoid the damaging impact collectors could have on rare species if left unregulated, thus helping to protect the wildlife of this very special fen for future generations.

Well over 9,000 species have been recorded on Wicken Fen between the early nineteenth and early twenty-first centuries, more than any other site in the country (see Appendix 1). These include at least ten species discovered on Wicken Fen that were completely new to science, plus a further twenty-five firsts for Britain. Turn back the clock a couple of thousand years and beavers would have been present (before being hunted to extinction), as indicated by a lower jaw bone found in the peat on adjacent Burwell Fen. Ancient whale bones and shark teeth have also been unearthed, and a 3,000-year-old human skull, as well as prehistoric reptiles from many millions of years ago.

Long before the peat was formed, gault clay was the uppermost stratum and formed the sea floor. In the subtropical seas lived the shark-like ichthyosaurus, the paddle-legged plesiosaurus and above them flew the bat-like pterodactyl. Fossilised bones and excreta of these reptiles are known as coprolites, derived from two Greek words meaning dung and stone. Their discovery on Burwell Fen in 1851 led to large-scale digging, rather like a gold rush. Being rich in phosphates, coprolites were used for the manufacture of fertiliser, superphosphate of lime.

An article published in the *London Evening Standard* on Saturday, 21 April 1900, paints a splendidly vivid picture of what Wicken Fen was like just a year after the National Trust's first land acquisition:

---

*   He was succeeded by his son Henry in 1946, assisted by his two others sons, Bill and Wilfred. The latter retired in 1987.

Enclosed by broad ditches ... it is overgrown with coarse sedge and sallow-bush. Rare plants and rare insects lurk in this natural sanctuary, and make a happy hunting ground for the botanist and entomologist. It has a charm of its own in a sense of indefinite vastness, and nowhere in England are the sunrises and sunsets more glorious, for a whole hemisphere of sky over-arches the place.

But the charm of the Fen is greatest when it is explored minutely. The swallowtail, perhaps the most beautiful of English butterflies, still lingers, though not nearly so common as formerly, when it was less hunted, and the food-plant of its caterpillar grew almost everywhere. Dragonflies dart to and fro like microscopic hummingbirds, the green snake writhes through the herbage, while rare birds still haunt the fens, though not in the abundance of forty years ago. Sometimes, however, a harrier or one of the scarcer hawks may be seen poised overhead. Dunlin, sandpipers, snipe, teal, ducks of various kinds, and in a hard winter wild geese visit the place, possibly even a whooper swan makes its appearance. But the drainage of the fens has gradually driven most of them away from East Anglia.

'Cock-Up' Bridge: Sunday, 4 August 2002

My parents' green Toyota Avensis heads slowly towards Factory Road. I have been a teenager for twenty-four hours and, bizarrely, this is what I am most excited about. Not a video game, not a gadget, not food, but crossing Ash Bridge and going to the end of Factory Road for the first time. Since my mysteriously fascinating experience at Judy's Hole in the spring, I have been strangely gripped by an intense intrigue relating to the nearby Fens. Travelling along this 1½-mile road fills me with suspense, as if it will lead to somewhere interesting and important.

Partway along, we pass a pylon, right by the side of the road. It seems enormous, part of a long line dominating the landscape. They look futuristic and yet dated at the same time. The progressively greying sky is heavily pregnant with rain. A downpour is imminent.

The drove reaches a T-junction at Priory Farm.* We head left, dip-
ping just below sea level and parking up on what is essentially the edge
of Wicken Fen nature reserve. Ahead, a grassy bank is visible. On top
of it are two bridges over Burwell Lode, one made of concrete and the
other an electric drawbridge held in the upright position. Known to
locals as 'Cock-Up' Bridge, a manual drawbridge (named High Bridge)
had stood on this site from 1848, tipping up to allow barges along the
lode and swinging down to let turf-diggers wheel their barrows across.
One of three drawbridges in the area, all were replaced with steep-
sided, humpback affairs in the early twentieth century. These were
also known as 'cock-up' bridges, despite being static. Just one of these
wooden bridges remains, over Wicken Lode, albeit completely rebuilt
in 1995. The bridge near Priory Farm was replaced with the current concrete construction in 1966.

My brother and I hop out of the car and walk up the bank for a closer
look at Burwell Lode. This waterway is one of many fenland canals in
the area, 'lode' deriving from an Old English word for way or course.
The oldest fen lodes are believed to date back to Roman times. This is
one of the more recent, dug by the Adventurers in the mid-seventeenth
century, replacing the Medieval 'High Lode' (later renamed Burwell Old
Lode) 500m to the north. Since that time, a combination of peat digging
and drainage has caused the ground level on either side of Burwell Lode
to drop by more than 2m.

Raindrops hit the surface, creating hundreds of tiny ripples. I take a
quick snap on the family digital camera, time-stamped 6.21 p.m., then
jump back inside the car to keep dry. We head back to Fenview 11, by
which time the rain has turned to hail, hammering on the conservatory
roof. While my family relaxes, chatting over a background soundtrack
of drumming precipitation, other families are facing the most challenging circumstances imaginable just 5 miles away after two 10-year-old
children go missing in Soham.

---

*   The name Priory Farm remains a mystery, being an unlikely location for a mon-
      astery, although possibly once owned by nearby monks from Fordham Abbey,
      Swaffham Prior or Ely.

Raindrops falling on Burwell Lode, 6.21 p.m. on 4 August 2002. (Ajay Tegala)

Ouse Valley: Monday, 14 November 2022 (Part Three)

I can hear distant skeins of greylag geese and whooper swans, but cannot see them through the greyness. A bird hide comes into view on the other side of the Old Bedford. This is strange, as I am quite sure my intended route does not pass any hides. In the disorientating murkiness, I have lost all concept of distance and completely missed a turning on the right. I spin around, walking briskly back on myself to find the path. 'This way,' I call out and Oakley immediately changes direction, too. Eventually making it back home to Fen View (named after Fenview, my grandparents' old bungalow in Burwell), I remove my wellies, peel off my sodden socks and lock the front door behind me, safely home for the night.

Exactly eighty-two years ago, my ancestors had a far-from-safe night. My grandad's father, Ernest Hector, and his father, Alfred Ernest, were both firefighters in Stafford. That night, they travelled to Coventry to help fight the massive blaze caused by heavy bombing, which killed over 500 people. Fortunately, the Haywood family all survived the war. On the twenty-fifth anniversary of the Coventry Blitz, my mum was born. Five and a half years later, the family moved to Fenview 11, Toyse Lane, Burwell. Eighteen years after that, my parents held their wedding reception at The Fox, on the same day as the Live Aid benefit concert. My dad's family had moved from post-partition northern India to southern England around the same time my maternal family moved from Stafford to the Fen-edge.

My dad being a Surrey schoolteacher, my birth was timed to coincide with the summer holidays. It also coincided with a new job at a different school, which meant moving house. A trinity of major life events. Delays getting keys to the Market Deeping house – on the nicely named Bramley Road – meant we stayed eleven nights with my grandparents at Fenview 11. Some twenty-nine Augusts later, I would drive down Toyse Lane in the National Trust's Land Rover for the first of many times (see Chapter 5), Fenview having led me to Fen life.

2

Finding the Fen

• First walk around Sedge Fen •
Management of Wicken Fen • Introducing Carol •
How to become a warden/ranger •
Scrub clearance •

Wicken Fen: Wednesday, 22 February 2003

Having an affection for waterbirds and a liking for pleasant countryside walks, I was eager to explore Wicken. With hindsight and poetic licence, this could be explained as a magnetic force, pulling me along Factory Road towards my future, the lure of the fen. During the February half-term holiday, the day finally comes. Our family sets off early from Market Deeping into a grey winter morning, arriving at the Wicken Fen car park for breakfast.

We walk slightly downhill along Lode Lane to the visitor centre. I spot a bearded man who gives the impression of someone born and bred in the Fens. This is warden Ralph Sargeant, who I will go on to meet properly a couple of years later. Walking through the doors of the visitor centre onto the reserve, we enter a lost landscape. Sedge Fen is in its winter shades of brown and gold, cloaked in the comforting cloudiness of lingering mist. Particles of water in the air create a definite wetland atmosphere, as moist as the peaty soil beneath the wooden boardwalk over which we tread.

Norman's Mill, Sedge Fen, 22 February 2003. (Ajay Tegala)

Ahead of us stands the famous windpump, a much-photographed emblem of the Fens. It is smaller than I expected. Known as Bill Norman's Mill, the windpump was originally located 1½ miles away on Adventurers' Fen. Alongside numerous others, it was built to drain and control water levels in turf digging pits. Wind would spin the sails, turning a shaft to drive a wheel that scooped water, transferring it into drains, which flowed into the Cam at Upware, then the Ouse and eventually out into the Wash. No two windpumps were the same, all hand-built from whatever materials were available. Some were weather-boarded, others skeletons, their internal workings visible. On very windy days, working too fast could sometimes cause them to catch fire. Norman's Mill was used in the 1940s to help drain land for wartime food production, before being abandoned. In a state of dilapidation, the pump was dismantled in 1955 and erected on Sedge Fen the following year, where it was lovingly restored. The sole working wooden wind-pump remaining in the Fens, it no longer drains away water but lifts it onto Sedge Fen.

Extending across the fen, a thin sheet of surface water sits on top of a grassy drove. Long and level, it looks like a lode, but the water is scarcely 2in deep. Heading anticlockwise around the boardwalk, we reach Wicken Lode itself, lined with reeds on either side. There is such

Cleared scrub on Sedge Fen, 22 February 2003. (Ajay Tegala)

geometry to the fen. Straight reed stems, droves, drains, ditches, dykes, lodes and roads all complement the flat horizon. Even the swans seem to be swimming in lines as straight as arrows.

The squelchy lodeside path leads us towards the most exciting aspect of the fen to a 13-year-old, the old tower hide. Ascending steep steps climbed by the Duke of Edinburgh half a century previously, we reach the top floor, open the shutters and behold the mere on Adventurers' Fen. Silhouetted ducks and geese sit on the calm, silver water. Four cormorants are perched on bare tree branches. We should have brought binoculars. A nature walk is always better with binoculars, especially if you are a budding young naturalist.

Looking at the photographs taken that morning, piles of chainsawed logs can be seen stacked in several places. This is the result of an ongoing clearance project, to keep the fen in optimum condition for its unique species, including various endangered plants and invertebrates.

Battling Scrub (Part One)

Keeping on top of encroaching bushy vegetation, known as scrub or carr, has been a recurring battle since G.W. Barnes became the reserve's first watcher. Leaving the fen unmanaged would result in a dense bushy cover of oak, birch, alder buckthorn and willows sucking water out of the ground, causing the fen to dry out. In time, the bushes would succeed into woodland and thus the open fen habitat, and its special species, would be lost.

Willow, birch and alder buckthorn are shrubs notorious for vigorous regrowth, thriving in wet conditions. Therefore cleared areas need to be cropped regularly to prevent them from 'scrubbing up' again. Stumps must be removed and cut material stacked carefully, burned or chipped. Willow poles are occasionally used as markers or fence posts on the fen. Pushed into peat, they frequently produce fresh leaves and have been known to grow into mature trees, as demonstrated by a row of evenly spaced willows on Sedge Fen.

The amount of scrub on the fen has fluctuated over time. A reduction of staff during the Second World War inevitably led to an increase in cover. Subsequently, countless volunteer groups have assisted with clearance. In the 1960s, forty young sailors from HMS *Ganges* cleared a huge amount from the field behind the windpump, known as the Ganges Field. The sailors also constructed their own accommodation, later used by the National Trust's working holiday camps before becoming the reserve's learning centre, its name changing from the Ganges Hut to the Wren Building.

The new millennium saw revived impetus to get on top of the scrub on Sedge Fen. Benefiting from the National Lottery Heritage Fund, the National Trust embarked on a five-year project to open up an ambitious 50 hectares. It would end up taking seven years and much hard grafting. Trials began in 1999 with 'Boris the big white digger' grubbing out roots. But cutting by hand, using chainsaws, was found to be the most effective clearance method. This was intensive, gruelling work and certainly not for the faint-hearted. A succession of young wardens were employed throughout the duration of the project. Among them was my future colleague, Carol.

Birth of a Conservationist

On the northern edge of the Cotswolds – 130 miles west of Wicken Fen – sits the small village of Aston Somerville. Home, in the 1970s, to Mr and Mrs Laidlaw and their young daughter Carol. Spring days would be spent gathering hundreds of peacock and small tortoiseshell butterfly caterpillars from nearby fields, rescuing them from certain death by pesticide poisoning. The family would also forage for moth larvae including 'hairy oobits'* and drinkers, which look like 1970s upholstery. Annual visits were made to a certain willow in the village. Growing in a hedge that was cut annually, the tree produced fresh new growth favoured by puss moth caterpillars. Named after the cat-like appearance of the adults, the lime green larvae look more like aliens when they rear up to fend off predators.

Rescued Lepidoptera larvae were kept in lots of little caterpillar-raising boxes and fed on nettle leaves. Twice a day, Mrs Laidlaw would don her pink rubber gloves to pick and wash fresh nettles. As lids were lifted, Carol's job was to stop the mad rush of hungry caterpillars from escaping. With a paintbrush, she would quickly but carefully knock them back into their boxes while the sharp-smelling nettles were refreshed. 'The rhythmic noise of 200 caterpillars munching on fresh leaves sounds like a crescendo of waves breaking on the shore,' she remembers fondly.

The butterfly and moth larvae would pupate on the glass lids, which were then balanced on any available surface in the spare bedroom. With windows left open, emerging adults were free to self-release themselves into the Worcestershire countryside and beyond. The Laidlaw family were soon to take flight themselves, heading north, returning to their native Scotland. Carol went on to study her other passion in life, English literature. In the final year of a Master's degree at Dundee University, she came across the Angus Council Ranger Service at a careers fair. With a love of nature and animals still very strong, this sounded like an ideal career. Sensibly deciding to test the waters before embarking on a new career path, Carol spent some time as a volunteer with the same ranger service. She absolutely loved it.

---

*   Scottish term for long, hairy caterpillars, usually tiger moths.

Ask almost any permanent warden or ranger how they came to secure their role, and they will likely tell you a similar story. All but a rare few begin their journey as a volunteer, eventually working their way up to a temporary paid contract, then another and maybe another, often in multiple locations. This was certainly the case for Carol throughout the second half of the 1990s. Summers would be spent in Scotland as a seasonal ranger. Winters would be based with her then partner in Cambridgeshire, working as a part-time waitress to support her voluntary warden work at none other than Wicken Fen. When a paid position became vacant, at the end of a three-year stay in Scotland, Carol applied. She was offered an initial two-year contract working on the scrub clearance project.

But was moving south, to the haunt of her now ex-partner, the right decision? It would mean leaving lovely Scotland for the faraway flat lands, many miles from family, friends and the coast. After two years extended to two decades, Carol tells me she is still homesick for Scotland, but has just learned to live with it.

Battling Scrub (Part Two)

The slowly rising winter sun is reflected in standing water on Sedge Fen. To the west, Verrall's Fen is masked in Monday morning mist. Frosted reed stems sparkle. Crows and rooks call out and jackdaws chatter as they fly from their overnight roosts. They are heading off to forage for the day. Three figures set off across the fen to clear scrub for the day. With them, they take chainsaws, fuel cans, chain-sharpening tools, flasks and food. Chugging along Wicken Lode, an old fen lighter* slows to a standstill. The three wardens disembark with their kit and the labour begins.

Before the starter cord can be pulled, the first cut must be contemplated carefully. Staring at a wall of scrub is like looking at a puzzle.

---

*   A type of flat-bottomed barge.

The wardens work out the best cuts to make in order to expend minimum energy for maximum gain. Carol likens the mass of interwoven branches to a sack of wool in which a herd of cats has been set loose. They must try to pick the individual threads out of this tangled mess. Not soft, clean wool, but prickly blackthorn, alder buckthorn and dense stands of willow. In the course of a day, each warden will probably clear a space of about 2m by 5m. Maybe double, if they are lucky enough to find a patch of silver birch, which cuts more easily, taking less of a toll on the cutting teeth of the saw's chain.

Early on in her scrub-battling days, Carol broke her first chainsaw when the piston sheered. The saw was taken to Peck's (agricultural machinery distributor) for repair, who concluded it had sheered because the saw had been overworked.

Chainsaws were pushed to their limits, working four to six hours a day, five days a week, eight months of the year. And wardens were pushed to their limits, too. Often, work would take place in ankle-deep water, cutting stumps as close to the ground as possible to reduce the chance of regrowth. Inevitably, saws would accidentally splash into water and plough into soil from time to time. At the end of a day's work, the scrub team would head back to the workshop with backs aching from bending down, safety boots chafing their legs and chainsaw trousers sodden and cold, 'like wearing a wet duvet'.

Some wardens quit, miserable, fed up, exhausted mentally as well as physically. Mark Lingwood lasted three years. But Carol was the longest serving, seeing the project to its end. What on earth kept her going for just shy of six years? 'Sheer bloody mindedness!'

There were small moments of joy, like 'when the chainsaw just worked'. Although the weather was often cold, there would be days with gorgeous blue skies or mist curling around willows like a magical, fairy-tale scene. And cake. Everything is better with cake.

Humour helped, too. Carol and Mark just clicked, sharing jokes and a similar attitude. Getting into a rhythm, laying the cut trees in a row meant they could be collected up easily and thrown into the burning trailer.* Fires on cold days can lift spirits ... and heat lunches. The thought of a coffee break would aid motivation, as would the promise of summer to come. Four blissful months with no chainsawing. Sounds of roaring machinery would be replaced with songs of breeding birds, petrol fumes** replaced by floral scents, the fen fizzing with beautiful butterflies and dragonflies.

---

*   Cut branches would be burned in a trailer, rather than on the ground, to avoid damage to the fen and chances of fire spreading.
**   Electric chainsaws and brush-cutters were introduced in 2023.

A Week at Wicken

• Teenage work experience • Sedge harvest •
Flora and fauna of the fen •
Beginning a career in conservation •
Studying and volunteering •

Wicken Fen: Monday, 18–Saturday, 23 July 2005

Being a teenager can be tough. There is a lot to deal with, physically and mentally. From the challenges of developing independence to coping with peer pressure. On top of this, finding an identity can be a struggle, as can choosing a career path to follow.

My teen hobbies included drawing, listening to music and watching the *Carry On* films. Learning about Kenneth Williams' diaries inspired me to start keeping my own. I also loved cycling in the countryside with my friends, being surrounded by open land and spotting wildlife. So, during the ten-week summer holiday before starting sixth form, my parents suggested I spend a week volunteering with the wardens of Wicken, staying with my grandparents in nearby Burwell. A rather good idea, it turns out.

Having started keeping a daily diary just a few weeks earlier, I recorded what my first day as a volunteer was like, sixteen days shy of my 16th birthday:

I was both nervous and excited about volunteering at Wicken Fen. Luckily, it turned out to be excellent. In the morning, I met wardens Kevin James and Carol Laidlaw and helped set up chairs in the Wren Building for a presentation when the Oak camp volunteers arrived. We cut sedge into the afternoon. James Selby, a full-time volunteer, taught me the names of various plants, which was very interesting. I am so glad I didn't miss this opportunity. The Oak campers are all great people and we enjoyed lunching under the summer sky, resting on a sedge stack.

It reads like an account of halcyon days, taking docky* in the sun, out in the fresh air with the Oak campers on their working holiday with the National Trust. But we weren't romantically picking strawberries, say, or gaily swishing nets around to catch insects. We were assisting with the tough job of harvesting sedge, trying our best to avoid horsefly bites and slicing our fingers. Cutting was not done with a scythe – as it had been done by the Barnes family until at least the 1960s – but a Mayfield croft tractor (a petrol-driven pedestrian mower with reciprocating blades, a bit like a heavy hedge-trimmer on wheels).

The wardens took it in turns to wheel this noisy machine up and down the edge of the field, cutting strip by strip from the headland. Freshly cut sedge was then forked into piles for us volunteers to tie carefully into bundles and stack neatly for sun-drying. We were lined up along evenly spaced wooden posts, wearing belts of orange baler twine. These lengths of twine had a loop at one end. We would lay the length on the ground, in front of our post, ready for a heap of sedge to be forked on top of it. Kevin would give his pitchfork a signature twirl before dropping the cut sedge onto the ground. The twine would then need to be wrapped tightly around the bundle, threading the end through the loop and pulling hard before tying a knot. Once dried, the sedge would be sold, generating a small income. That autumn, most of the harvest was used to re-thatch a roof on the High Street in Wicken.

---

* Cambridgeshire Fen term for morning break taken by agricultural labourers, so named because pay would be docked.

Wardens taking docky, Sedge Fen, 18 July 2005. (Ajay Tegala)

This otherwise toilsome task was fulfilling due to blissful surroundings and a strong sense of camaraderie. The presence of the wardens' dogs, Zed and Keeper, provided occasional distraction and relief. Intermittent wafts of water mint and meadowsweet filled the air. These are two of the most fragrant wildflowers that grow on the fen. Throughout the week, James tested my memory of the various fen flowers to which he had introduced me. These included hemp-agrimony, with its square-edged stem; comfrey, with its hairy leaves and clusters of bell-shaped flowers; two species of loosestrife, purple and yellow; and flag iris, also with yellow flowers.

Despite head warden Martin jocularly warning me I wouldn't want to come back for a second gruelling day, I arrived on time next morning, with equal enthusiasm and a slightly larger packed lunch. We headed along the grassy drove to carry on where we had left off. Some of the Oak campers were now sporting blue plasters bound around their fingers for protection. To cover my arms, I wore some of my dad's old long-sleeved cotton shirts.

Carol had run a moth trap overnight, sharing her findings with us out on the fen. My instant favourite was the buff-tip, with silver and

Buff-tip moth on my hand, 10 June 2021. (Ajay Tegala)

beige wings held against its body. It looks remarkably like a snapped birch twig. I was impressed by its cunning disguise, never having seen anything like it before.

Finishing our allotted area early in the afternoon, Kevin took us on a walk around the nature trail. I was fascinated by the Godwin Plots, which demonstrate the process of plant succession on the fen. These plots are cut at different intervals – annually, biannually, triennially and quadrennially – except for one section left uncut since 1927. It put perfectly into perspective what we were achieving with the sedge harvest, clearing strips of vegetation on rotation to disturb the natural process of succession in favour of creating diverse habitats. 'Playing God', if you will, but with good purpose, desperately trying to conserve species humankind has made rare through centuries of habitat destruction.

I added a new bird species to my list on the Wednesday. Lifting up the shutters of West Mere Hide, I felt a tingling sensation, hardly believing what was in front of me. There, on the edge of the water in plain sight, were two little egrets. Not listed in my British bird guide, the species had spread north from mainland Europe since the book was published in the mid-1980s. Like white herons, but half the size, they were close enough to show up reasonably clearly in the photograph I took with my little point-and-shoot camera. It was in the trees on the mere that Cambridgeshire's first breeding pair had been proven the previous summer.

Thursday's new bird was to be very distant. On the usual morning journey across Sedge Fen, James pointed out three distant marsh harriers in flight. Although far away, I could see how much bigger they are than kestrels, the only bird of prey I was familiar with at the time. I had often longed to lay eyes upon large raptors and, although distant, seeing marsh harriers was an exciting moment.

At the end of the week, one of the friendly staff in the visitor centre, Jenny, asked if I was interested in a career in conservation. Until that week, I didn't even know what conservation was. I had learned a lot in my five days at Wicken. The enlightening experience ended with a Saturday morning trip along the lode ... and a life-changing realisation:

On the boat trip back, Kevin said he thinks he is one of the luckiest men alive, to work as a warden at Wicken Fen, and he explained how it is such a pleasure to work there. James had actually come out to visit the fen on his day off, which showed how they all love their work so much. This made me realise that this is also the job for me. It would be that job where it is a pleasure to wake up on Monday mornings with a whole week of fun work ahead. A job that is not just work, but that is my pleasure and interest. I would love to work at the Fen ... I started the week not knowing where my life was going and, after six days at wonderful Wicken Fen, I realised what I want to do with my life. There is nothing I'd rather do for a job.

So, the answer to Jenny's question was a resounding yes. And not just for the fun of working outdoors in a beautiful place, but to be able to help habitats and species in need of protection. To be able to make a difference for fragile and vulnerable wildlife.

Back at my summer job in the Market Deeping Tesco store, Wicken seems like a world away. But it is very much on my mind. I write in my diary that, 'I know what I am aiming for in life now. For the first time ever, I know for sure what I want to be when I'm older.' None of my friends know what working in conservation is or really understand why I want to do it. But my A-Level geography teacher does and so does a friend of my dad's, offering advice. I also receive a helpful email from the Wicken wardens with some useful tips on the road to becoming a ranger or warden.

Their wise words warn that volunteering is the only way to acquire experience. The wider the range of experience that can be gained, the better. Patience is a quality needed in abundance and the determination not to get disheartened on the often long journey. A countryside qualification is key, a degree being the top requirement. I have to prepare myself to face disappointment, do lots of waiting and not expect to become rich. I am warned that the work is physically hard and the results are often slow. Sometimes, the end of a project will be several decades in the future. But, with commitment and motivation, there will come a sense of achievement and satisfaction.

So, my journey starts. I begin regular volunteering with the Lincolnshire Wildlife Trust at Deeping Lakes nature reserve, a Site of Special Scientific Interest just 3 miles from home. My first session at Deeping Lakes is the day after Boxing Day, in thick snow. Over the course of the day, my feet become so cold that I put my gloves on them in a desperate attempt to warm numb toes. I soon learn to dress appropriately.

I also go on to learn how to identify trees and more wildflowers, thanks to warden Dave and enthusiastic volunteers Norah and Brian (it was Brian and Norah who kindly lent me a spare pair of socks on that cold December day). I also return to Wicken for another week's volunteering in the summer of 2006, again in 2007 and once more in 2008.

My journey takes me to the rural Nottinghamshire hilltop campus of Brackenhurst, overlooking the minster town of Southwell. There, alongside like-minded students, I complete a degree in Environmental Conservation and Countryside Management – including a dissertation on the wildflower areas we were creating at Deeping Lakes – incorporating a placement year on the Norfolk coast's Blakeney National Nature Reserve to broaden my experience, always keeping in touch with the team at Wicken and hoping to one day work there.

The road is long and I am fortunate in being able to afford to volunteer full-time for several months. After graduating, I secure a seasonal visitor-focused position on the fen, which financially supports further volunteering with the wardens. Nine months later, I gain my first paid position in conservation, a seasonal assistant ranger role back at Blakeney. Another two six-month contracts follow before I secure a permanent coastal ranger job with the National Trust in 2013. After a rich and varied half-decade on the Norfolk coast, I transition into a grazing ranger on Wicken Fen, fulfilling my dream of thirteen years.

4

Rewilding

• **Extinction of the swallowtail** • **The Wicken Fen Vision** • **Defining the term 'rewilding'** • **Returning farmland to fenland** • **Grassland and wetland birds** • **Death and rebirth of Burwell Fen** • **Arrival of the Koniks** • **First foal on the fen** • **Arrival of the Highland cattle** • **Other British rewilding projects** •

The Wicken Fen Vision

On 1 May, two birthdays are celebrated on the fen, ranger Carol's and the reserve itself. In 1999, the National Trust marks 100 years since purchasing its first 2 acres on Sedge Fen. During the lead up to the Wicken Fen centenary, decades of management and monitoring are reflected on and the next 100 years are contemplated. This is a time of dreaming and ambition, of planning and preparation.

One might reasonably expect a century of conservation to produce an improvement in habitat quality and an increase in diversity. Almost every nature conservation project aims to increase biodiversity or, at least, prevent its loss. Naturally, a truly vast amount of knowledge and experience was gained on Wicken Fen throughout the twentieth century. But its fragility was known from the very start and time has shown the challenges presented by its isolation. While scrub clearance prevents the fen from succeeding into woodland, keeping it wet enough is a constant challenge. Sedge Fen is an island of wetland surrounded by drained land. It sits 2m higher than the farmland surrounding it and more than 4m above the water table, as can be seen by the water level in the adjacent farm ditches during summer. Despite the best efforts put into protecting the fen, not all of its unique species have been able to thrive.

The extinction of the swallowtail butterfly from Wicken is a classic example. The food plant of its larvae, milk parsley, has declined in tandem with inevitable drying of the fen since the nineteenth century. Swallowtails eventually became extinct at Wicken in the early 1950s. Pinned specimens from the first half of the twentieth century demonstrate a decrease in wing size over time. This is a very visual indication that the larger-winged, stronger fliers, which flew further into the surrounding landscape, were not able to survive there due to the absence of milk parsley. So it was only the weaker fliers, those that never left Sedge Fen, that managed to reproduce, thus resulting in shrinking wings over time.

During the spring and summer of 1955, fifty adults and 200 larvae were reintroduced to the fen, brought over from the Norfolk Broads (the only place in Britain where the species breeds). This reintroduction was unsuccessful due to poor growth of milk parsley, which had failed to colonise suitable areas. A major planting operation was undertaken in 1974, followed by the introduction of 228 swallowtails the following summer. But plant numbers decreased, and the butterfly became extinct again within half a decade. A third reintroduction was attempted in summer 1993. This was also unsuccessful. It became clear that reintroduction was not the answer.

In their 1967 book *The Theory of Island Biogeography*, ecologist Robert MacArthur and biologist E.O. Wilson established that recovery of species at risk of extinction required conservation areas to be large enough.

Indeed, it was the limited amount of suitable habitat that resulted in the extinction of the swallowtail at Wicken. Time needed to be turned back in an attempt to restore lost wetland on a landscape scale. The reserve needed to be made much bigger. And 1999 seemed the perfect time to start. The government's Countryside Stewardship Scheme had been set up at the start of the decade, providing subsidies and grants to help improve environmental management. The National Trust had acquired former farmland on Baker's Fen in 1993 (part of Priory Farm) and, thanks to positive hydrological management, the reedbed on Adventurers' Fen was increased successfully. The stewardship scheme also enabled more scrapes to be created, increasing suitable lapwing habitat, reversing a decade-long decline.

So the Wicken Fen Vision was born, an ambitious 100-year plan to create a bigger, better, more joined up and diverse landscape for wildlife and people, stretching across 33 square miles (the size of almost 12,000 football pitches), east of the River Cam from Wicken to the northern edge of Cambridge. This was the brainchild of property manager Adrian Colston. Long-term conservation on a landscape scale can help increase the survival of rare species by creating spreading space for wildlife alongside a growing number of people. Early on, the project faced criticism for taking 'prime' farmland out of production and there was a misconception that the National Trust wanted to flood vast areas.* But, within just six years, the reserve more than doubled in size thanks to the purchase of adjacent farmland, a flying start to this epic journey as pioneers of what would later become widely known as rewilding.

Just shy of a decade before the Wicken Fen Vision was launched, an article, titled 'Trying to Take Back the Planet', appeared in the New York magazine *Newsweek*. It reported how environmental activists wanted to 'take back and "rewild" one third of the United States'. This was the first time the term rewilding appeared in print, certainly to a global audience.

---

* This led to an unsubstantiated fear that the project could bring malaria to the area.

Twenty years later, it had become more widely used, defined as the returning of land to a wilder and more natural state. The often divisive topic has been much debated by scientists, students, conservationists and landowners. I remember debates at university, especially in relation to reintroduction projects. Proposals to release wolves in Scotland – to control the overpopulation of red deer that have a significant impact on ecosystems – raised widespread concern and negative voices in the media. Another popular ongoing debate is how to define the terms 'wild' and 'natural', words used with increasing frequency and casualness. I dislike the much-used word 'biodiverse' as it sounds grammatically incorrect to me, I think 'rich in biodiversity' sounds better.

There is a very valid argument that it is impossible for Britain to ever become truly wild again, humankind having had such an irreversible impact. But, the important thing is that positive actions are being made. In 2011, the organisation Rewilding Europe was founded, followed by Rewilding Britain four years later. The latter defines rewilding as 'the large-scale restoration of ecosystems', seeking to 'reinstate natural processes' and sometimes introduce missing species in order to shape habitats and landscapes. Subsequently, the definition has become much broader, covering a spectrum of scales without necessarily having to return land to a defined historic baseline.

In its broadest sense, rewilding can mean making land or water more suitable for wildlife, no matter how small the area or simple the methods – such as creating a small nature pond or miniature wildflower meadow. Rewilding Britain outline five principles, all of which apply to the Wicken Fen Vision project:

- Reconnecting local communities with wild nature and enriching their lives.
- Seeking to reinstate natural processes, letting nature lead.
- Finding opportunities for nature-based economies that enrich and thrive alongside nature.
- Restoring ecosystems with space for nature to drive changes and shape living systems.
- Leaving a positive legacy of long-term benefits for future generations.

Wicken Fen can easily be classed as one of the very first rewilding sites in Britain, having started with ecosystem restoration on Baker's Fen in 1993 (or, arguably, as far back as 1953, when part of Adventurers' Fen, reclaimed for wartime agriculture, was returned to nature). One year after the launch of the Wicken Fen Vision, 2000 saw the reinstatement of natural processes on more former farmland thanks to the acquisition of 100 hectares adjacent to the reserve, known as Guinea Hall Fen. A year later, the Vision project continued apace with the purchase of another piece of adjacent fenland, this one much loved for its wildlife before being drained in living memory.

From Wetland to Dry Land ... and Back Again

The last of the Cambridgeshire Fens to be drained were reclaimed for agriculture during the early 1940s. These included Swaffham Prior Fen and Adventurers' Fen, the latter adjacent to Wicken, lying within the parish of Burwell. The southern part of Adventurers' Fen – now known as Burwell Fen – had been the favoured haunt of renowned naturalist and wildlife artist Eric Ennion since moving to Burwell in 1904, when his father succeeded Charles Lucas as the village doctor. Ennion's gorgeous book, *Adventurers Fen*, is full of beautiful sketches and lovely tales of wildlife watching. But, be warned, a happy ending it has not!

This 165-hectare triangle of fen – enclosed by the banks of Burwell and Reach Lodes (sides of the triangle) and the commissioner's drain (base of the triangle) – had faced a variety of pressures and exploitation throughout the nineteenth century. Decades of turf digging had removed vast quantities of peat, the diggers and their dogs causing too much disturbance for many birds to nest safely. Demand for turf fell in the early twentieth century due to the modernisation of stoves and fireplaces, and the First World War prompted a conversion to agriculture. The 1920s then saw agricultural regression and nature began to claim back the fen as it became progressively wetter.

A great flood, in the winter of 1936–37, filled the fen with enough water to withstand future droughts, transforming it into a vast reedy wetland. A farmer's nightmare but a naturalist's dream. Tens of thou-

Burwell Fen, July 1934. (E.A.R. Ennion)

sands of starlings and hundreds of sand martins roosted in the reeds. As Ennion recalls, 'Short-eared owls and harriers were ever on the prowl.' In 1938, a pair of bitterns nested, the first to breed in Cambridgeshire for almost a century.* A pair of black-necked grebes also bred, the first nesting record in all of East Anglia.

But the days of this wild, watery wonderland were to be short-lived. Ennion's closing chapter paints a picture of his 'last look round' before drainage commenced in 1941. Without bitterness, he writes how the kingfishers he watched would find other places to fish. 'It must be so … nature goes on elsewhere.' I wonder whether he ever imagined that a day might come when nature could reclaim his beloved lost fen?

Interestingly, former fen drainage commissioner Charles Lucas had written, back in 1930, that the land between the Wicken and Reach Lodes should become derelict. He proposed it 'be taken out of drainage and given to the nation for scientific purposes, when it might become a sanctuary for birds and what not'.

* Sadly, a bittern was also shot 'by mistake' on Burwell Fen the same year and a hen harrier, too. Ennion and gamekeeper Ernest Parr worked hard to protect hen harriers wintering on Burwell Fen.

Sixty years after diggers and draglines had drained it, South Adventurers' Fen – subsequently known as Burwell Fen Farm – came up for sale. The National Trust became the owners of this previously iconic triangle of land in autumn 2001. Adjacent to the nature reserve, this was the logical next piece in the Wicken Fen Vision puzzle.

For a decade, it was relatively uninspiring rough grassland, grazed by tenant cattle. I once overheard it referred to by visitors as 'waste ground'. However, plans were afoot to increase biodiversity. An interline takes water, drained from farmland to the east, through the middle of the fen, underneath Reach Lode and into the Cam at Upware. Any plans to re-wet the fen would have to be designed carefully to avoid water simply ending up in the interline and draining away. The answer was to build a clay bank and make the south-western half of Burwell Fen into a self-contained reservoir. Clay was dug from a borrow pit** on the fen.

But before the first drop of water was added, magic started happening. The rough grassland was a great habitat for voles and other rodents. This healthy population of small mammals formed a rich larder for the fen's resident kestrels, hovering and swooping to catch their prey.

From September 2011, I cycled along the edge of Burwell Fen several times a week, commuting between Wicken Fen and Anglesey Abbey, 8 miles south-west, along the newly opened Lodes Way cycle trail. Having graduated in the summer, I was continuing my quest for full-time employment in nature conservation by volunteering with the Wicken wardens alongside paid work in both the visitor centre and newly opened cycle hire centre, as well as Anglesey Abbey's gift shop. Living in National Trust volunteer accommodation at the latter,*** I had the pleasure of cycling between the two, soaking up the scenery.

A Saturday evening in mid-October is particularly memorable. After carrying my bike up and down the concrete steps of 'Cock-Up' Bridge, I hop back onto the saddle and freewheel down the lode-bank. Where the

---

** A pit formed by the excavation of material to use for embankments.
*** Anglesey Abbey and Wicken Fen were part of the same National Trust portfolio at this time.

track turns to the right, a long-winged bird catches my attention. It pivots on its axis and drops down into the grass. An owl. Its wings too long to be any of the three species I am familiar with – barn, little or tawny – it emerges from the field, wings beating slowly, its piercing yellow eyes fixed forwards. The pale underwings first caught my attention, but now I can appreciate the mottled browns and gold on its back as it powers into the night.

What an awesome sight. An unexpected surprise. I had only ever seen one short-eared owl before, from a distance among the sand dunes of Blakeney Point. This up-close encounter fills me with excitement and appreciation, which I convert into pedal-pushing power, speeding the remaining 6 miles home to tell my housemates, 'The Abbey Girls', about my wildlife wow. This is just the first of several 'shorties' I will see in the following two months due to an influx arriving on the east coast from Scandinavia. Word soon spreads in the birding community, 'Cock-Up' Bridge becoming a favoured lookout point from where a maximum of fifteen owls are recorded in flight at one time.

The following autumn sees more short-eared owls on Burwell Fen. And, with the bank complete, the fen is flooded for the first time in seventy-one years. I am now working for Natural England on the Northumberland coast, but see the new year in with my friends at Anglesey Abbey. A New Year's Day trip to look at Burwell Fen is essential.

Barn owl and short-eared owl, Burwell Fen, 24 February 2023. (Kenny Brooks)

Cycling over Reach Lode bridge, I gaze out over the fen. Deep blue sky and grey-white clouds are reflected in the water. Tussocks of grass poke through the otherwise perfect mirror to the sky. This is a tantalising glimpse of a bright new future, reminiscent of the past. Shallow depressions have remained imprinted in the ground even after drainage and cultivation. These dormant pools have been reawakened, heralding the rebirth of Ennion's beloved fen. Part of a palaeochannel* weaves through the middle, it too having been resurrected with the lifeblood of the Fens.

Come spring, I am stationed back on the north Norfolk coast, where news from the fen reaches me. It is a privilege to be party to some confidential news. Amazingly – and perhaps symbolically – as well as Ennion's pools returning, so too does one of the special species that once nested in them. A pair of black-necked grebes breed in the very same corner of the fen that the species had done pre-drainage. A wonderful, almost incredible coincidence. And an even rarer waterbird makes a breeding attempt, the black-winged stilt, appropriately named with its tall, thin legs. Another lanky, pied wader species actually manages to raise chicks. Avocets, with their delicate upturned bills, are noted for colonising new wetland habitat with small islands. They are also known for not necessarily returning the following year, as turns

---

* The remnant of an inactive river.

Winter floodwater on Burwell Fen, 1 January 2013. (Ajay Tegala)

out to be the case on Burwell Fen. One more brief breeder is the black-headed gull, forming a short-lived colony. Their dives and squawks bring bustle to Burwell, noisy nature proving the value of the Vision. Create suitable habitat and wildlife will find it.

But creating and managing suitable habitat does not just involve re-wetting. There is the ongoing battle to prevent precious open fenland succeeding to woodland. With the reserve growing in size, a naturalistic approach is needed.

Koniks Come to Wicken Fen

Twenty-four hooves patter on the peaty ground of Verrall's Fen. Spring 2001 sees the first Konik polski – an Eastern European breed of pony[*] – set foot in the Cambridgeshire Fens. Aged between 10 months and 7 years, the six geldings begin to explore their new home. The Fens are not too dissimilar to the Norfolk Broads, where they have come from, nor indeed the northern Netherlands, where their parents hail from. Most of these horses will go on to spend over two decades living permanently on this 55-hectare quiet corner of fen, enclosed by a watery boundary of dyke and lode. Their coats are various shades from mousy grey to fox red, blending in with the fen vegetation but occasionally delighting walkers on the other side of the water who are lucky enough to spot them.

The small herd spend their days nibbling on vegetation, rooting for rhizomes, drinking from drains, sheltering in scrub, rolling in the soil and ring-barking a large tree (known subsequently as the dead oak and later the fallen oak). Alongside some practical management by wardens, these equines will help to create a vibrant patchwork of diverse habitats. The following year, they are joined by another six Koniks from Norfolk, two of which will go on to spend more than twenty years as conservation grazers on Verrall's Fen alongside 'the originals'.

---

[*]   'Konik' is Polish for small horse (therefore 'Konik pony' effectively means 'pony pony' in two languages).

Opposite: Grazing Koniks. (Joss Goodchild)

The National Trust chose Konik polski after an extensive consultation, with approval from the government's then adviser for the natural environment, English Nature. Animals introduced into a minimal husbandry system must be tough and hardy to thrive in a wetland environment year round. Needless to say, the decision to introduce naturalistic grazing was certainly not taken lightly. Academics, experts and livestock grazing practitioners in Britain and abroad were consulted. Careful consideration was given to factors including temperament when left unhandled as well as adaptability to the environment.

With their proven history as robust conservation grazers on similar wetland habitat in mainland Europe, thorough research identified Koniks as the breed most suited to the Fenland landscape. With no native fen pony type available, the Konik appeared highly suited to living in a wetland environment under extensive, naturalistic management conditions. The long-term plan was, of course, not just to have a dozen geldings on the ancient fen, but a free-roaming, breeding herd to play a key part in restoration of the wider landscape.

First Foals on the Fen

The first foal is a long timing coming. In 2003, a group of four mares and two stallions from the Netherlands are introduced to Adventurers' Fen. All twelve of the previous males on the fen were geldings, but these intact stallions are a bit sparkier. The younger of the two, Kors, gets pushed out of the group by the older one shortly after arrival. There are high hopes for lead stallion Adonis. Alas, despite his name, he has rather small testicles and may be sub-fertile.

Early the following year, a further four mares and three stallions are brought over. From this group, a dark-coloured, pretty-faced mare named Oriola produces what the press enthusiastically (and slightly inaccurately) announce is the first wild foal born in Britain since the last Ice Age.

Carol finds the newborn foal on her birthday and names him Harry Konik (setting the wheels in motion for there to be a Harry Konik Jr* at some point in the future). She describes the arrival as somehow feeling 'weirdly non-eventful' for such an historical moment. It is all so smooth, 'horse does what it is supposed to do'. But there is a strong sense of rightness. At last, the herd is functioning properly, producing young. It is a landmark moment in the Vision project.

A second colt soon follows, named Hanty, and another four foals are born the next spring. The tenth foal to be born is the first from the original breeding group, after Kors was actively sought out by some very fed-up mares. Unlike the previous births, this one is to be a bit more complicated.

Eric, son of Kors, is born to Krieka in May 2006. The arrival of this group's first foal prompts immediate envy in the lead mare, Nanja, who begins hectoring him. Next morning, a member of the public reports a foal outside the grazing enclosure. The wardens attend, finding Eric calling for his mother, having been booted out by bossy Nanja. In certain circumstances, foals can be quite elastic during their first twenty-four hours or so. Provide a calm, reassuring presence and a lost youngster will tend to follow, enabling a person to fulfil a loosely parent-like position. This plays to the wardens' advantage and they coax him back to the herd. Carol stays a while to keep an eye on Eric, and it is a good job she does. Clearly still jealous of the foal, Nanja pushes him boldly into a ditch. If left unassisted, the day-old colt is likely to die a horrible, watery death.

As a young mare, Eric's mother happened to be a particularly friendly individual and 'a glutton for a bum scratch'. Carol, on her lunch break, once decided to time how long she could scratch said bottom before Krieka grew tired of it. Needless to say, Carol grew tired long before Krieka! But, with a new foal at foot, Krieka becomes understandably protective. Carol knows she must get into the ditch to rescue the foal, but this will require her head being at the height of its protective mother's hooves.

---

* A reference to American singer Harry Connick Jr, son of attorney Harry Connick (Sr).

The safety of the foal paramount in her mind, Carol must act fast. With no dry suit or waders to hand, she removes keys and mobile phone from her trouser pockets, takes a deep breath and wades into the cold, waist-deep ditch. What happens next amazes Carol, who tends to be cautious of non-scientific animal behaviour theories and anthropomorphism. Perhaps, from Carol's body language, Krieka seems to recognise that no harm is meant. The previously defensive mare quietly stands, allowing Carol to lift the foal out of the ditch, place him on the bank and move gently away. A strong sense of euphoria and relief ensues. Getting into a ditch was absolutely worth it to reunite mother and foal. Such is the strong impact these special animals have on those who work with them. Being part of their lives instils a great care and affection, a dedication to their welfare.

Eric and Krieka clearly need separating from Nanja. So the rest of the day is spent splitting the herd. The following week, another mare

Eric aged 2 weeks, by the mere, 28 May 2006. (Carol Laidlaw)

gives birth and Nanja displays the same behaviour. So this pair are also removed from the herd for their safety, joining Krieka and Eric in their separate area. A week later, at last Nanja gives birth to her own foal. This finally causes her foal envy to evaporate and all is well with the reunited herd, the wardens having gained a raw insight into breeding herd dynamics.

Highlands in Fenlands

Four years after the arrival of the first Koniks, Highland cattle are introduced to the reserve. This is the next big moment in the restoration project, to have naturally fluctuating numbers of two large herbivore species grazing over large areas. Like the Koniks, Highlands are hardy, placid and well-suited to life on the fen. Equipped for life in the wilds of Scotland with their thick, shaggy coats, they have little trouble weathering English winters. Cattle on the fen are essentially fulfilling the role of the aurochs, a native species of cattle extinct in Britain since the Late Bronze Age. An aurochs skull was actually unearthed on Burwell Fen with a Neolithic axe-head embedded in its cranium (the discovery was deposited in Cambridge's Sedgwick Museum).

Having Koniks and Highlands together offers diverse grazing characteristics. Horses graze selectively, favouring sweet spring grass, then exploiting tougher rush, sedge and scrub in winter. They snip with their incisors, creating a patchwork of short-cropped grass mixed with taller vegetation. Koniks also browse on brambles, docks, nettles and thistles, assisting with weed control. To extract sufficient nutrition, they eat large quantities of vegetation. Cattle break down tough, fibrous vegetation by 'chewing the cud' to extract more nutrients. Unable to graze as selectively as horses, the cattle pull and tear vegetation with their tongues. They occasionally browse on scrub, preventing it from completely engulfing the fen, but leaving some patches and thus creating a mosaic of habitats supporting a wealth of species.

Ewan aged 3 years, Baker's Fen, 17 October 2006. (Carol Laidlaw)

Eight Highland cows and a bull arrive on Baker's Fen between the spring and autumn of 2005. These cows have come from the Isle of Mull and the bull, Ewan, from Oban on the adjacent Scottish mainland. The day she first sets eyes upon 2-year-old Ewan, Carol thinks to herself, 'F***, he's big!' But, after a few years managing the breeding herd, she will look back at pictures of young Ewan and think how cute and little he looked. In fact, the original nine Highlands are from a domestic background, so are tolerant of touch. Wendy loves a back scratch. If the daily welfare checks have to be done in a hurry, it is best not to approach Wendy, who will pester wardens for a scratch 'and a guid blether'.*

The following spring sees all eight cows give birth. Ewan is clearly a very proactive bull (although, some of the cows were already in calf when they left Scotland). Every one of the fen's animals has an individual personality. Ewan and two of his sons develop a habit of affectionately resting their chins on Carol's shoulder. If stressed and wanting to calm down, she will sit with the cattle, finding their earthliness 'really grounding'. After six incredibly tough winters of scrub clearance, Carol's commitment is rewarded by morphing into the grazing warden position, a role that hits all of her passions and enthusiasms.

---

*   Scottish term meaning a good talk or gossip.

As a child, Carol was fascinated by animal behaviour. Aged 6, she saw the film *Watership Down* and then read the book by Richard Adams. This sparked a love for literature, seeking out stories in which animals communicate with people. Her childhood favourite fantasy novels included *The Horse and His Boy* by C.S. Lewis and Edith Nesbit's *The Phoenix and the Carpet*. Unbeknown to Carol at the time, this early interest would provide a firm foundation for her future career. Finally becoming a permanent ranger, she and the Wicken Fen grazing project have grown together – while many similar rewilding ventures have been set up across the country.

Wider Rewilding

Since the start of the Wicken Fen Vision in 1999, several other rewilding initiatives have been established in Britain. Two years later, the Great Fen Project was launched 30 miles north-west of Wicken with very similar ambitions (and also conceived by Adrian Colston). A collaboration between five organisations,** their vision aims to restore 14 square miles of Fenland habitat, connecting Holme and Woodwalton Fens. Further north, the Lincolnshire Wildlife Trust's Bourne North Fen is a third project aiming to restore peatland and create wet fenland.

One of the best-known English rewilding projects is Knepp Wildland in West Sussex. The estate's former dairy pasture, arable and parkland was converted into a diverse area of 'wilderness' by its owners, the Burrell family. Work began in 2001 with Countryside Stewardship funding. Summer 2003 saw the introduction of twenty Old English longhorn cattle as conservation grazers to gradually remove vegetation and create a mosaic of habitats. Hedges were left uncut and expanded, eventually attracting record numbers of nightingales. Tourism really took off at Knepp, too, raising awareness, spreading inspiration and helping generate income essential for perpetuating the project.

** Including the Wildlife Trust for Bedfordshire, Cambridgeshire and Northamptonshire.

Another family-run estate, Wild Ken Hill, rose significantly in profile when it became the home of *Springwatch* in 2021. National television exposure inevitably created great interest in the Norfolk estate. As well as showcasing rewilded habitats and the array of species inhabiting them, the popular television series also praised the regenerative farming done on the estate. Ken Hill Farm produces food sustainably alongside its nature conservation practices, setting a powerful example to other farmers and landowners.

Back in 2000, the Royal Society for the Protection of Birds (RSPB) purchased Hope Farm, in Cambridgeshire, to undertake nature-friendly farming and monitor its benefits, sharing their techniques with farmers. As well as becoming pioneers of wildlife-friendly agriculture, the RSPB have also converted intensive farmland into prime wetland habitat. In 1995, they created Lakenheath Fen nature reserve in north-west Suffolk, planting reedbeds and establishing wet grassland on former arable fields, just as the National Trust had done on Adventurers' and Baker's Fens. Merely 2 miles up the road from Wicken, 1995 also saw the creation of the privately owned Kingfishers Bridge nature reserve, another project transforming farmland into wetland. Koniks were later introduced to Kingfishers Bridge, to act as naturalistic grazers. Since then, other former farmland in the Fens has been rewilded, such as High Fen near Methwold in south-west Norfolk, managed by the company Nattergal to recover biodiversity and reinstate functioning natural processes.

Three decades after becoming rewilding pioneers, Wicken Fen is in great company. Ideas and knowledge are shared between the many similar projects across the country and beyond. Indeed, Carol spends many hours sharing her expertise to help a variety of land managers make the best livestock choices for their rewilding journeys. With biodiversity in crisis and nature facing profound pressure on a global scale, rewilding is a ray of hope, a growing movement of positive action gaining increased interest, support and momentum.

5

Carol, the Cattle, the Koniks and Me

• **First day as a fen ranger** • **New Forest Eye** •
Cattle handling • **Meeting the herds** • **Ear-tagging**
calves • **Livestock management** • **Horse behaviour**
• **Our relationship with the horse** • **Euthanasia** •
Naming • **Dung sampling** • **Ada gets stuck** •
Mare crosses river • **Gale gets out** • **Vasectomies** •

Burwell Fen: Tuesday, 14–Saturday, 18 August 2018

The atmosphere is tense. My new colleagues are on edge. Preparation prevents panic. And preparation for the day ahead is the focus of our weekly team meeting. I wave goodbye to any hopes of a cheery welcome, rightfully so. Today will not be remembered as my first day as a Wicken Fen ranger, but the day we deal with New Forest Eye. At least, that is what Carol suspects it is; the vet will be able to confirm in a couple of hours.

Over the previous two days, a number of the younger bulls have developed weepy, pinky-red eyes, resembling conjunctivitis. Research points towards the highly contagious disease known as New Forest Eye (or Infectious Bovine Keratorconjunctivitis), one of the most common conditions affecting cattle, but never before encountered in Wicken Fen's free-roaming Highland herd. It is spread by bacteria carried by flies and in dust, both of which have been prevalent in summer 2018's prolonged spell of dry weather. Cattle with this disease can suffer extreme pain. If untreated, it can cause ulceration of the eye and lead to blindness.

Alongside all members of the ranger team, several volunteers are present at the 8.15 a.m. meeting, which promptly evolves into a briefing. Carol, having carefully prepared a list of equipment and roles overnight, speaks calmly and clearly. She gives an overview of the situation and assigns roles. We are warned there will be periods of patient waiting interspersed with episodes of intense activity where we will have to work dynamically and at pace in order to corral the rarely handled herd efficiently. We are encouraged to ask questions and offer ideas throughout the day, but requested to pick appropriate moments.

A cattle crush (or 'squeeze chute') is hitched to the back of the tractor. It is notably wider than the domestic crushes I am familiar with, in order to contain Highland horns. Some of the volunteers hop on bikes and ride 2 miles cross-country to the middle of Burwell Fen. I am assigned the Land Rover, its paintwork thoroughly scratched by the teeth of countless inquisitive, nibbling Koniks. We load hurdle pins, ropes, head collars, shackles, sticks, towels, tarpaulins, buckets, sacks of ready-mixed cattle feed, water for hand-washing and a hefty heap of snacks to fuel the workforce. Happy that everything on the list has been loaded and the trailer is hitched correctly, I hop behind the wheel, turn the key in the ignition and begin a journey almost 8 miles further than the cyclists, to get to the same spot by road. My predecessor, Maddie – who I have a one-week handover with – sits in the passenger seat to give directions, although I know the route well, via good old Toyse Lane. On the journey, Maddie offers helpful tips on how to get the most out of this opportunity to see the herd up close. It will be full on, but ideal for learning lots, a baptism of fire – or, rather, fur and horns!

Carol calls in the cattle. Hands cupped to her mouth, she shouts, 'Come on! Hup-hup-hup!' so loudly it could cut through the rowdiest sports crowd. Hearing her vowelly yodeling from across the fen, cattle begin trotting enthusiastically over. Some of the cows look surprisingly elegant, lifting their legs daintily while holding heads high. The herd has been trained to associate this call – alongside honking of the Land Rover horn – with food. The corral, a relatively small enclosure, is baited with piles of feed (a mixture of flaked barley, sugar beet pellets and cattle nuts). Seasoned adults lead the way, some tossing their horns as they bound eagerly along. The four calves, born in spring, haven't yet got a taste for the food, but run instinctively with their mothers. It is quite a sight to behold. As well as a slight apprehension at how fast they move and how close to us they come, I feel tingling excitement that this is my new job.

Meanwhile, the crush is moved into position at the end of the race (a narrow corridor adjoining the corral, designed for cattle to run along). I am shown a lever that operates the yoke, for securing animals once they are in the crush. Pulled too early, horns can get stuck, causing unwanted stress. Pulled too late, front legs can get caught or the cow can escape too soon. Timing is crucial. Time is also particularly precious in the hot conditions, as the cattle can only be held so long before they may start to overheat. Towels can be soaked with ditchwater and placed on animals' backs to cool them.

A vehicle pulls up by the old corrugated barn. Having travelled from Bressingham in south Norfolk, the vet and her assistant get out and begin filling a bucket with disposable gloves, syringes and needles, plus various antibiotics and sedatives in small glass bottles.

Unbeknown to me at the time, Carol is carefully sorting the order of animals as they are filtered from the corral through a swinging gate into the race, one by one. Understandably, mothers and calves need to stay together to remain calm. Also, certain bulls must be kept apart due to a hierarchy within the herd. Put the wrong two bulls next to each other and a fight can break out in an enclosed space, wreaking havoc and resulting in potential injury. This is why Carol has warned us she may shout instructions for us to follow immediately. If an opportunity presents itself, it must be taken, as it could save a lot of time repositioning individuals. This intuition takes time to develop. So Carol, normally calm and collected, knows she must be clear and concise with instructions for the relevant team members to play their key role at the right moment.

My role is scribe. We need to record which individuals are given antibiotics. Every animal has a tag in each ear with a unique six-digit code, a legal requirement. But dense Highland hair can often hide the numbers on these tags. Every animal also has a name and Maddie knows all of the twenty-six cattle personally. I will also be expected to, in time. So she introduces me to each animal and tells me a handy fact or identification tip as they come through the handling system.

A few females are first, advancing with caution and requiring gentle encouragement into the crush. Their eyes are mostly fine, it is the bulls that have the symptoms. However, one has a weepy eye, a dun cow named Ailie-Belle. The vet takes a good look and confirms that her symptoms indeed look suspiciously like New Forest Eye. We wrap soft ropes around Ailie's horns and hold her head still, while she is held in the yoke. The vet then squirts an antibiotic gel under her eyelids. Ailie thrashes her head in discomfort. Fortunately, the vet manages to get the full dose of thick, creamy liquid into her eye, closing the lid and massaging the gel around the eyeball to spread it over the cornea. I take an instant shine to Ailie and feel sympathy for her condition, sincerely hoping she will make a swift recovery having played a small part in her treatment.

The final step of the process is very important. Before we release her from the crush, we put a big pile of feed under her nose then step back out of her personal space. She tucks into her reward. The hope is, next time we run her through the race, she will associate it with a great big pile of tasty feed, rather than having liquid squirted into her eye. Ensuring cattle have good first experiences of new things is important. If something hurts them, they will be reluctant to repeat it, understandably.

Many of Carol's adopted handling techniques have been inspired by American animal behaviourist Temple Grandin, whose books Maddie recommends to me. Seeing from an animal's viewpoint is the key to humane and effective livestock handling. As a child with autism, Grandin noticed that cattle were calmed by being held in a crush, which inspired her to create the hug machine, a stress-relieving device to calm hypersensitive people. Cattle become less stressed when they are restrained, unable to thrash around. Reading animal behaviour reveals when they are stressed. Something as simple as a shadow or object in their path can worry them, prompting a reaction such as calling out, trying to jump, defecating or merely refusing to walk any further forwards. Cattle will also feel uneasy if they are being made to walk on a slippery surface. Once unsettled, just like a person who has been involved in a traumatic experience, they will need time to calm down.

The design of the race on the fen follows Grandin's designs, who found that curved chutes work better than straight ones. The curve prompts cattle to think they are returning to where they came from, to the herd, rather than going to an unknown place. Curvature also encourages their natural circling behaviour as well as hiding people from view. Indeed, we make sure we stand behind the cattle we are trying to move, rather than blocking their way forward.

As the herd are run through the race, four bulls and another cow are identified with the disease. I can see that a couple of the bulls have more serious symptoms, their eyes having become cloudy. George, a 3-year-old black bull, appears to have a pinky-white spot in the centre of his glazed eye. The vet will have to return at least once for subsequent treatment over the next week.

Some of the males are less cooperative than Ailie-Belle, so they are injected with sedative, making them easier to handle and ensuring a less stressful experience for them. The last bull is the most challenging. Three-year-old Binky is named after the fictional white horse in Terry Pratchett's Discworld book series, due to his quirky coat colouration.[*]

---

[*] Binky was born the year fantasy author Terry Pratchett died. Having been a fan of his work for more than twenty years, Carol wanted to name a fen animal after one of his fictional animals. In 2022, I would name an animal Wight in tenuous tribute to Yes drummer Alan White, of whom I had been a fan for over two decades.

He is the lowest-ranking bull in the herd's hierarchy, possibly due to his appearance or some other difference that the other cattle can sense. Although Binky responds to feed, he will not come to the corral. This is due to his dislike of other cattle in his personal space. He spends a fair bit of his time in the far corner of the fen, avoiding conflict while finding his status. A recent altercation with another bull may well have been how he contracted New Forest Eye.

The vet has now been here a fair few hours and the clock is ticking. There is little hope of leading or pushing Binky all the way to the corral, where most of the herd are lingering. So we load four hurdles onto a trailer and take them over to him. A makeshift pen is erected around the bull. Without the aid of a crush to hold him, he is injected with sedative. We try to push him into a corner to secure his horns and hold his head still. But we have to wait longer for the sedative to kick in. His adrenaline levels are high and he might use his horns to flick the hurdles out of his way.

In the team, we have varying levels of experience, but are united in determination to achieve our goal. Animal welfare is at the forefront of our minds, along with our own safety. With my wedding just eleven days away, I am particularly keen to avoid being punctured by a horn, trapping my fingers between hurdles or generally getting injured in any way.

As Carol had indicated in the morning meeting, there would be moments of frantic activity and periods of patience, holding nerves. We eventually finish work three hours late, exhausted but with a strong sense of accomplishment and relief. Driving home, I reflect on the day, later summarising in my diary how 'the strong team feeling came across, with good organisation, support and recognition'. Thanks to the support of volunteers, we achieved a lot. Having met twenty-six cattle up close and personal in somewhat of a whirlwind, I am keen to get to know them better over the coming weeks.

One week later, the vet makes a third and final visit. Thankfully, the antibiotics have been working. All affected cattle are improving and no new individuals have developed symptoms. Things could have been much worse, especially had we not reacted so promptly. We just have to be prepared that George may not recover full vision in one of his eyes.

Strudel receiving eye treatment, Burwell Fen, 21 August 2018. (Ajay Tegala)

During my five-day handover with her, Maddie shares many tips, experiences and anecdotes. With a deep love for the fen and its livestock, she is clearly sad to see the end of her ranger days, but is very motivated to fulfil her ambition of becoming a secondary school teacher. Helping me identify individual animals, I can see how teaching is something that comes very naturally to her. Mallow is one of the first horses I meet, easily identifiable by a white star on his forehead and a pink stripe on his lower lip. He has a habit of curling his upper lip, exposing gnashers in comedic fashion. While showing teeth can be a sign of aggression, curling back the upper lip helps horses, and cattle, to smell chemicals in the air, pheromones in particular. This is known as the flehmen response, from the German word meaning to bare the upper teeth.

Mallow is one of the more sociable of the horses, actively approaching us. Maddie explains, when a horse comes over and presents their head near to yours, blowing very gently on their nose is like saying hello.

But blow too hard and it will come across as aggression rather than friendliness. She smiles, recounting how horses grazing on water mint have fresh breath. Ever inquisitive, some have learned to undo coat zips. They love to chew on almost anything, from clothing to bikes, vehicles to the aerials of our two-way radios. But, unlike the cattle, they are not motivated by a bucket of feed. So, unlike domestic horses, they cannot easily be given medicine hidden in food.

Walking through the herd of twenty-six horses (there is an equal number of horses and cattle on Burwell Fen at the time), I feel a bit like a plus-one at a party of strangers. Some horses offer a warm greeting, like Mallow, while many are engrossed in their established social groups, or too intent on grazing to take any notice. But, as broadminded as I am, I have never been to a party where defecation or copulation has taken place so overtly!

After completing our Saturday morning check of the Burwell Fen horses, we sit for a minute in the old barn. Last night was Maddie's leaving do, held at the Maid's Head in Wicken. Inevitably, she had been bought several pints of cider, making her feel a little fragile this morning. I offer a restorative banana, which is well received.

Mallow showing his teeth, Burwell Fen, 10 November 2018. (Harry Mitchell)

Burwell Fen: September 2018

Fresh from honeymooning on the Canal du Midi, I settle in to my new working life on the fen. This involves a plethora of tasks, from familiarising myself with the various machinery and equipment in the tractor shed to becoming accustomed with a bundle of keys and the quirks of countless corresponding locks across the reserve. Between learning where all the culverts, potholes and fences in need of fixing are, I spend a few mornings with Carol, getting to know the livestock better and hoping to soak up as much of her knowledge as I possibly can. Having just completed a Master of Philosophy degree in the behaviour of the herds, after almost eight years of work, Carol has a little more time to spare and a wealth of information to share.

Back on Burwell Fen after a fortnight away, I am impressed to see how George's cornea has improved. The affected eye looks brighter and he can evidently see us through it. Thankfully, all of the cattle have recovered well from New Forest Eye, with no further spreading or flareups. The robustness of the herds will become increasingly apparent over my months and years to come. So too will a growing catalogue of animal experiences ranging from the sublime to the hilarious. On our first proper stroll around the fen together, Carol smiles as we chat about breeding biology, assuring me I will soon be talking casually about cow vulvae and stallion scrota!

I meet the fluffy teddy bear calves, born between April and June. Munin is named after one of Odin's ravens[*] because he is the son of a black cow called Raven, Gilliflower is the daughter of Apple and so was named after a variety of the fruit, and Hoolie was born to Gale on a windy day (when it was 'blowin' a hoolie'). The young calves are a little wary of people. Sitting calmly in their vicinity, while having docky, will gradually help them relax around rangers, becoming easier to handle. Carol explains how, of all of the many placement students over the years, everyone attracted to Wicken by the horses invariably goes on to love the cattle just as much, if not more.

---

[*]   In Norse mythology, Munin (Old Norse for 'memory') is one of a pair of ravens. The name appeals to Carol's sense of humour, going on to spell it 'Moo-nin'.

I am looking forward to getting to know both species and already feel increasingly confident around the bulls, following my initial reservations regarding their size and horns. Many people have a wariness of bulls bred into them. Caution is always sensible when in the vicinity of not just bulls, but cows with calves also. As a Wicken ranger checking on the herd, I am able to approach each animal safely, providing I treat them with respect. This, Carol tells me, is key, being considerate when entering their personal space, not intruding on it too hastily, or for too long, and never standing directly in front of them (as they have a blind spot between their widely spaced eyes). To avoid surprising any cattle or horses, we talk to them on approach. Hearing our voices alerts them to our presence, so as not to startle them when we walk gently towards them. We can say anything we like, it is the way in which we speak, move and act that they pick up on, communication through body language. Although they almost certainly recognise the sound of Carol's voice ... and will soon become familiar with mine, too.

We take a look at the four Belles. This bovine quartet was introduced into the herd during the previous December in an effort to add genetic diversity. Being a small, closed herd, there had been concerns of an approaching genetic bottleneck. The patchy white markings on recent bulls, Binky and Socks, are a possible indication of inbreeding. Purchasing four fresh cows, from Lancashire, provided the solution. Their arrival had been greeted with enthusiasm by the Burwell bulls. A few months on, a couple of the Belles are displaying pregnant bulges. Due to the wild nature of the herd, mating dates are not known. Carol explains that a good look at their rears can give a clue whether calving is imminent. 'Flobbiness' is the term she has devised to describe the blancmange-like looseness a cow displays ahead of giving birth, which the cattle do in the field, unassisted. Another clue is swelling of the udders as they fill with milk in preparation to feed a calf. When a cow is about to give birth, she will usually take herself away to a quiet spot. They generally prefer to have their calf alone, in peace, rather than among the herd.

Mindful she has imparted a large amount of ungulate information, Carol gently steers the conversation away from work. I share that Harry and I met in Norfolk and she reveals how she and Gez met Morris dancing. We return to our bikes, left locked by the open-sided old barn. Carol's faithful rescue German Shepherd, Tic-Tac, is sat by the barn, waiting patiently for her. Cycling back to base, I imagine how interesting the coming months will be as I experience all aspects of herd life, from the excitement of birth to the sadness of death.

Baker's Fen: September 2018

Comfrey, like most of the early cows born on Adventurers' Fen, is named after a plant. In her case, a characteristic fenland flower and one of the first plants I learned to identify on Sedge Fen. She is to be the first of the fen's animals I will witness being put humanely to rest. Daily checks have identified a foot problem markedly affecting her mobility, meaning she lags behind the rest of the non-breeding group. The distance between her and the eight others is a clear sign something is wrong, as well as the way she is limping, nodding her head with every step. When stationary, her rigid posture and slightly sad expression indicate discomfort. While the other cattle munch on grass and chew the cud, Comfrey stands stiffly, tensely.

The vet is called out. He examines the foot carefully, treats it with antiseptic spray, dresses it in a sort of boot for protection and gives her an antibiotic injection in the rump. A daily oral treatment for pain and inflammation is prescribed, to be given over the course of the next week. Seeing her getting used to the dressing, I can't help but think she looks sorry for herself.

Being qualified to administer veterinary medicine, Carol is able to give Comfrey further antibiotic rump injections on alternate days and feed her painkillers cunningly hidden in a bucket of feed. Experience gives Carol serious doubts that this treatment will be enough to cure the ageing cow of her affliction. As predicted, a week passes without improvement. Sadly, this means euthanasia is the only option. An equine specialist by training, our new vet has not put a cow to sleep before. And I have not witnessed any large animal being put to rest.

We construct a pen around the cow, using four hurdles first and then removing one to create a triangle, gently squeezing her into a corner. I wonder to myself whether she has any sense of what is about to happen. A lethal dose is injected into the neck, causing her to fall quickly to the ground. All the time acting with respect and dignity, the vet reaches for his stethoscope, nods sombrely to us and gently strokes her coat.

Watching life disappear in a few seconds seems like such a huge thing to me. But I feel reassured that the process is completely humane. The combination of her age and condition meant there would have been no coming back. She lived a great life on the fen, far longer and freer than most cattle. For Carol, there is greater emotion. Comfrey was the fifth calf born on the fen, daughter of Ewan, the original bull. She has known the cow all its life, just over twelve years.

A phrase often gets quoted at Wicken, as it did that day: 'you have livestock, you have dead-stock'. A common saying among those working with animals, often quoted by long-serving late warden Ralph. It may sound blasé, but it is strangely comforting. Death is a fact of life. Of course, it is never a decision taken lightly, even when it is clear cut. Philosophical thoughts fill my mind as I drive the livestock trailer back to base.

Despite our wild-type management, animal carcasses are removed by a licensed contractor, as is the case for all domestic and farmed animals in Britain. There is an argument that our herds are part of the landscape and should remain part of the ecosystem in death – like wild deer, for example – providing food for scavengers from beetles to red kites. However, practical, moral and legal considerations prohibit this approach.

I had decided to assign each of our wedding guests the name of a Wicken animal, on the back of their table place cards. After dinner, one was pulled out of a hat (a cow named Speedwell), and the corresponding guest given a prize. My mother-in-law had been assigned Comfrey. Being a cattle farmer herself, she took it in good humour when I passed on the news that her cow had been put to sleep exactly one month after the wedding.

Burwell Fen: Saturday, 24 November 2018

Ailie-Belle was one of the very first cows I met on the fen. It now looks like she could be the first to calve on my watch. Yesterday, I noticed she had taken herself away from the main herd, which aroused suspicion she might be gearing up towards giving birth. After grabbing my radio and bike from base, I cycle along the Lodes Way to 'Cock-Up' Bridge. Locating the cattle through binoculars,* I make a beeline towards them, wading through the rough grass, burrs clinging to my clothing. As predicted, Ailie is not with the rest of the cattle. Mindful I have a guided walk in a few hours' time, I trek hastily across the fen on my wild cow chase, later recording in my diary what happens next:

> It was a relief to find her relatively easily. I noticed she was a bit bloodied at the back end and looked distinctly slimmer. On closer inspection, she had a tiny red calf in front of her. Carol and Gez sped over in the Land Rover and met me. We managed to get the calf – a male – into the back of the Landy calmly. Carol gave me the tags, thinking I'd done it before, and I went for it. The whole process went smoothly and successfully. Although Gez said the Land Rover was rocking like in some tacky 1970s sitcom.

And so the sixty-fourth calf born on the holding was tagged, albeit a tad askew in my debut attempt. I chose not to record in my diary how my hands were shaking during the process. Punching the tags into the ear of a newborn animal reminds me a bit of firing a rifle. Before pulling the trigger, one should be completely happy they are on target. In terms of a calf's ear, the correct spot is the middle third. Tags too near the tip of the ear can snag more easily. But closer to the head there is thicker cartilage, so the tag may not punch all of the way through and potentially be painful for the animal. Additionally, the veins in the ear are best avoided. Having located the appropriate place

---

* A slightly battered pair – not my prized birdwatching optics, which are too precious to risk being nibbled by curious Koniks.

for the tag, the applicator can be squeezed. I liken the sensation to a cross between using a nutcracker and stapler. The surprise and sensation prompts some calves to thrash around, even call out, whereas others instinctively keep very still and quiet – an early indication of their personality.

I go on to grow in confidence with increased experience, although the excitement of finding newborn animals never dims. Nor does the satisfaction, and relief, of completing a successful tagging. In the field, it can be a somewhat frantic process.

The Land Rover is used for staff safety. Mother is distracted with a heap of feed while calf is scooped up and carefully bundled into the back of the vehicle. The younger the calf, the better. Ailie's calf was still wet with afterbirth, not yet having taken its first steps or had its first colostrum (the nutrient-rich first milk produced after birth).

Not all ear-tagging experiences on the fen are this straightforward, although most are. Calves that have had their first colostrum sometimes have to be walked steadily around the field and tired out before they can be picked up and tagged. Some mothers are more defensive than others. Carol is pleased that Ailie-Belle is apparently good at calving and displayed no aggression towards us during the tagging process. Punching identification tags into both ears is a legal requirement. All cattle in Britain have to be recorded and issued with passports. This is for traceability, to prevent and control disease outbreak.

On the fen, the Highlands display natural behaviour, usually caching their calves for the first few days. This is instinctual, protecting their newborn from predators while they are vulnerable. Staff and volunteers learn to read cow behaviour and appearance. If the mother looks agitated on approach, it is likely her cached calf is somewhere nearby. With a bit of experience, the appearance of udders can indicate whether they have been fed from recently. Within a week, the calf is usually integrated into the herd. If it survives its first seven days – which almost all do – they are given a name.

Being my first calf, I am granted the opportunity to name Ailie's bull. I choose Tyto, from the scientific name for barn owl, *Tyto alba*, because I found one in the grass a few metres away from the newborn calf.

Nineteen days after Ailie gave birth to Tyto, the second Belle calves. Carlie also has a red calf. Her first birth goes well and she behaves very calmly during the ear-tagging. The Belles are looking to be ideal calvers, which is great news. My second tagging attempt goes much better. Knowing what to expect this time, I make sure both halves of each tag are lined up before I squeeze the applicator. We take a moment to examine the anatomy of the calf so I can be fully confident for the future. This one is a heifer (female). Naturally, it is important we record the correct gender of every calf. All births have to be registered with the British Cattle Movement Service within forty-eight hours. I always enjoy registering a new birth on the system as well as recording it in the paper herd log.

A week later, I name the heifer Flame, being red, born twelve days before Christmas and also in memory of my grandad, who passed away the day before she was born – he lived in nearby Burwell for forty-four years of his life.

Carlie is unique among the cattle in that her horns are slightly inward turning, a bit like a halo. As Flame grows up, her horns will turn ever so slightly inward at the ends, a genetic feature inherited from her mother, albeit on a lesser scale. The rough rule is that female Highland horns point upwards, like Harley-Davidson handlebars. In contrast, bull horns curve slightly forwards, enabling them to be used like a weapon during fights with other bulls. As well as defence, horns are needed for thermo-regulation and cooling, contributing to natural biology and immunity. Some of our bulls are identifiable due to chipped ends of their horns.

Ear-tagging is one of a small number of legal and moral obligations the National Trust has in order to comply with welfare legislation. This prevents the Wicken Fen Vision conservation grazing from being fully naturalistic. However, animals are not given supplementary feed – except in very rare circumstances – nor are they treated with worm-ers or antibiotics as standard and are not rounded up regularly or have their hooves trimmed. They are allowed to form their own social groups and, when not limited by space, breed freely. Hooves chip naturally, like those of wild deer. The fen provides them with the food, water and

Highland cow with slightly exaggerated 'handlebar' horns! (Ajay Tegala)

shelter they need, even in winter. However, during prolonged frozen periods, we may have to break ice so that water can be accessed.

We obviously have a duty to prevent any unnecessary suffering, utilising veterinary support where appropriate. Animal health and welfare is extremely important to us. Day-to-day management of the herds involves robust daily welfare checks, looking out for behavioural and physiological clues to an animal's state, with emphasis on breeding animals and known issues. As my experience grows, I take on the monthly conditions checks, monitoring the body and hoof condition of each individual carefully and scoring them out of ten, five being prime condition. Carol meets with the vet each year to undertake a written health report.

Facilitating the most naturalistic behaviour possible is key to our management. Due to the impracticality of microchipping horses kept as wild, we have an exemption from DEFRA.* One of the conditions attached to this derogation is that we record and are able to identify each individual. For every animal, we keep detailed records of their appearance as well as any distinctive behavioural traits. My early weeks on the reserve include many hours spent leafing through the identification guides.

No two horses are the same. A few stand out easily due to white markings on their face, dark patches on their shoulders, or even a pale patch on a hoof. Coat shades range from dark to light, mousy to golden. Some manes hang predominantly to the offside (their right), some on the nearside (their left), or a mixture of both. Forelocks (fringes) may be long or short. Legs have different levels of zebra striping and dorsal stripes vary in thickness. Small, dark spots may be present on one or both cheeks. Another feature are whorls, tiny spirals of hair usually on the forehead, which may be central, slightly higher or lower than the eyes, a little to the left or the right. Some of the horses have whorls on their neck, occasionally in a line of upward feathering. A few have double whorls, either side by side or one above the other. Scars and lumps can also be distinguishing features and some stallions have split nostrils from being in fights. A few of the older individuals even have patches of grey hair on the foreheads, although often concealed by forelocks.

For a selection of Koniks, personality trumps physical features. Percy, for example, is particularly sociable and is usually the first to come over and say hello. His occasional tendency to make friends with visitors contradicts our efforts to keep people away from the herds. Too much human contact can detract from their unique, natural behaviour and interactions with the landscape. We never hand-feed the Koniks for this reason as well as not wanting them to associate people with being fed, which could lead to them pestering visitors and even biting them.

Just like people, some individuals click better than others. While Percy is generally friendly to everyone he meets, other horses may

---

*   The government's Department for Environment, Food and Rural Affairs, responsible for environmental protection, food production, agriculture, fisheries and rural communities in the United Kingdom.

get on better with some staff or volunteers than others. As a regular checker, it is a lovely feeling to earn respect and build relationships. I learn that, just like humans, horses have good days and bad. One of my favourite mares is Cygnus, or Brownie as I affectionately call her due to her dark coat. She often loves a good scratch under her chin, wobbling her lip and wriggling with satisfaction. If I move off too soon, she may follow me a short distance, hoping for more attention, which I find hard to refuse. But, some days, beloved Brownie just wants to carry on grazing and not interact with me, aloof on the hoof. Secretly disappointed at being rejected, especially if I feel in need of a bit of fuss, I console myself that it is actually wonderful to see these animals exercising free will.

I have found the best way to identify a horse is to memorise one key feature that stands out. Learning the lead stallions is most important. That way, if there is a hard-to-identify mare with an issue, the pool of possibilities can be narrowed down by her stallion. Juveniles are notoriously difficult. While young foals usually stay close to their mothers, when they grow up they may leave their natal group.

Watching the herd as one entity is fascinating. They may be grazing or resting together, trotting across the fen or whipped into a frenzy by sparring stallions. This is one of very few herds able to interact freely the way it does, horses actually behaving like horses. Identifying harems and individuals leads to an intimate understanding of the herd. Lead stallions frequently round up their mares, head down, snaking in a circle to keep them tightly together. Otherwise, a plucky younger male may attempt to mount or steal one of his mares.

The sex ratio is fairly even in the herd. While some males form bachelor groups, a few harems contain multiple stallions. One such group contains stallions Boxer and Spod and four mares. Boxer is the lead stallion, but one of the mares is in fact his mother, Wren. So, while Spod may largely be denied the opportunity to mate with most of the Boxer's mares, he almost certainly sires Wren's foals at least!

Being able to point out individuals by name and share a fact about their history or temperament usually impresses visitors and friends. But, again, just like humans, temperaments can sometimes change over time as a result of life experiences. Some mares have become less affectionate in their later years, such as Krieka, whose 'glutton for a bum scratch' days had passed by the time I got to know her. Also like humans, foals may resemble one of their parents in appearance or personality.

The foaling period generally runs from March to May, although early and late foals may occur, often to first-time mothers. One such foal was Talitha, born on 31 July. Being born later means grass nutrient levels are lower, which can affect the richness of a mare's milk and therefore stunt their foal's development. So we gave tiny Talitha extra attention during our daily checks of the herd. Consequently, she became used to human contact, which led to her becoming a bit pushy, craving attention and demanding fuss if she didn't get it.

A young moody mare can be a problem for staff and potentially visitors, running the risk of being bothered or even kicked by petulant youngsters. Carol encouraged us to assert gentle but firm boundaries to avoid Talitha getting too cocky. But the filly then went the other way and became nervous of us. A skittish horse is just as undesirable as a boisterous one when it comes to handling. So we further fine-tuned our behaviour to encourage the most ideal response from Talitha. I found this is a fascinating learning process. It also highlighted the need for all members of the team to demonstrate consistent behaviour towards the animals. We do as much as we can to encourage cattle and horse herd dynamics that are as 'wild' as possible while also relatively easy to handle on the occasions that we have to. This comes back to the original choice of Koniks and Highlands, the combination of hardiness and placidity that both possess.

Fairly quickly, I found my perceptions were changing. I am sure most people, given the opportunity to experience herds interacting with each other and displaying social structures, could not fail to be influenced by such a fascinating insight into animal behaviour. One of my earliest joyful childhood memories is of feeding carrots to the horses and ponies in the stables at the Horseracing Forensic Laboratory* in Newmarket, where my grandad worked as a research chemist. I loved learning the names, sketching their faces, carefully hand-feeding them and occasionally sitting on the backs of what I assumed were happy horses. Of course, they had a high standard of welfare with sufficient exercise, shelter, access to food and water and freedom from fear, distress, discomfort, pain, injury and disease. But domestic horses do not experience the degree of freedom that the Koniks in the Wicken Fen herd do.

Having been lucky enough to grow up around horses, Carol had dreamed of having her own horse to ride. But, having worked with Koniks, watching them interact as family groups, 'being themselves' and acting as a fundamental part of the landscape, she would now find it difficult to have a pet equine. Horses are celebrated in our society, inspiring such an emotional, visceral response to their beauty, elegance and grace. Historically, the horse has done so much for humankind, helping create empires, fight battles, farm land and industrialise. We have such a bond with them. They are important, loved and give us so much. But, Carol asks, 'has anyone considered what we have done for the horse?'

On the fen, horses can be seen actually behaving like horses and cattle being cattle. In the western world, we are conditioned to think about the latter differently, as walking burgers and steaks (although, in other cultures, cattle are considered sacred). The richness of their personalities is often under-appreciated. At Wicken, the Highland cattle are able to develop rich, vibrant social lives. They display generational communities, with grandmothers and aunts helping to look after calves. In both species, the experience of elders benefits the herds, spreading knowledge down the generations and maintaining herd equilibrium. I have found that, looking beyond the surface and challenging my mindset, there is so much to explore.

---

*   Leaders in anti-doping analysis and research, to prevent racehorses from illegal drugging to artificially increase their chances of winning races.

Burwell Fen: Tuesday, 1 January 2019

A third Belle is heavily pregnant as we head into the festive holiday period. I wonder whether Anna-Belle might end up calving at Christmas. Arriving back at work on New Year's Day, I check our grazing diary to see whether Anna has given birth yet. She has not, so, naturally she is my first port of call. I cycle along the Lodes Way to Burwell Fen, accompanied by Harry, who has come along for the day to volunteer and see what my job involves. Searching along the edge of the reeds, we excitedly spot a red cow, Anna, with a newborn red bull calf by her side.

Carol and Gez head straight over in the Land Rover – just as they had done when I found Ailie had calved – and my third ear-tagging follows smoothly. According to my diary, 'Carol said she would be happy I could cope without her next time. A great start to the year.' Being born on the first day of a new calendar year, Harry's mind sets off in search of a fitting name for the calf. He suggests Prospero in the hope of a prosperous new year and kick-starting a Shakespearean naming theme for the 2019-born calves.

Naming themes for the calves, like the foals, had started when annual births first exceeded ten. This year, we are expecting eleven cows to give birth. In fact, we end up with twelve calves, because Anna-Belle calves again in December. The gestation period for a Highland cow is just over nine months, compared to eleven months for the Koniks. Coming into season about every three to four weeks, Anna must have become pregnant in late February, enabling her to produce both the first and last calves of the year. From *The Tempest* to *A Midsummer Night's Dream*, her second calf is a black bull named Bottom. Indeed, red cows can give birth to black calves and vice versa.

For a calf to be black, one of its parents must have the black gene. Red coat colour is recessive to black, which means a red cow and red bull cannot produce a black calf, whereas a black cow and black bull may yield black or red calves. A gene that dilutes red and black coat colour enables red animals to produce blonde (one dilution gene) or white (two dilution genes) calves and black animals to produce dun (one dilution gene) or silver (two dilution genes) calves. A seventh colour of Highland is the brindle, when an animal has streaks of both red and black in its coat.

Burwell Fen: Wednesday, 9 January 2019

When he reached a week old, Prospero was 'officially' named and Wicken's marketing and communications officer Julia* put a feelgood press release out. Two days later, at 8.00 a.m., I meet Ben from Radio Cambridgeshire at the end of Factory Road to chat about Prospero and the role of our Highland cattle on the fen. After recording our conversation, he speeds off in search of sufficient phone signal to send the sound file back to the studio. Meanwhile, I cross 'Cock-Up' Bridge onto Burwell Fen for a distinctly less glamorous task.

Donning a thick winter hat, two fleeces, coat, gloves and over-trousers for added warmth, I trudge across a fen swept by biting wind, alone. Wisely, the Koniks are sheltering in the old barn. Three weeks later, this structurally unsound ruin will be demolished. For now, I am grateful to be out of the wind as I peel off my gloves to grip the wad of empty food bags stuffed into my coat pocket. The herd are close together and moving around, making it a challenge to keep track of individuals. I study their faces, still learning the names of some of the mares.

I also study their other ends, guessing who will be the next to defecate. Strange as it may sound, this is my job for the morning. After a couple of minutes, one of the mares lifts her tail in preparation. Lumps of warm digested grass pop out, forming a steaming pile on the barn floor. I must bag the dung as soon as I can, while it is fresh, before any invertebrates may find it. Because our animals are not treated for parasites, bi-monthly fecal egg counts are conducted to monitor intestinal worm numbers. Stallions often display competitive dunging, leaving their mark on top of another's, resulting in some sizeable heaps, but I must keep individual animals' dung in separate bags.

After sourcing the allotted number of Konik samples, I head back out into the cold wind. The cattle are sat down, resting. While the

---

*   With a Master's degree in Shakespeare and Theatre with the Shakespeare Institute, Julia was very enthusiastic about the year's cattle naming theme!

horses spend about sixteen hours a day grazing, the cattle graze for around eight. Gently, I encourage one of the older cows to stand, by entering her personal space, partly bending my knee and leaning slightly towards her. Bramble responds by slowly rising to her feet and taking a few steps away from me. I back out of her flight zone, having successfully got her up and moving. Rising after a rest and beginning to walk often prompts the cattle to eject what I require from them. By comparison, the Koniks poo beautifully, cleanly, almost with a sense of elegance. But the cattle produce runny pats that sometimes spatter their hind legs. There is a great sense of relief when I have finished bagging the final sample of strong-smelling slop. Time to head to the fridge.

Naturally, we have a separate fridge for dung samples (although owl pellets for dissection frequently find their way into the same space as staff sandwiches!). When time allows, small samples of dung are mixed with solution and dropped onto slides with a pipette. Through a microscope, worm eggs can be counted. After almost two decades of analysis, it was concluded we had sufficient data to show that a worm burden is not a concern for our stock. Despite seasonal fluctuations, the data show no correlation between ill health or poor condition and the number of intestinal worms.

'Never work with children or animals' goes the old show-business adage, because they may behave unpredictably. Animals may behave unpredictably anywhere, at any time. Occasional unexpected moments are to be expected on the fen, but their timing cannot always be foreseen. When we spot the possibility of an incident, we respond accordingly, therefore 'animal adventures' are rare and few. On the whole, the livestock spend their time where they should be, doing what they are supposed to do, mostly grazing. Exceptions to the norm tend to be memorable and inevitably get recorded in my diary. A trio of top 'animal adventures' follow, providing an insight into atypical antics of the mostly placid livestock.

Verrall's Fen: Saturday, 2 March 2019

It is nearly the end of the working day. Cycling back to base along the Lodes Way, a message comes over the two-way radio. 'Chloe to Ajay.' The duty manager informs me of a report she has just received from a visitor. Apparently, there is a pony in the lode with only its head visible. It turns out to be a 2-year-old mare, named after mathematician Ada Lovelace:

> When I arrived on the scene, she was stuck in a muddy, reedy patch on the edge of Verrall's Fen. With no other rangers or volunteers on site, I had to head to Carol's. Her and Gez were in the garden and thankfully free. We loaded up the RTV*, drove down, Carol and I donned dry suits and hopped in beside Ada. We placed soft-but-strong ropes under her belly and sides, then Gez pulled with the RTV, getting her out sideways. Exhausted and shaking, her rear legs had been firmly gripped by the mud. We made wisps from dead vegetation and brushed the water off her legs. Then we had to get her to rejoin the herd. Not far away, but a bit of soft mud lay between her and them. Understandably she was nervous but eventually made it across.

I have a tendency to simplify things in my personal diary entries. Getting ropes around a horse in a cold, reedy ditch is no mean feat, especially when her legs are stuck in the mud. We had to feel our way around the horse, making sure ropes were positioned carefully so that no harm was inflicted when we pulled her out with the RTV. The experience was another important learning curve, as well as a demonstration of effective teamwork and my colleagues' unshakeable dedication to animal welfare.

---

*   Rough Terrain Vehicle (a small, open vehicle with four large wheels – or tracks – used to drive over rough ground).

Guinea Hall Fen: Friday, 19 July 2019

The breeding season is a time when lively behaviour is more likely. Escapees have included one or two tiny calves slipping through small gaps and occasional mares wanting to avoid stallion attention. With enough adrenaline, a mare being bothered can clean jump a 4ft fence.

During my first few summers working with the Koniks, I experience a couple of cases of a horse getting out onto the grassy drove south of Guinea Hall Fen. With a couple of gates along 'the green mile', they can usually be returned fairly quickly when adopting the appropriate fieldcraft. An optimal recovery team will include someone near the gate, ready to close it when required (either when the escapee has walked through, or to prevent any other horses from wandering out). Another person, positioned beyond the gate, can hold up their arms to stop the horse going past it. A third person, behind the horse, can then coax them gently towards the gate. Telepathy and good reading of body language are the magic ingredients.

There is always a strong lure back to the herd. I have never known any of the Koniks to travel far if they have ended up on the wrong side of a fence. They will instinctively stay near the herd. The further away from the herd you have to push them to reach the nearest gate, the harder it will be. So, in some cases, cutting through the fence is our only option, repairing it swiftly afterwards. But what if the boundary a horse has crossed is not a fence, but a river?

Guinea Hall Fen checks with Louise. We were making good progress until we spotted a mare on the opposite side of New River. She was about half a mile from the nearest bridges in both directions. The farmer was contacted to open his gate over the bridge near the old barn. But she wouldn't walk to it, not wanting to leave the herd. The decision was made to get the vet out to sedate her. I stayed and watched for a few hours until the vet arrived. Whilst watching, waiting and anticipating, I found myself literally pulling hairs out of the back of my head.

Mare on wrong side of the river, 19 July 2019. (Ajay Tegala)

The mare in question had a foal back on the other side of the river. This meant there was absolutely no way she could be coaxed half a mile away from it. There also seemed to be no way of encouraging her to cross the river. So a plan was formed to put her in a trailer and drive her back. Due to the nature of the herd, any such movements of our Koniks are usually near impossible without sedation. Unlike the cattle, who will follow food into a trailer, the Koniks are very unlikely to walk into a dark, metal enclosure of their own accord. Pushing them too hard can become a welfare issue, especially if they are already stressed.

'As the RTV arrived with the vet, the mare decided to just cross the river herself, which she did with relative ease, reuniting with her foal.' So we were not charged for any sedative, just the call-out fee and vet's travel time from Bressingham and back. It was a bit embarrassing, but ultimately a relief to have solved the problem, and with minimal additional stress applied to the mare, her foal or the herd.

Burwell Fen: Thursday, 25–Saturday, 27 July 2019

Six days after 'mare crosses river', we are greeted with 'cow jumps fence'. Gale has always been a crafty character. Not one to submit if she isn't in the mood for mating, even if she is in season and her pheromones smell irresistible to all the bulls. Fortunately, like most of our mature cattle, she is a sucker for a bucket of feed. So luring her off the cycle track and back onto the holding is a fairly simple operation. Knocking in extra wooden posts to make the fence stock-proof is quite wearing for place-ment student Josh and I due to the 38°C conditions.*

Next morning, we find Gale has somehow managed to get out on the cycle track again. More fence repairs follow. This time, Josh and I are grateful for a 10° drop in temperature. The following morning – hoping for a quiet day ahead of a week in Dorset filming *Inside the Bat Cave* with the BBC – I find Gale has conquered the fence for a third time in as many days:

> Managed to get her back through the gate on my own. Around midday, there was a call about a Konik out. Alone again, I somehow managed to get her through a gate back onto Guinea Hall Fen. Quite tired at the end of this week.

I was certainly chalking up my animal-handling experiences, whereas Gale was chalking up reasons to be moved out of the breeding herd. Always a feisty and independent character, she was at this time heading into old age. Her efforts to escape were mostly likely driven by a desire to avoid the importunate mating attempts of the younger bulls. This was taken into consideration a few months later, when similar behav-iour was displayed. She was brought temporarily to the peace of the paddock before a more permanent move to the non-breeding herd on Baker's Fen.

You might think she would take the welcome chance to rest, but not Gale. During her first night in the paddock, she tests the perimeter fence and finds a weak spot. Unbeknown to the sleeping residents on nearby Lode Lane, a cow is trampling down the road and behind the cafe. Over the course of the night, dearest Gale manages to trot all of the way over to the far side of Sedge Fen, right by the gate onto Verrall's grazing area.

---

*   That afternoon, at Cambridge Botanic Garden, the country's then highest tem-perature was recorded, 38.7°C. Cambridge would reach 39.9°C three years later.

In a swift recalculation of previous plans, the gate is swung open and Gale joins the trio of non-breeding cattle living in this quiet corner of the fen. She has inadvertently chosen her own destiny, which turns out to be ideal. Over the following few weeks, she improves in condition, her escapades cease and she settles into a comfortable, quiet lifestyle, slowly associating with her new field-mates. Subsequently, there have been no further notable cattle escapes on the reserve for a run of multiple years.

Perhaps my most memorable animal handling experience relates not to cows, but stallions. Back in 2012, the grazing tenancy ended on Burwell Fen, providing the opportunity for Wicken's growing livestock herds to graze a wider area. The National Trust's original plan was to construct a bridge over the lode, allowing animals to move between Adventurers' and Burwell Fens. One thing I have learned working for the Trust is just how expensive building bridges can be. Especially when they are designed for use by cattle and Koniks. With sufficient funding for a bridge not forthcoming, management of the herd was adjusted.

July 2014 saw the creation of a non-breeding herd on Burwell, consisting of a carefully selected group of stallions and their mares from Adventurers' Fen. Vasectomisation was chosen over castration so that males could retain their breeding behaviour. This way, they could still hold harems, hopefully keeping the mares active, instead of becoming lazy and large – and subsequently more likely to develop laminitis.[*]

Alongside the vasectomised stallions on Burwell lives Peat. Burwell's sole gelding, 'Peat the Eat', as he is affectionately referred to, is the porkiest pony on the fen. Each month, when all animals have their condition assessed, Peat consistently scores at the weightier end of the spectrum, but he wears it well. The other males all fluctuate around the mid-point, averaging prime condition, but the mares tend to be a tad chunkier, like Cetti, who comes close to being the female answer to Peat.

---

[*]   Painful inflammation and damage to the tissue between the hoof and underlying pedal bone.

Burwell Fen: Wednesday, 23–Thursday, 24 October 2019

Five years after the first round of vasectomies, the herd of Koniks on Adventurers' Fen had risen to over seventy, with twenty foals born that spring. There was a need to reduce the breeding herd to avoid over-grazing. So, in late October 2019, we set about the task of moving twenty-seven horses and vasectomising ten stallions in two days. An event such as this requires careful preparation with room for flexibility, as the animals inevitably spring surprises and chuck challenges our way.

In the lead-up, vets are booked, volunteers lined up and hurdles collated. All horses to be moved are dotted with animal marker paint for ease of identification. We are moving two intact family groups, so it is important that foals travel with their mothers. The day before the move, I close various field gates on Baker's Fen to shut the herd out of the wetter areas. This will make loading them into our livestock trailer easier, reducing the risk of it getting stuck in soft ground. Numerous trailer journeys will be required between Baker's and Burwell Fens, so we are very grateful to the Environment Agency for allowing us to lower their electric drawbridge over Burwell Lode. This cuts a 4-mile journey down to less than a mile (giving us the rare pleasure of driving over 'Cock-Up' Bridge).

I am stationed on Burwell Fen to receive the horses that Carol rounds up and loads with the help of vet nurse Kat and her tranquiliser darts. Mere minutes into day one, we face our first dilemma. Not to be restricted by the field gates that were closed to limit their range, the herd have somehow crossed a ditch into the very wet part of Baker's Fen we wanted to keep them out of. The 'on-the-hoof' process of encouraging them back to the drier areas unsettles the herd. Not ideal. But luck soon heads our way. Before we really have time to look up, our focused and intense day reaches its end with all planned horses moved, plus two extra from tomorrow's list:

Day two went smoothly. Despite dreaming about them escaping overnight, everything went really well and we got all moves and operations done ahead of time. Great teamwork. An amazing feeling to have achieved what has been weeks in the planning. Always fascinating to have these hands-on days with the animals.

Fascinating indeed, not to mention the eye-watering experience of witnessing ten vasectomies in the middle of a field. I have nothing but respect and admiration for the vets, seeing them working carefully on the stallions. Due to the fiddly nature of the operation, stallions are put under general anaesthetic. Myself and the volunteers help by holding limp legs out of the way while vets Georgie, Eduardo and Sole make their incisions and snips. If we feel any twitches in the legs, we notify Kat, who increases the drip. It may look and feel a bit haphazard, due to being in a field, but the vets are true professionals. Some stallions take longer than others, depending on how much they fight the drugs and how easily accessible their spermatic cords are. Once successfully snipped, I am spellbound as the skin is sewn up skilfully with speed and dexterity. I am also surprised, prompted by the occasion, how openly some of our older male volunteers talk about their own vasectomies!

Each stallion must be kept in its own pen, formed of four hurdles, while the anaesthetic wears off. This is important for their welfare. Stallions, like bulls, will actively exploit perceived weakness or vulnerability in others. Another male's semi-unconsciousness is an

Vets vasectomising a sedated stallion, Burwell Fen, 24 October 2019. (Ajay Tegala)

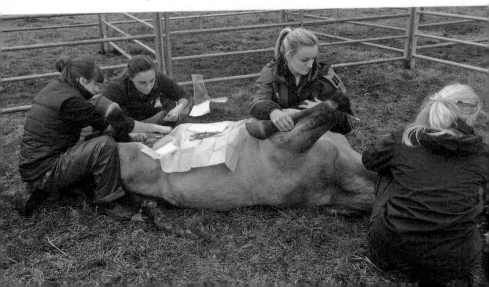

opportunity to even up the status quo (in fairness, females will also get the boot in, given the chance). And such exertion is not advisable just minutes after surgery!

One of the males – named Big Tiny Little after the late American musician – seems determined to pick a fight with Gypsy, three years his senior. Big Tiny is incredibly determined, he just won't give over. We continuously have to keep him away from Gypsy. In contrast to the cool control we have maintained over two days of handling the herd, suddenly the horses are back to being wild. And wild is certainly the word for Big Tiny's behaviour. It feels like he is unstoppable, as if the anaesthetic has transformed him into a completely different character, with twice the energy and self-confidence.

Despite Big Tiny Little's big drama, all ten males heal well, helped by the lack of flies at this time of year. No wounds become infected or reopened. But this does not mean our mission has been accomplished. The nature of moving family groups out of the breeding herd presents two future tasks. Firstly, four of the foals moved are males and will therefore require vasectomising the following year, prior to reaching sexual maturity. Secondly, some of the mares are likely to be pregnant. This doesn't just mean the possibility of more colts, but jealousy from the other mares who haven't set eyes on a foal for several years.

I find it interesting how quickly some of these mares change allegiance when new males appear on the scene. The desire to reproduce is innate. Aware they have not managed to achieve this with their current stallion, some mares decide to try their luck with the fresh meat, unaware these new stallions are also incapable of reproducing. Big Tiny Little, with his sidekick Gulliver, work as a pair to try and steal mares. The duo work well together and manage to form their own harem with admirable persistence – the move to Burwell Fen has certainly revealed Big Tiny's persistent side!

Towards the end of February 2020, the first mare gives birth. Naturally, this provokes a reaction from the established Burwell mares, who haven't seen a foal for half a decade. One of the higher-ranking mares attempts to steal the baby, whipping up the whole herd into a frenzy. Carol has to make like a mare, stealing the foal back and literally shouting at her, 'MINE!' The message is understood. Peace returns and the young filly returns to its biological mother. Fortunately, none of the subsequent seven foals born that spring face the same drama. It is only the first that causes such a stir.

6

Nature Takes Over

• Pandemic • A glimpse of the past •
'Lockdown' life • Corncrake surprise •
A difficult birth • Reopening • Bareback riders •
An evening dip • Selling horses • Cutbacks •
Making hay • Christmas Eve • Selling cattle •
Springwatch • Oakley • Water vole at Judy's Hole •
Invasive non-natives •

London: Saturday, 29 February–Sunday, 1 March 2020

It is not often that a ranger finds themself in a John Lewis store in a work capacity. I have been approached with an opportunity to spend a weekend in the capital to promote a new collaboration between the National Trust and Barbour. Maker of the iconic wax jacket, Barbour was founded a year before the Trust. A portion of the sales from the clothing range they are launching will help fund some of our conservation projects.

Having been one of the 'real models' for the National Trust's collaboration with Cotswold Outdoor the previous year, my name had come up. Debating whether two days of my ranger time can be justified, my line manager John decides it seems such an off-the-wall opportunity that it should be embraced with enthusiasm and good humour.

Good humour is indeed needed, truth be told, as the majority of shoppers on Oxford Street, it turns out, are not particularly interested in attending an in-store ranger talk. However, I am able to have some one-to-one chats. It is hard to quantify the success of a conversation, you may never know whether you have inspired someone to give more thought to conservation. That weekend, I may have inspired someone, or maybe not at all. It feels more like the latter to be honest. But part of the unease I felt that weekend was not so much whether I had wasted my time, but whether it had been worth the risk of being in busy London with all the talk of coronavirus.* I had grown tired of hearing about the quarantined *Diamond Princess* cruise ship on the news every morning, little knowing it was to be more relevant to my life than I imagined.

Wicken Fen: Sunday, 15–Saturday, 21 March 2020

A fortnight after my weekend in London, life back at Wicken was changing. The beauty of keeping a diary is that one can look back at key events and read exactly what they were doing, thinking and how they were feeling.

15.03.20

Spent the last half hour of the work day sanitising computers, telephones, door handles and such. These are the latest measures to reduce virus spread. One wonders what the next week will bring?

18.03.20

Forty-eight hours after the prime minister asked all over-seventies to 'self-isolate' and people to work from home where possible, avoiding 'mass gatherings', and life is quite different. Yesterday, the cafe and visitor centre at Wicken closed. We are still using volunteers for livestock checks, those under seventy and without health concerns.

---

*   At the time, there had been seventeen confirmed cases in England, since the first case four weeks before.

They are heading straight out and texting in their observations. I am just doing all I can to stay clean and healthy so that I can continue to work and check/protect the livestock.

21.03.20

Late in the evening, news filtered through that Wicken will be closed to the public from tomorrow due to high visitor numbers preventing safe social distancing on the boardwalk.

Ouse Valley: Monday, 23 March 2020

Such a surreal day. All National Trust properties are now closed to the public. Last night, Carol messaged to say the new volunteer I inducted last Monday is isolating with 'a sneezy cold'. In case this is the virus, countryside manager Martin wants me to stay at home for seven days, to make sure I have not come down with anything. I am absolutely fine. After seven years of continuous employment without a single sick day, I feel frustrated not being able to go into work but am able to return the following day.

Of course, it is only the five countryside staff who will be working on the fen over the next few weeks (Carol, John, Luke, Martin and myself), all other staff are staying at home. With 110 horses and forty-seven cattle – including up to thirty pregnant females – spaced over 340 hectares, it is essential that rangers are on site for animal welfare reasons. As it happens, we are to have a fair share of difficult births and broken fences to deal with over the following few months. The need to work safely prevents us from travelling together in the same vehicle and requires us to constantly maintain a minimum 2m distance between each other, as well as sanitising all surfaces and tools after use. Despite the unnatural physical distance, a stronger bond develops between us, to the point where we become a bit like a family.

At home on that first Monday, after a few hours of homeworking at my laptop, I get my bicycle out of the garage. In the sunshine, I head over to Welches Dam, following the Old Bedford Barrier Bank towards Welney. 'Lovely to be out in blissful isolation.'

By the Ouse Washes, my first small tortoiseshell and peacock butterflies of the spring bring joy. 'I can hear more skylarks than planes, see more redshank than people and more whooper swans than cars.' And there are only a few whooper swans, most of the wintering population having already set off northwards towards their breeding grounds. As much as our human lives are changing, bird migrations will not be any different this year – although they will share the skies with significantly fewer aeroplanes.

It is comforting to see natural patterns unchanged by the pandemic. Spring continues to spring forth. I am more alive to it than ever, as it dawns on me that this is a privileged glimpse of a world I never dreamed I would see. It feels as if the clock has been turned back to a time before planes, before cars. These Fenland cycle rides are to provide solace in nature (and frequent excuses for arriving late to family video calls!).

24.03.20

Back on Burwell Fen today. Fairly quiet everywhere after the prime minister's address to the nation last night, which has enforced strict ruling on the few reasons to leave home.

31.03.20

Eighth working day in a row. Dropped by Ely Tesco on my way home. Very surreal, queuing to get in, with the two-metre social distancing rules in place. No pasta. Petrol has dropped to £1.04½ pence per litre.

Wicken Fen: April 2020

As the days of 'lockdown' roll into weeks, nature slowly takes over Sedge Fen. With zero footfall on the boardwalk, vegetation grows up between the boards, creating an eerie, post-apocalyptic atmosphere. Carrying out essential duties only, we do not cut the grass, allowing paths and verges to grow wild. Typically brazen muntjac deer develop even greater confidence, spending more time in the open, their barking more audible. Without fear of disturbance, two marsh harrier nests appear a mere stone's throw from the usually busy boardwalk.

Overgrown boardwalk, Sedge Fen, 29 June 2020. (Ajay Tegala)

Skylark nest on Guinea Hall Fen, 29 June 2020. (Ajay Tegala)

Above the visitor centre, I hear snipe drumming for the first time. Such an unearthly sound, created by two outer tail feathers vibrating as the male bird speeds and dives. A lapwing pair nests on Verrall's Fen and goes on to fledge young. I come across two skylark nests in the grass near Guinea Hall. With reduced air pollution, the scent of hawthorn blossom seems more pungent. My nose becomes more sensitive. When occasional cars pass with open windows, I get wafts of perfume, deodorant, shampoo, fabric conditioner, marijuana. With the roads so quiet, it is safe for me to cycle to work, which I first do on Good Friday. By the autumn equinox, I have cycled to work and back seventeen times, totalling 735 miles.

On Burwell Fen, Carol hears a distinctive bird call, like the sound of a coin being rubbed against the fine teeth of a comb. Surely there is only one bird it can be? I head to the spot, near 'Cock-Up' Bridge, and listen eagerly. Sure enough, I hear the unmistakable 'crexing' call of my first corncrake. We knew there had been a reintroduction project

30 miles away, on the Nene Washes,* for several years. But we did not know that birds had been turning up even closer, on the Ouse Washes near Welney. This is probably where the Burwell bird had come from. It was heard calling for more than a week, before eventually moving on, presumably due to the absence of a female to breed with.

Ranger life on the fen may have had its birding highlights – a privilege, considering most of the population were not able to visit nature reserves, unless they lived near one and were able to take daily exercise there – but the livestock management certainly kept us on our toes.

On 1 April, a foal is born on Burwell and seems very unsteady on its feet. Concerned about possible lameness on her nearside rear leg, we keep a close eye on her. Fortunately, after a couple of days, she improves markedly and a vet visit is not required.

The chosen naming theme for foals in 2020 is 1920s jazz musicians and this first filly is named after saxophonist Peggy Gilbert. One week earlier, a newborn colt had rolled into a ditch no fewer than three times while trying to stand. Thankfully, the experience had been character-building, not detrimental, and he went on to become perfectly strong and healthy by the end of his first week. Due to his ditch-rolling experience, the colt was named after Jelly Roll Morton (prompting us all to listen to 'Jelly Roll Blues' at our respective homes after work).

On 18 April we receive our first vet visit during the pandemic. Our grazing diary entry for the previous day describes how 2-year-old cow Gilliflower looks restless and uncomfortable with 'mucus at vulva, possibly gearing up to calve'. While checking the herd next morning, I find her away from the other cattle. Something doesn't seem quite right somehow. She is distressed and has what looks like a calf's leg protruding from her rear. Watching from a distance, I soon suspect the calf is

---

*   The corncrake had become extinct in England, as a breeding species, by the late 1930s. This was due largely to changing farming practices leading to large-scale destruction of hay meadows.

likely to be stillborn. I radio through to base and a phone call is made to the vet. While waiting from them to arrive, I manage to secure Gilli by gently coaxing her onto a culvert over the main drain, closing the gates on either side.

Social distancing proves challenging when you are trying to retrieve a stillborn bull from inside a cow! Concerned for Gilli's welfare, we put all our effort into retrieving the calf. It is hard to get a firm grip and, at the same time, pull with sufficient force. But between us we eventually succeed at our task. The vet gives Gilli an internal examination and fortunately finds no issues. However, we must monitor the cow closely in case of future infection.

Three days later, the vet is back. Not for Gilli, who has made a good recovery, but this time to assist with a stillborn foal. On the whole, stillbirths among our livestock are relatively rare. It's just strange how, in all manner of aspects of life, dramas often cluster. The next morning brings happier happenings on Burwell Fen, with the birth of a healthy heifer. My diary records that Luke and I tagged her in the back of the Hilux (the malfunctioning Land Rover having been confined to the workshop). Scooping up Raven's dun heifer from the grass, I 'didn't realise until afterwards that the calf must have been sat in a patch of nettles'.

While I was spending time outside in the fresh air getting my hands and boots dirty, I did sympathise with those stuck mostly indoors, the heroic healthcare workers and those facing financial difficulties or domestic violence. My neighbours were both working in supermarkets, often facing verbal abuse from customers. On Easter Sunday, Harry and I hid some foil-wrapped chocolate eggs in their front garden, which happily brought them some cheer after the stresses of their work.

Wicken Fen: Monday, 18 May 2020

There is a slight feeling of apprehension about today. After being closed to the public for eight weeks, the car park is opening for thirty-six cars per day so that local residents can visit for pre-booked, socially distanced exercise. Carol, Luke, Martin and I are transitioning our shortened 8 a.m. to 1 p.m. working days to a '9 to 5' routine and are being supported by a small number of visitor welcome staff so that we can continue to focus on livestock and infrastructure. Isabel, Chris, Julia and Kayley return from furlough leave, swapping time in their homes for time in the car park. It is good to see them again.

We are aware the increase in visitors elevates the likelihood of us coming into contact with the virus. But the team continue to take everything in their stride – although daunted about the possibility of redundancy on the horizon – agreeing to be extra vigilant. We wear gloves when opening gates and only cross narrow bridges when no members of the public are on them. I find it frustrating, although not unexpected, how selfish and inconsiderate a small number of visitors can be. But what happens one Friday evening is a complete shock.

Burwell Fen: Friday, 22–Saturday, 23 May 2020

Back in March, we had foreseen the possibility of theft, our tractor shed and workshop being remote and vulnerable. So we increased security, blocking access with bulky felled tree trunks. We also foresaw possible illegal gatherings in our isolated car parks. But we were totally surprised by a report received in late May. A local resident had reported people 'riding the Koniks' on Burwell Fen. It sounded absurd. If true, it was extremely concerning that people were harassing our horses.

The following morning's checks of the herd are extra thorough. Thankfully, the horses appear relaxed, calm and unharmed. All fences and gates are undamaged, with no signs of vandalism, just a pile of discarded empty bottles and snack packets by one gate. Was this someone's idea of fun? Picnicking and riding unbroken ponies in a seemingly remote spot? Concerned this could develop into a regular occurrence, Carol and Gez take an evening dog walk along Burwell Lode-bank to cast an eye over the herd from a safe distance.

To their shock and disbelief, they spot three young men in with the herd and three young women lingering nearby. All three men have goes at leaping on the horses bareback, prompting them to move at speed across the field. Recounting the tale, Carol admits that, despite being very angry, she has a small element of sneaking admiration for their skill. These are clearly people with knowledge and experience of horses, able to sit astride untamed equines. Presumably, it gives them a thrill and, perhaps, impresses the accompanying ladies. But, on their second night, they have been spotted, unnerved. Car registrations have been noted down, although the police cannot really do much. We shudder to think how far this could go.

Upware: Friday, 29 May 2020

Having been angered and deeply concerned by the shameless bareback riding of our Koniks, staff local to Burwell unofficially keep a casual watch on the herd in the evenings. A week after it first occurred, I take an evening trip to Upware with Harry, walking along the lode-bank to check on the horses and at the same time enjoying an evening picnic. This is our first joint journey beyond our home village in almost ten weeks. Harry, working from home, has travelled no further than the farm shop 3½ miles from the house.

With the horses untroubled – there are to be no further disturbances to them – we enjoy the sunshine. It almost feels like being on holiday. At the junction of Reach* and Wicken Lodes, the water is clear and inviting. By the wooden 'cock-up' bridge, I climb into the water. On touching the bottom, my feet sink a couple of inches into the soft, silty bed of the lode, releasing an earthy smell. Dragonflies and damselflies dance overhead as I swim. Shoals of small fish dart away downstream, while

---

*   The section of lode, between the Cam and the point where Burwell and Reach Lodes split, is known to some as Burwell Lode and others as Reach Lode. I tend to favour the latter as it was dug several centuries earlier.

An evening swim in the lode, Upware, 29 May 2020. (Harry Mitchell)

aquatic plants on the surface stick to my shoulders, forming a foliage necklace. Two common terns fly above, emitting their sharp calls. How I adore that sound. One of them dives into the water like an arrow, emerging with a small fish in its bill. After a few minutes of floating, I pull myself back onto the bank, emerging refreshed and invigorated by the glorious wild swim.

Wicken Fen: June–July 2020

With the gradual easing of restrictions, planned Konik moves and sales can now take place after being on hold for several weeks. Early June also sees the arrival of two crew from Silverback Films, who spend almost three weeks filming the breeding herd with state-of-the-art equipment. We are told the footage will form part of a blue chip British wildlife programme to air in about three years' time (this turns out to be the *Wild Isles* series).

In the non-breeding herd, there are four yearling colts to remove, to prevent it becoming a second breeding herd. A local statutory body had expressed an interest in purchasing eight young Koniks and we are now able to arrange the sale and transportation of our four males along with four yearling fillies. The only catch is that they want non-breeding Koniks, to form a 'flying herd' that can be moved around multiple sites in Norfolk. This means castrating the four young stallions before they leave the fen, which had not been possible during the first two months of strict 'lockdown' as it was not deemed essential work.

Summer is not the ideal time to perform such operations, as flies increase infection risk to healing wounds, and all four horses go on to show some level of swelling or weepiness after their operations. However, within a fortnight they have healed enough to travel. It never ceases to impress me how quickly horses can heal. Locally based horse transporters Mel and Maggie do the transportation honours.

July sees four more males transported, this time up to Aberdeenshire. These include one of my favourite horses, Dyson (named after inventor James Dyson, that year's naming theme having been British scientists). A cheeky yet friendly young male, he and I had bonded during my first weeks as a fen ranger. Dyson was one of the first horses I had the opportunity to engage hands-on with.

In order to graze some small, isolated fields near the visitor centre, Carol planned to head-collar train a couple of Koniks so they could be moved easily between each area. The approachable Dyson and his best pal Darwin (named after Charles) seemed to be the best candidates. The process began with a move to the paddocks followed by castration, in autumn 2018. Fortunately, this did not dent Dyson's sociability with the team, nor did it stop his adolescent tendency to push the boundaries! He had a habit of waving a front leg around to gain attention, slightly annoying and potentially painful when standing close to him. So, whenever he displayed this behaviour, backs would be turned and attention halted. We would re-engage with him when he behaved more gently. A smart individual and a thinker, he soon learned. Another part of the training involved introducing the pair to random objects and noises – including wheelbarrows, a vintage rubber horn and even a space-hopper – so that they would not be startled by anything when being led on public tracks between grazing areas. Darwin was wary of new things, but Dyson was ever inquisitive. Ultimately, the pandemic put an end to their training and it made sense to send some of our friendliest horses to a new owner. Even so, I was sad to see Dyson leave, vowing to one day go and visit him in his new home.

More horse moves follow later in the year with five mares going to a Norfolk farmer for his private rewilding project and three individuals heading to Yorkshire. Footage of this trio appears on *Winterwatch*, which sparks the pro-British native horse debate. The National Trust receive a few letters questioning why we do not have British natives grazing on Wicken Fen. All writers are sent polite replies explaining that, after twenty years of experience with Koniks, we have found them to be very well adapted to conservation grazing on the fen. Consultation with vets has affirmed they are the ideal horse species for this specific reserve. We also point out that the majority of National Trust properties with horses do have native equine breeds. Our grazing programme is profoundly different to any other Trust property and we are the only one that has Koniks.

Mid-June sees a return to mowing, which, I confess, makes me feel slightly uncomfortable. I have enjoyed watching nature take over, seeing unmown verges and path-edges brimming with butterflies and buzzing with bees. This undisturbed wildlife seems so right to me that I feel terrible for destroying its habitat. Of course, I understand the need to conserve footpaths, but I have a renewed yearning for greater harmony with nature. Truth be told, I have started to resent seeing people back in the places that have been used solely by wildlife for several weeks (and having to share the roads with a growing number of cars, speeding uncomfortably close as they overtake my bike).

Seeing what I have seen, on a reserve with no visitors, has undeniably demonstrated what a negative impact man has on nature. Our mere presence is enough to stop some birds from nesting, namely the marsh harrier. By July, I am monitoring the two nests on Sedge Fen carefully from the roof of the boardwalk hide. On the 1st, one brood has three confident fliers plus a fourth less agile, while the second nest is less advanced with no sign of any juveniles yet. Martin resists pressure to open the boardwalk, rightfully urging that this will not be possible until all the young harriers are fully fledged.

Next summer, there will be no harriers nesting near the boardwalk. They will be forced to the remoter parts of the reserve with less visitor pressure. But that is the beauty of Wicken Fen, it has just about enough space for both people and wildlife. With an economy needing to rebuild itself through travel and tourism, it is important for people to have access to nature, because with access comes appreciation. And with appreciation comes much-needed support for conservation.

Alongside the uncertainty and worry of isolation came a heightened awareness and appreciation for local nature. More people became bird-watchers, more gardens were made nature-friendly, more naturalists were born. For Wicken Fen to build funds back up, it needed people to support the reserve. At the end of July, an inevitable consultation is launched. It proposes the loss of two and a half ranger days per week, the closure of our gift shop and the complete loss of our learning team. Like many other people across the globe, National Trust staff now face the threat of redundancy.

Loss of the fen's education department would be tragic. Young minds are shaped at Wicken; a pond-dipping session can change a life, exciting someone about weird and wonderful creatures in our natural world. Take away these opportunities to experience nature and our environment faces further threats. Fortunately, staff and volunteers stand up and feed their thoughts back constructively. We are listened to. The learning team are kept, the shop is saved and only one ranger day per week is lost (I am the ranger chosen to take the hit). Additionally, operational budgets are greatly reduced.

Lode Lane: Sunday, 20 September 2020

As a necessary result of limited funds, all spending is controlled tightly. Other than vet visits, we barely buy a single thing for the reserve, gradually using up our supply of posts, staples and wire for fence repairs. Hay has become hard to acquire and is needed for bedding out the livestock trailer, now that we are able to go ahead with horse moves. Just as we had grown salad and vegetables in our respective gardens throughout spring and summer, Carol and Gez set about producing hay using environmentally friendly methods (Tom and Barbara Good* would eat their hearts out!).

After a day's work on the fen, I cycle up Lode Lane to the paddock and hop over the fence into what feels like the nineteenth century. For the last few warm, dry evenings, Carol and Gez have adopted a routine of scything then cider. Hand-cut grass lies in rows, which they are now forking into piles. The next step involves their handmade contraption, an impressive bit of kit constructed from recycled wood resourcefully engineered by Gez. Carol stuffs handfuls of dry grass inside the wooden cuboid. Gez pulls a lever, which slides a square panel to compress the grass inside. This is repeated until a dense bale of hay is formed in the chamber.

The pair now thread orange baler twine carefully between the planks, pulling tight and tying. As they repeat the process, the first bale emerges from the now open end. Next, it is my turn. Repeating what I have observed, useful tips are offered at each stage. A few minutes later, I lift my first bale triumphantly onto the pile. What a feeling, to have produced something useful and sustainable in idyllic surroundings with a carbon footprint of practically zero. My euphoria is shared

---

*   Characters from the 1970s sitcom *The Good Life* who escape the 'rat race' and become self-sufficient.

Carol and Gez making hay, Lode Lane, 20 September 2020. (Ajay Tegala)

by Gez because I have just proved that his invention can be used by another person. The feeling of satisfaction sustains my smile for most of the 22-mile cycle ride home.

Burwell Fen: Thursday, 24 December 2020

Throughout autumn, travel restrictions continue to be lifted slowly. The Wicken Fen cafe reopens and the number of visitors permitted onto Sedge Fen each day increases gradually, following a one-way circuit around the boardwalk. After the October half-term holiday, restrictions have to be increased in response to a growing number of coronavirus cases. So the cafe has to close again. Christmas Eve brings heavy rain, flooding a number of homes in the county and part of the A1. In Wicken, a power outage leads to failure of the sewage pump. The resulting effluent floods around the visitor centre and creeps unnervingly close to the edge of the nature reserve.

Meanwhile, we rangers are busy with Binky, a bull in a bad way on Burwell Fen. With impaired mobility, things are not looking good for him. A provisional vet visit was booked yesterday and confirmed this morning. During my first day on the fen, we had penned him for New Forest Eye treatment. Today, due to unrelated injuries, we pen him again. The vet confirms euthanasia is our only option. Never an easy call to make, but the welfare concerns are crystal clear justification. Minutes later, I drive the livestock trailer back to base. Just like saying goodbye to a friend, many memories come floating to mind. Having such a different coat colour to any other animal on the fen, he received more attention and interest than the rest. Reserve staff and volunteers who didn't work with the livestock would still know Binky if ever they spotted him on the fen, as would many regular visitors, some of them giving him their own names. One such walker was passing that morning and shared our sadness.

Next morning, Carol completes the daily livestock checks before heading home for Christmas dinner. I too am checking cattle, with my father-in-law on the family farm in east Norfolk, fuelled with roasted chestnuts fresh from the Aga (before returning home to the Fens that evening, as per the government ruling).

Wicken Fen: Wednesday, 6 January 2021

The start of the year is slightly stressful on the fen as we navigate our way through a third national 'lockdown'. The first Wednesday of January is somewhat chaotic. My diary records that, starting work for the day at 8 a.m., we are told the fen will be closing. Forty minutes later, a message comes over the two-way radios to say we are actually going to stay open. But, by the end of the day, it has been decided the fen will need to close after all. The team understands there is both pressure to generate income and an important need to be safe and responsible. But we still find the changes tiring, having been through so many over the past ten months. There has been so much hurried roping off – and un-roping, then re-roping – of access paths and seemingly endless rushed printing and positioning of posters and signs.

From the second half of 2020 into 2021, a number of residents from the surrounding towns and villages began visiting Wicken Fen for the first time. I thought it was really great to see a fresh new audience enjoying the place. Seeing people appreciating the reserve always makes me happy. Finding that some of our new audience were unfamiliar with the countryside code, we wanted to encourage a greater understanding, to prevent littering, dog fouling, stock-proof gates being left open and to avoid the chances of visitors clashing with livestock.

While the vast majority of our Koniks and cattle are placid, all have unique personalities and occasionally individuals may be slightly more bold or confident than the rest. For both livestock welfare and visitors' peace of mind, we occasionally choose to move the more spirited animals away from public areas. Any breeding cattle we have even the slightest behavioural concerns about are put on a 'to move' list. For example, Strudel, son of Apple, was a bull all rangers and volunteer checkers felt slightly cautious around. Tyto, who I had a soft spot for (being the first calf I had ear-tagged), also found his way onto the list. Some of the more boisterous bulls, we noticed, came from the same maternal lines. This contributed to a change in our management, introduced in early 2021.

With nine of our ten 2020-born calves being male,[*] the sex ratio had become unbalanced. In order to reduce the number of bulls henceforth, as well as slowing down herd growth, we begin the practice of castration at birth by banding bull calves. This bloodless method of castration is humane and effective, if done correctly. An elasticated band must be fitted on the scrotum, above both testes. If the testicles are retracted, the banding will obviously not have the desired outcome and could cause serious future problems, especially if the urethra (the tube connecting the bladder and genitals) is mistaken for a testis.

My first experience of banding is on a red calf named Canute, son of Carlie-Belle. With some successful bandings now under her belt, Carol offers lyrical advice. It is, she says, 'like trying to feel for two broad beans inside a felt purse'. After a bit of guddling,[**] I locate both 'beans' and manage to secure the band in the desired location (after it pings off the applicator the first couple of times, we learn to dampen the band slightly).

To further decelerate growth of the breeding herd, we move a selection of cattle to new homes over the course of the year. In spring, three cows and their castrated calves (steers) are moved to the Norfolk Broads. A further seven steers are sent there the following June. Most conservation grazing projects prefer non-breeding cattle to intact bulls.

I manage to find a lovely home for one of our young steers, Sugarloaf. A delightful lady named Liz, at Joe-on-the-Donkey Cottage near Saffron Walden, got in touch because she had inherited a retired show cow who she felt needed some company. A few months later, volunteer Hugh and I transport Sugarloaf over to his new home. Six months on, we drive

---

[*]   The Trivers-Willard hypothesis states that parents in good condition bias their offspring sex ratio towards 'the sex with higher variation in reproductive value'. It is possible that good grazing on Burwell Fen resulted in higher bull births. Whereas previously, on Harrison's Farm where grazing was slightly poorer, more heifers were born.

[**] Scottish term for groping with hands, usually to catch fish (rather than testes!).

another young steer to form a Highland trio on Liz's smallholding (Canute is later moved there too), now a regenerative farming project with an agenda of stewardship of the land to increase its biodiversity.

In contrast to a decreasing number of bulls on the reserve, the number of dog owners increases greatly, many of them with puppies that have had minimal socialisation due to 'lockdown' restrictions. Numerous owners are not necessarily mindful of nesting birds, oblivious to the disturbance that can be caused by dogs running free through grass, scrub and wetlands. This is brought to the attention of the nation by *Springwatch* in May 2021. At Wild Ken Hill, one of the remote cameras captures a loose dog running across the freshwater grazing marsh, greatly disturbing breeding avocets with vulnerable chicks.

Wild Ken Hill: Monday, 24 May–Saturday, 12 June 2021

Every once in a while, a great opportunity presents itself. I am over-joyed when my television agent rings to say the BBC Natural History Unit have offered me an interview for a placement position. But this exciting news also presents a dilemma. If successful, I will require three whole months away from Wicken. Timing is unfortunate, with one of the ranger team having just handed in their notice. I would feel guilty leaving the other two rangers to do the work of four. But, if I don't take the opportunity, I will probably regret it for years to come. Confiding in Carol, she agrees neither scenario is ideal, but says I must do what I feel is right for me. It is still a really tough decision, as I know leaving the fen for twelve weeks will make life tough for my colleagues after an already challenging twelve months. And there is the chance I could end up without a job to come back to.

A few weeks later, granted unpaid leave from the National Trust, I head to north-west Norfolk for three weeks on location as part of the *Springwatch* team. Fully immersed in the teamwork of making a live tel-evision series, life is fun, full-on and sometimes surreal. One minute I could be preparing hot drinks for the presenters, and the next I might be talking to the regional television news about the experience of being part of team *Springwatch* at Wild Ken Hill. During the live shows, I might just as likely be helping Lucy Lapwing assemble props as frantically holding up an aerial to secure signal for the outside broadcast. Most of the time, everything is slick and professional, but the nature of making live television from a Norfolk field means there is always the chance of something going wrong.

I always felt a sense of both excitement and relief at 8.59 p.m. as the end credits music plays through my headset, having made it through another show. Sometimes, we would be rewarded with the sight of a dramatic orange sky, other times, we might even spot a spoonbill flying silently by. Most of the crew were staying in a hotel near King's Lynn and, returning there after work, a few of us would head to nearby Dersingham Bog and listen to nightjars churring, occasionally glimpsing their kestrel-like silhouettes.

Minimal time was spent sleeping, as early morning is the best time to go birdwatching. And we had the privilege of an elite kind of birdwatching, facilitated by forty remote cameras, giving us intimate views of nesting species ranging from avocet to buzzard and shelduck to swallow. One of my responsibilities was to monitor these live cameras between 4 a.m. and 2 p.m. over the weekends. Inside a truck parked in the barn, two of us would stare at a big screen onto which the cameras fed. I watched wader chicks hatch, identified the prey items fed by adult raptors to their young and counted how often the parent passerines (songbirds) fed their young, capturing countless clips for potential use in the next show.

It was fascinating and fun but there was also tremendous pressure, needing to secure quality footage of key moments that could happen at any time with little or no notice. Panning and zooming had to be smooth, brightness and colour consistently balanced and the correct cameras had to be recording at the right time (a maximum of ten could record simultaneously). The most eagerly awaited moment was the hatching of the shelduck chicks. Deep in the safety of a former fox den, multiple cameras enabled different views of the hole, ready for their emergence. It was during my last morning shift that the chicks finally appeared. Excitement was matched by genuine fear, as camera positions were tweaked frantically to follow the fluffy black-and-white brood being led across an open field onto the marsh. The satisfaction of seeing our footage in the next show was gargantuan.

As well as gaining live television experience, networking, developing my naturalist skills and forming friendships, another highlight was having access to Ken Hill and gaining an insight into its management. The Buscall family embarked on their Wild Ken Hill project in 2018 to gain greater benefits from their land. Their two principal motivations are to future proof their operations from commercial challenges and to address both the biodiversity and climate crises. To achieve this, their land is classified according to its agricultural productivity potential and its existing level of other benefits, principally for conservation, but also for public value, including carbon sinks.

Like at Knepp, they have ceased the farming of unproductive arable land, allowing natural processes to return, improving biodiversity and sequestering carbon. Rewilding. This is the same land management approach the National Trust has been following on the former farmland surrounding Wicken Fen since 1993.

On the productive arable land at Ken Hill, farming practices have been adjusted to regenerative agriculture. Just like in the rewilding areas, the aim is to sequester carbon and boost biodiversity, as well as repairing soil health and delivering sustainable crop yields using minimal chemical input. This is better for not only biodiversity and the climate, but also quality of food and the long-term sustainability of their farming business.

On a walk around the estate, along with two BBC producers and two fellow *Springwatch* researchers, we are shown some of the practices adopted on the farm. We learn how their weather stations monitor and analyse specific fields to inform when and if fertiliser should be applied. Money has been saved on fungicide by only applying it where and when it is needed, rather than blanket application on a set date. I can really see the business sense in this, as well as the environmental benefits. Being able to demonstrate that environmental wins can also be financial gains is a very powerful message. My in-laws being farmers in the Norfolk Broads, I have first-hand experience of the need to make ends meet as well as the rewards of creating wildflower margins and wader scrapes alongside arable fields.

Another simple technique adopted at Wild Ken Hill is making all fields rectangular, avoiding fiddly little corners and patches under pylons that take time, effort and money to access when they can instead contain wildflower mixes to benefit crop-pollinating insects. I am also impressed by their focus on soil protection. Minimum tillage avoids releasing carbon and destroying soil structure. Using cover crops also protects soil from fertility loss through run-off. I feel inspired by what they are achieving and optimistic seeing them share evidence that farming – producing food – can work hand-in-hand with nature recovery. Thanks to *Springwatch*, Wild Ken Hill was elevated as an ambassador of regenerative farming across Britain and beyond.

I meet lots of new people during my placement. When introducing myself, I invariably mention that I am also a ranger, assuming that most people will have at least heard of world-famous Wicken Fen. But I soon realise that many have not, even big lovers of British wildlife. This is definitely in the back of my mind as I return to ranger life in the second half of June. After twelve weeks away from the fen (except for two visits to catch up with Carol and meet the newborn livestock), I find returning to ranger life relatively easy. There are several things to catch up on but no big surprises. Outside of work, however, this summer is to have a life-changing event in store for me.

Fen View: Monday, 2 August 2021

Harry has wanted a dog since long before we met. I have a real fondness for Labradors but also a few concerns about the practicalities of becoming a dog owner. Harry has been trying to talk me round for quite a while ... and I am running out of excuses!

News has come through that a friend is trying to home the last in a litter of eight Labradors. We have often discussed what we might name a dog, always assuming it would be a 'she'. Mabel, Bluebell, Hazel, Teasel, Bramble. The last two are also names of cows on the fen. But the puppy in question is a 'he'. Tomorrow is my birthday and we have plans, so we agree to meet the 6-week-old pup the day after. Plant and tree names appeal to us. But, looking around the garden for inspiration, everything seems predominantly feminine, like Apple, also a fen cow. 'We need something masculine-sounding. A bit like Oak. But two-syllable names are best.'

'How about Oakley?' I suggest, thinking of my third great-grandfather, Edwin Oakley. Perfect. A two-syllable name, not too common but not too unusual or difficult to pronounce. And also a tree linked with the National Trust. When we meet the puppy, it is love at first sight. Eleven incredibly long days later, we bring Oakley home and training begins. Determined to mould an ambassador to other dogs visiting nature reserves, the pressure is on. But it is a labour of love and we are lucky that he is calm and good-natured, as well as inquisitive and sometimes cheeky. Privileged in being able to bring him to work with me occasionally, Oakley lives the life of a fen hound without contradicting my conservationist values.

Judy's Hole: 20 June 2022

Just a few weeks before I became a dog owner, the third national 'lockdown' officially ended on 18 July 2021. Some eleven months later, the virus finds its way to our household. With only mild symptoms, I do as much work as I am able to from home. Four consecutive days of negative lateral flow tests are required before I can reintegrate with my colleagues. So I do livestock checks remotely, travelling directly to Adventurers' Fen, then straight back home afterwards, just like I had done on 24 March 2020 at the very beginning of the pandemic.

The Summer Solstice Eve is a gorgeous day. Heading back along Factory Road, I feel drawn to pull over by Ash Bridge. Remembering my first visit to this special spot some two decades ago, I take a brisk stroll beside the stream to Judy's Hole. The bank by Folly Bridge is thick with tall grass, nettles and docks. Beyond it, the shallow river water is clear. I gaze at it a while before thinking about walking back to the car. A small, brown mammal catches the corner of my eye. I stay still and keep quiet. It doesn't notice me and continues to go about its business, which involves slipping into the stream with a characteristic plop and swimming across. Keeping its back and the top of its head above the surface, the water vole paddles away, long dark tail held straight and trailing just beneath the water. This intimate view of a charismatic rodent makes my day.

Throughout the 1990s, Britain's water vole population fell by almost 90 per cent. This rapid decline was due to the spread of American mink, which make easy meals of them. Not having co-evolved with mink, they have no strategies to avoid them. The voles were not helped by the canalisation of so many of the nation's river networks. With so little river-edge habitat, mink did not have to search far to find voles. Long-serving Wicken Fen visitor operations and experiences manager Isabel[*] remembers how, in the late 1990s and early 2000s, visitors to the fen would often be delighted to spot what they thought was an otter.[**] In actual fact, it was mink they had seen.

American mink were brought to the country for their fur, with escapees going on to thrive in the British countryside, reproducing prolifically. In 2003, the Norfolk Mink Project was set up to stop them

---

[*]   Isabel is Wicken Fen's longest-serving member of staff since the Barnes brothers, having worked over twenty-five consecutive years.

[**]   Otters returned to Wicken Fen in 1998.

causing water vole decline. The project has expanded over time, with Waterlife Recovery East striving for a mink-free East Anglia. Their definition of eradication success is a twelve-month period without evidence of breeding mink within a 3,000-square-mile area.

Inquisitive by nature, American mink cannot resist exploring covered spaces and climbing onto floating objects. Taking advantage of this, the Game and Wildlife Conservation Trust invented a method of live trapping comprising of a raft with a tunnel on top, containing a cage trap. Should a non-target species enter the trap, it can be released unharmed. Thanks to the development of trap alarms, instant electronic notifications can be sent – by text message or email – whenever a trap door closes. I helped locate four traps across Wicken, Adventurers' and Burwell Fens (baited with mink pheromones as an additional lure). Encouragingly, a lack of activity points to an absence of mink on the reserve.

A much harder to eradicate invasive, non-native species is *Crassula helmsii*, also known as New Zealand Pigmyweed. This Australasian aquatic plant can form dense mats on the margins and surfaces of ponds, shading out native plants. Since arriving in England in the mid-1950s, it has spread into every county. And it is present across the wider Wicken Fen nature reserve. Cleaning footwear can reduce the chances of accidental transfer between sites. However, it can also stick to birds' legs. On some localised spots, the weed can be uprooted or covered to block the sunlight it needs to survive.

On Burwell and Baker's Fens, the parts of the reserve where crassula is most abundant, fluctuating water levels throughout the year help reduce it spreading. The change in growing conditions, between winter inundation and summer exposure, seems to prevent it from thriving. Fortunately, this seems to be enough to stop it outcompeting important fen flora. Interestingly, the livestock have no interest in grazing it.

Aerial view of Wicken Fen and Adventurers' Fen, 16 April 2023. (Simon Stirrup)

Burwell Fen, 9 April 1933. (E.A.R. Ennion)

Pair of common cranes over Wicken Fen, 28 March 2013. (© Richard Nicoll)

Bittern, Adventurers' Fen, 17 May 2015. (© Richard Nicoll)

Male and female marsh harrier above Wicken Fen, 22 April 2019. (© Richard Nicoll)

Male hen harriers squabbling, Sedge Fen, 25 January 2016. (© Richard Nicoll)

Reed warbler tending to 16-day-old cuckoo chick, Wicken Lode, 24 July 2013. (© Richard Nicoll)

Newly fledged cuckoo with wing and tail feathers still growing. It characteristically waves one wing as its reed warbler host arrives to feed it with a common darter dragonfly. Reach Lode, 30 June 2014. (James McCallum)

Male emperor dragonfly perched on a reed stem, 5 July 2012. (© Richard Nicoll)

Swallowtails collected on Wicken Fen, June 1916.
(Oxford University Museum of Natural History)

Clockwise from top left: Glow-worm, Sedge Fen, 23 June 2023. (Simon Stirrup); Grass snake on the fen, September 2006. (Carol Laidlaw); Orchids on Sedge Fen, 22 June 2020. (National Trust Images/Mike Selby); Ragged-robin, Sedge Fen, 28 May 2006. (Carol Laidlaw)

Clockwise from top left: Old Tower Hide, Sedge Fen, 20 January 2019. (National Trust Images/ Mike Selby); Norman's Mill, Sedge Fen, 13 December 2022. (Kate Amann, 'Fen Photographer'); Humpback 'cock-up' bridge over Wicken Lode, 23 July 2019. (National Trust Images/Mike Selby)

Cattle and Koniks on Verrall's Fen. (Joss Goodchild)

Koniks herd on Guinea Hall Fen, 7 June 2022. (National Trust Images/Mike Selby)

Koniks interacting. (Joss Goodchild)

Napia with newborn foal, Guinea Hall Fen, 5 April 2023. (Simon Stirrup)

Clockwise from above: Highland cattle on Baker's Fen, 9 November 2007. (Carol Laidlaw); Ear-tagging Cordelia, Burwell Fen, 9 November 2019. (National Trust Images/Mike Selby); Giving Toby a scratch under the chin, Burwell Fen, 18 August 2019. (Harry Mitchell)

Clockwise from top left: Dyson aged just under 3 years, Guinea Hall Fen, 4 May 2020. (Ajay Tegala); Flame aged 21 months, Burwell Fen, 30 September 2020. (Ajay Tegala); Carol with a selection of Highland bulls, Harrison's Farm, 17 March 2021. (Mike Selby)

Oakley's first visit to Wicken Fen, 16 September 2021. (Rick Johnson)

Rangers Carol, Dan, John and I reenacting a 1950s sedge harvest, 4 July 2022. (Mike Selby)

Above: Filming *The Wild Life* with Ade Adepitan, 20 February 2023. (National Trust Images/ Paul Harris). Watch online at: www.youtube.com/watch?v=r_bbzNmHFVI.
Below: Carol with Tim, Verrall's Fen, 22 March 2023. (National Trust Images/Mike Selby)

Early morning at 'Cock-Up' Bridge, Burwell Fen. (Di Cope)

Sunrise over Monks' Lode, 20 January 2024. (Kate Amann, 'Fen Photographer')

Sunset, Wicken Fen. (Di Cope)

Aurora Borealis over Norman's Mill, 27 February 2023. (Kate Amann, 'Fen Photographer')

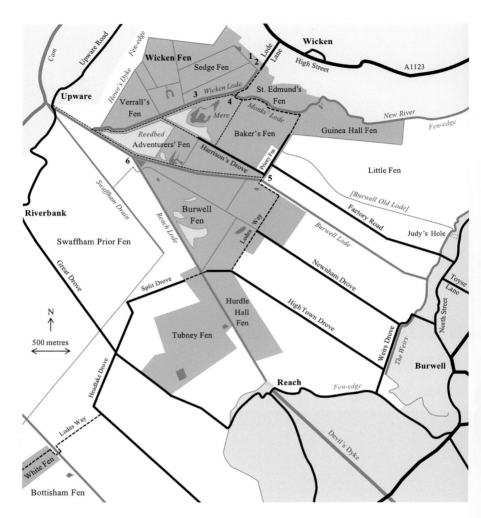

Map of Wicken Fen and Burwell Fen with selected place names. (Ajay Tegala)

1. Norman's Mill
2. Visitor Centre
3. Old Tower Hide
4. Norman's Bridge
5. 'Cock-Up' Bridge
6. Pout Hall Corner

Wetland Management

Baker's Fen: Tuesday, 15 November 2022

A fountain of frothy white water rises. Last week, the ditch was murky and lifeless, just a shallow layer of grey liquid lying on top of rank-smelling earth. Now, it sparkles and flows. Rangers rejoice. On Sunday, Carol turned the key and grinned when she heard the crashing sound that followed. Water – rising from the Newmarket chalk hills and flowing north-westerly along a 6-mile stream named the New River – spills freely from the 6in pipe. It seeps into ditches and drains, travelling across the fen like lifeblood through its veins. Turning on the Baker's Fen water is a milestone in the ranger calendar.

The ponds and scrapes have been dry for almost six months, mud having baked and cracked in the summer heat. An abstraction licence from the Environment Agency permits 120,000 cubic metres of river water to be taken between 1 November and 31 March each year. We always save a portion of that quota for the last week of March in an effort to keep the scrapes wet throughout spring. It seldom lasts to the end of summer; an array of fast-growing plants drink it up, the sun dries it out and relentless wind accelerates evaporation.

Returning after four days away, I know what to expect. But that does not dent the joy one bit. Oakley and I cross Norman's Bridge, over Monks' Lode,* then turn left. Through the trees, I glimpse the shining silver of standing water on Baker's Fen. A few footsteps further and my ears detect the whistling of wigeon. These ducks breed in Iceland, Scandinavia and Russia, migrating to Britain for its milder winters. Extending from their grey bodies, the chestnut heads of the drakes stand out, with their golden-yellow crowns. Looking through binoculars, I scan left to right. Around the tussocks of rush, more and more can be picked out. Block counting, I hope for a hundred. There must be over three hundred, alongside scores of mallard, the green heads of the drakes almost upstaging the wigeon. But not quite. A six-month absence makes wigeon the more special.

There have been wigeon in other parts of the county for a few weeks already. But they only come to Baker's Fen when there is water. Turn on the tap and they come. Literally overnight. Like magic ... although, really, it is quite simple. The more wetland habitat the fen can provide, the more wildfowl, waders and other waterbirds it can host. Not so long ago, until 1993, Baker's Fen was arable farmland, part of Priory Farm. Unlike ancient woodlands and rainforest, it can take just a few years to create new wetlands. Restoring drained peat to hold water as it should, however, takes a bit longer. Former countryside manager Martin described the first few years of re-wetting Baker's Fen as creating a peaty 'soup' that the water just flowed through, rather than being absorbed.

---

*   Named after the monks of Fordham Abbey, who did much banking in Medieval times.

Winter water and wigeon on Baker's Fen, 6 February 2020. (Ajay Tegala)

Swaffham Prior Fen: Tuesday, 15 November 2022

Oakley leads the way. He has not been to this part of the reserve yet, but knows to follow the long, straight track. He spots a selection of sticks at the base of a hawthorn and field maple hedgerow. Layered in waterproofs with my hood up, I am managing to stay mostly dry despite the driving rain. But it is becoming sweltering under all these layers in the mild, 12°C conditions. Choosing the appropriate number of layers is a careful choice and usually needs altering multiple times throughout the ranger's day.

'All right then, we can play fetch.' I toss Oakley's chosen stick into the air. Not my best throw, it veers off-piste and crashes through the middle of the hedge. He dives straight in. Five seconds later, he emerges, stick in mouth. 'Well done, boy.' I put him on a lead as we push through the kissing gate. A tenant farmer's sheep are grazing in this field. The grass looks richer now than it did all summer. We brush past some spindly blackthorn, heading to the water control point. I lift the upturned bucket and begin to attach the water meter, which I have lugged with me along the track, following its service and calibration. 'Balls!' The wide selection of Allen keys stuffed in my coat pocket are all redundant. I should have brought sockets and spanners, the bolts are too tight to undo with fingers. Turning on the Tubney Fen water will have to wait until tomorrow.

Tubney Fen, a 101-hectare former turf farm* west of the small village of Reach, was purchased by the National Trust in 2005. I have to admit, Tubney took a bit of time to grow on me, seemingly less beautiful or interesting than other parts of the reserve. Most of my work there seemed to involve repairing fences (to keep the tenant farmers' cattle and sheep contained), pulling ragwort and topping thistles (to prevent seed spreading onto neighbouring land). It just felt like a few grassy, weedy fields with little to get excited about. The mere is pleasant enough and attracts a respectable selection of water birds. During a lunch break, from the hide I could watch little grebes diving beneath the surface, trying to predict where precisely they would pop back up. One summer afternoon, I spotted fluffy lapwing chicks, blending in with the mud when they kept still. And on a spring morning during 'lockdown', a sound like jangling keys could be heard, the call of a corn bunting.

But it was the winter wetland management that finally ignited my excitement. An old irrigation system for filling livestock drinking troughs was adapted to top up the mere and create other areas of standing water. There is something very satisfying about choosing where to add water, watching it flow and then seeing wildlife benefit from your action.

Simple as that may sound, every element of management involves a level of logistical planning. Sometimes you find yourself a lone ranger, as was the case when I once had to move ten long pipes across Tubney Fen to fill up a low area in the northern field. To transport these 6m aluminium pipes, I wound down both front windows of the Hilux and popped two through at a time. I then squeezed in behind them and drove carefully, every rut causing them to bounce around and clatter, bumping my elbows as I steered.

*   Turf as in grass for lawns, rather than peat for digging, drying and burning. However, it was used for the latter before the former.

I achieved my goal. Returning a few days later, an oasis had formed, drawing in dozens of wigeon, a few greylag geese, some black-headed gulls and seven little egrets. With this bustle of birds benefiting from the standing water, I saw the place in a different light. Nature was returning and taking hold, thanks to a gentle nudge from us. Any area can become a haven for wildlife with the right ingredients.

I load Oakley into the back of the Land Rover. We travel slowly along the bumpy back roads, from the open-edged Split Drove on to Headlake Drove with its hedgerows on either side. A flock of medium-sized birds emerges from the cover on the western edge, flying over the road into the eastern hedge. A glimpse of grey rumps contrasting with dark tails confirms these are fieldfares. I wind down the window and listen to their chattering calls. A winter visitor from Scandinavia, they have flown over 800 miles to get here to gorge on berries and apples.

Ding, ding, ding. Mobile phone reception improves and a string of messages come through on our ranger work chat. These include a report of the first dead swan of the autumn followed by the latest Avian Influenza guidance from DEFRA. It turns out we only need to report dead swans if we find three or more. This winter, we will find just two – much to my relief, fearing wildfowl decimation on a scale similar to the gannets and Sandwich terns in seabird colonies over the summer.

My next stop is White Fen. This 20-acre strip of former farmland was acquired by the National Trust in 2008 to facilitate a national cycle route through the Wicken Fen Vision area to the neighbouring property of Anglesey Abbey and on to Cambridge. The underlying geology here is not peat and the surrounding land is farmed intensively, so it was decided White Fen would be an appropriate place to plant a community woodland (led by John during his early warden days). The survival rate of the trees was much higher than expected, forming dense cover. Somehow, a sea buckthorn was planted and flourished, its bright orange berries outshining its neighbouring red haws and dark purple sloes.

Oakley is having a great day, this is his third walk of the morning. The current stick of choice is a spindly length of willow. He trots along gleefully as I inspect the recent extension to the woodland, on the southern edge. In 2021, the National Trust launched its Blossom Together initiative and team Wicken discovered we were eligible for central funding to buy trees, guards and tools. Our proposal was given the green light to make White Fen greener.

Naturally, the tree planting was a great opportunity for community involvement and associated social media. We are careful with the content, tone and wording of all our online posts, but had not foreseen some people would see 'Wicken Fen' and 'tree planting' in the same sentence and wonder why on earth we were planting trees on prime peatland (considered detrimental to the valuable peat, trees compromising hydrology and actually storing less carbon than the soil). Of course, we were not. We spend hours every winter removing trees and scrub from the ancient fen to conserve it. But we relished the opportunity to create a patch of blossoming trees in an appropriate location.

Back in the Landy, the hound and I return to base, bumping along Headlake Drove. Ranger John Hughes calls it Headache Drove because it is so uneven to drive on. Beneath the road, peat expands and contracts, creating dips, bumps and cracks in the tarmac. At a staggered crossroads, a section of the drove heads vaguely east towards Reach. John calls the first 500m of this drove 'the worst bit of road in Cambridgeshire' due to a dense succession of massive dips. Speed along here in a car and it could easily end up a write-off.

John is a Cambridge man who started volunteering at Wicken in 2006. This led to a seasonal warden contract in the following year, alongside Gemma, who became his girlfriend that summer. The pair were married a few years later. John has got to know every corner of the fen and come to understand the little quirks and tricks that can save time or get you out of a muddle. Like all of the team, he is no stranger to the occasional 'tractor in a ditch' episode, which has become a ranger rite of passage. Ever diplomatic and pragmatic, if a vehicle does get damaged or stuck, John will know what to do or who best to call. After his family and the fen, Cambridge United Football Club is John's great passion.

West of the 'worst road in Cambridgeshire', Great Drove heads through Swaffham Prior Fen to the hamlet of Riverbank, made up of just six households, including two farms and an old chapel. Trees have been planted along the sides of the road to form a windbreak. However, their roots suck water out of the peat, worsening the condition of the road. Allegedly, some of these dips contain tarmac almost a metre thick due to repeated resurfacing efforts.

Although these droves may seem treacherous, they are nothing compared to what they were like in the nineteenth century. In *The Fenman's World*, Charles Lucas describes the dangers of travelling these routes by horse and trap. He recounts how the unguarded drains on either side of the droves 'gave rise to some anxious moments to those traversing the way by night'. Because 'everything was black', deviation from the centre of the 40ft-wide droves could easily lead to 'getting suddenly landed in the drain'. This would mean waiting until daylight for assistance as 'it was next to impossible to pull the horse or trap out of the water without ropes and men'.

Deep wheel ruts held water during winter, making travel by trap 'perilous' and so 'everyone rode on horseback if possible'. Lucas recounts accompanying the messenger 'who rode a typical Fen horse, suitable for Fen work'. The messenger's horse tripped, throwing its rider 'with a splosh right into the middle of the river'. He pulled himself out of the water, 'remounted his nag, and rode off again with vigour ... before we reached our destination, he had not a wet thread on him'.

Another anecdote shared in his book tells how 'a short way from the Manure Factory' his horse 'suddenly sank into the earth up to the girths'. Fortunately, the mare 'very cleverly negotiated the difficulty' and managed to land him safely on terra firma. He concludes that 'a pre-Fen water-course must have crossed the Drove at this point'. Knowing the location of a palaeochannel that crosses Factory Road, I am confident I know the exact place to which he must have been referring. From certain angles and in aerial photographs, a wide, shallow depression is visible across Little Fen and there is a subtle dip in the tarmac road. I often think of Lucas and his horse when I pass along this particular part of the drove, as I certainly did one February morning after a particularly rainy few days.

Little Fen: Saturday, 13 February 2021

It is my weekend as duty ranger. This means keeping check on the reserve and being on site should any issues arise. It is a sunny Saturday with blue sky, a change from the recent deluge of rain and smattering of short-lived snow showers. But there is still standing water in some farmers' fields. I drive along Factory Road in the Hilux, feeling cheerful.

About halfway along the drove, it pays to decelerate as the surface becomes progressively uneven. It then narrows to become a single-track road. I can see water in the field to the right. It is lying in the palaeochannel. Many centuries have passed since it was an active watercourse, but the subtle topography has remained. This dormant river has filled up with rainwater to recreate history. The farmer, I notice, has hand-dug a grip to drain the standing water from his field. He must have been somewhat disgruntled. In contrast, I feel privileged to have a rare glimpse of the past.

Palaeochannel after heavy rain, 13 February 2021. (Ajay Tegala)

Adventurers' Fen: Thursday, 17 November 2022

Kitted out in wellies, waterproof trousers and overcoats, long-serving volunteer John B, relatively recent ranger Dan and I bundle into the RTV. I steer along the grassy track beside the Lodes Way, crossing Norman's Bridge. The track drops down the lode-bank and runs beside it. This section becomes notoriously wet and sticky after autumn rain. I daringly leave the RTV in two-wheel-drive and we slide through the mud, emerging on the firmer ground unscathed.

I decide not to drive on to Baker's Fen and stick to the track beside the lode-bank. Surveying the fen as we drive alongside it, we see how wet it has become in the four days since the water was turned on. Around the corner, we approach the maltings, a historic name relating to two ponds dug about a century ago, presumably to soak grain in.

'Hello Poppy.' I alert my passengers to the red Highland cow poking her head over the stock fencing. We certainly chose the right route. Our first job is to check the livestock and the seven cattle are hidden in the scrub around the maltings. We probably would have missed them had we followed the main route through the middle of Guinea Hall Fen. The second leg of our journey takes us on to the subtly higher part of that track, in our search for eighty horses.

The ruined remains of Guinea Hall Farm are frequented by the herd, especially when seeking shelter. Next to a large horse chestnut tree, two sides of the old farmhouse still stand, surrounded by debris from the fallen walls. I find the pale bricks particularly attractive (and have even gathered a few, with permission, to arrange around our garden pond at home). Known as Burwell Whites,* the bricks were produced from clay dug and fired in the old factory just half a mile away. Parts of the building were also constructed from clunch,** a chalky limestone rock

---

*   Produced until 1971, many local buildings were made with Burwell brick and also Sir Winston Churchill's underground wartime offices in Whitehall, London.

**   Clunch was used in eastern England and Normandy when stronger building materials were not available.

mined locally. The Koniks like to lick, crunch and munch on the clunch. It provides them with minerals and microbes beneficial to digestion, forming a small part of their balanced diet, alongside the vegetation they graze on. Chewing the chalky clunch sometimes gives them the amusing appearance of wearing pale grey lipstick.

A stone's throw from the ruins stand two 25 sq m enclosures, protected by 2m-high deer fencing. They were erected immediately prior to livestock arriving on the fen, serving as control plots to monitor the impact of grazing on plant diversity. Indeed, they have proved that grazing increases diversity. Because our animals are not wormed, their dung is free of chemical residues and can therefore support a great number of invertebrates and fungi. A survey recorded 120 species of beetle associated with dung on the fen, with dozens of specimens in each pile. This does not happen when animals are treated regularly with wormers. Our animals also spread seeds in their dung – some species are able to survive twelve days in a horse's stomach – helping important plants to recolonise the former intensively farmed land.

Despite being within 50m of each other, the eastern enclosure is full of dense hawthorn bushes, yet the western one contains no scrub at all. The underlying geology is identical and yet these two neighbouring plots look so extraordinarily different, proving that experiments don't always produce the results you expect. A theory is that the grass grew quicker in the western enclosure, shading out any hawthorn seedlings before they could establish themselves. But why did the grass grow faster in the western enclosure? Was this flourishing of growth just a random coincidence? Sometimes nature acts in ways we are not able to control or explain. This is one of my fascinations with rewilding, seeing natural processes follow their own course, sometimes in ways we do not fully understand.

Opposite: Knocking in a fence post with John B, Burwell Fen, 14 February 2019. (Luke Underwood)

The enclosure fences have fallen inwards in places, several wooden posts having rotted, some snapping when livestock have scratched against them. We had recently done some 'godfathering', knocking in new posts in an admittedly botched effort to hold the fence up. It is functional, for the time being at least. There are miles and miles of fences on the fen and hundreds of wooden fence posts, all slowly rotting at varying rates. With a limited supply of replacement posts, the perimeter fences are given highest priority along with gateposts, which have a habit of shifting. Consequently, gates frequently have to be tinkered with to ensure they self-close and remain stock-proof.

During the interwar years, there were orchards on Guinea Hall Fen. Apples were harvested and taken to a nearby cold store along First Drove, located halfway along the railway siding that connected Burwell's brick factory to the main Ely–Newmarket line. The fruit trees were all cleared during the Second World War in order to grow crops, which were considered more valuable. The farm was never connected to mains power and was only accessible by off-road vehicles. I once led a guided walk for Burwell Women's Institute and among the group was Mary, who had grown up in the neighbouring dwelling to Guinea Hall, Hundred Acre Farm. She shared memories of summer swims in the river and cycling 3 miles on bumpy tracks to get to school in the village. During winter, bicycle tyres would become caked in thick clay, while walking back from school was a long trek, sometimes arriving home in darkness.

There they are. Eighty horses, all spaced into their respective groups, their coats dampened dark by the rain, blending in well with their surroundings. They are resting. It is their quiet time of year, the breeding season long since over. All have been in good shape for several weeks now, no injuries inflicted between jostling stallions. The herd is calmly dozing, post-graze, enabling a careful head count to make sure all are present. They are.

It is 8°C but feels much cooler as we drive into the west-south-westerly wind, rain coming in from the open sides of the RTV. I tense my shoulders and tuck in my neck, only moving my hands and wrists to steer the wheel. Winter will get far colder than this, but autumn has been so warm, reaching 20°C as late as Hallowe'en.

John and Dan hop out to unlock and open a succession of field gates as we head north-west to Lapwing. This compartment is named after Lapwing Farm,* one of a small number of nineteenth-century dwellings long since gone in all but name. Others include Pout Hall, at the junction of Burwell and Reach Lodes, which allegedly 'collapsed into a jungle of nettles' around 1900, and the ironically named Ragamore Castle. The latter stood on Baker's Fen near Monks' Lode and was still inhabited during the Second World War.

I hop out of the RTV, wading through reed and thick grass to reach the Softrak harvester. This specialised machine has revolutionised our management of the fen. Having tracks, rather than tyres, enables it to work on delicate, wet ground without leaving ruts in the soft, peaty soil. It was purchased in an effort to advance and modernise the management of Sedge Fen. Following the scrub clearance project, there were an extra 50 hectares of open fen to manage. The days of working holidays had passed, making it a struggle to cut a third of the fen each year within the narrow window after the end of the breeding bird season and before the fen becomes too wet. The Fen Harvester made this important management task not only possible, but far more efficient.

The hours of ranger time spent raking and forking were no longer necessary. A mower at the front of the harvester fires cut vegetation through a chute into a bin at the back. The bin is mechanically emptied at appropriate locations, creating piles known as Duffey heaps, named after arachnologist Eric Duffey. His research revealed that piles of litter (cut material) benefit invertebrates, the warmth of the rotting biomass creating valuable habitat for species not to be found elsewhere on the fen. With commercial harvest of sedge and reed

---

* A large family lived there in the 1860s and '70s. It was so damp in winter that they lived upstairs, seldom leaving the fen except by boat on Burwell Lode. After ague caused a death, the family moved to Burwell village.

Operating the harvester on Sedge Fen, 11 September 2021. (National Trust Images/ Mike Selby)

no longer financially viable, creating Duffey heaps not only benefits wildlife, but eliminates the cost – and carbon footprint – of removing tons of litter from the fen.

The harvester also powers a woodchipper. This has proven a very efficient way of processing felled trees and brash. The chipped material makes an ideal path dressing, protecting soil from heavy footfall in the wet months. Harrison's Drove becomes notoriously churned up each winter, thick clay sticking to walkers' boots. When clearing encroaching scrub from either side of the drove, we feed cut branches into the chipper and spread the output straight onto the drove, often with the help of corporate work parties who swap office for fen on their annual 'green day'.

Today, I will begin cutting the reedbed. In 2019, we reinstated a rotational management regime in which a section is cut every four years (compared to three on Sedge Fen). This prevents the reedbed from becoming overgrown with bushes, securing suitable habitat for nesting and roosting birds of international importance, namely the marsh harrier.

Running on tracks enables the harvester to operate in a few inches of standing water. But there are hazards to negotiate as I steer the machine into the Four Pools, becoming engulfed by dense, tall reed.

There are various levers, switches and buttons, but no pedals. Acceleration and braking is all done with my right hand, operating a joystick. Push it away to move forwards, pull it backwards to reverse, let go and you stop moving instantly. Directing the joystick left and right enables steering and two tiny buttons increase and decrease speed. Unlike the RTV, Land Rover or our various vintage tractors, the harvester boasts air conditioning, functioning windscreen wipers, a radio and even a USB connection. Luxury!

But this is not a time for bopping along to favourite tunes. That time will come when a working rhythm is entered. First, I must become familiar with my surroundings. The Four Pools reedbed was created in the mid-1990s, each pool roughly half a hectare in size. The gradient slopes gradually, pool four being the deepest. All are surrounded by deep ditches on each side.

After finding the culvert across the ditch into pool one, I must locate its centre. Using an aerial photograph, my phone and best guesswork, I navigate through the jungle of tall stems and occasional willows. Bingo. An old Duffey heap marks the centre, where the last three years' cuttings have been heaped. Orientating into the quarter in need of cutting, I switch on the mower and increase engine speed.

Drive too fast and you risk clogging the chute with reed and potentially heading into a ditch beyond the 'point of no reverse'. Angle the mower too low and you suck up mud, which can also block the chute. I set the mower at what I think is the correct height and advance cautiously towards the ditch. Soon, the ditch edge comes abruptly into view, thankfully before the harvester plunges nose-first into it, my biggest fear (and a horror I will go on to face 13 months later). Orientated, I gradually relax into a rhythm.

Unlike the immaculately straight edges and lawn-like even mowing of the Sedge Fen strips, I am liberated to leave patches and create wonky edges. This will create habitat for wildlife. Even turning too quickly on the tracks and churning up a bit of bare mud is a good thing. This suits my sometimes more-creative-than-practical mindset. Visions of bearded tits and bitterns* benefiting from this management fill my mind as I sit comfortably in the cab, warm and dry, protected from the rain outside. Managing reedbeds wasn't such a comfortable experience eighty odd years ago. Life on Adventurers' Fen was profoundly different in the early 1940s.

During the Second World War, reduced availability of imported food and harsh rationing brought about the need to grow more crops in Britain. The Ministry of Agriculture set up the 'Dig for Victory' campaign, transforming open spaces into allotments and reclaiming land for agriculture. In 1939, Alan Bloom, a Cambridge plant nursery owner, purchased Priory Farm on Adventurers' Fen. His honest and insightful book *The Farm in the Fen* documents the admirable efforts that went into converting overgrown and flooded fen into arable farmland, including a large part of the National Trust's land. Destruction of wildlife habitat** was necessary in order to stop the nation from starving. Great areas of scrub were chopped and sawn by hand, the roots then dragged out using Allis-Chalmers and Case tractors. Huge bog oaks in the soil had to be blasted with explosives, the longest oak encountered was 108ft (found where the Four Pools were later created). New ditches were dug and droves concreted. Swathes of reedbed were burned.

Bloom explains how 'nobody wanted reeds for thatching just then, and we wanted them out of the way quickly before the new shoots grew too high'. So permission was sought and gained to burn the reed in the old turf pits south of Wicken Lode. Successful to a point, sizeable patches remained unburnt, showing that the water level was too high for ploughing. Tractors had become bogged in this area in 1941.

---

*   In fact, bitterns prefer deeper pools among the reed, which is probably why they tend to nest in the main reedbed rather than the Four Pools, although they have been observed flying in and out of the latter.

**   Sedge (including Verrall's) and St Edmund's Fens, however, continued to be managed for wildlife throughout the war.

Two years later, beet and potatoes were being grown in the same triangle of fen between Burwell and Wicken Lodes. The King and Queen visited in 1942, to see the 'magnificent work' being carried out, from oaks being blown up to Fen-men digging dykes and Land Girls from Manchester sawing trees and driving tractors.

The core part of Priory Farm has continued to produce beet, wheat and silage ever since. Following the end of the war, the National Trust's land gradually returned to nature, reeds taking over the northern part of Adventurers' Fen. Excitement felt by the National Trust team when a pair of marsh harriers bred in 1981 matched the elation Alan Bloom felt thirty-eight years previously, when beet and potatoes were harvested from the very same piece of land. Nearby reverted farmland was to provide me with excitement a few months into my time as a Wicken ranger.

Burwell Fen: Saturday, 26 January 2019

It is 7°C at 7.30 a.m. as I drive to work, complaining of a headache despite having consumed no alcohol for almost four weeks. An hour later, my spirits are lifted.

At 8.30 a.m. I became aware of a bird call over the Sedge Fen ... cranes! I saw a pair flying towards Adventurers' Fen. A couple of hours later, I was doing the livestock checks on Burwell Fen when two flew in and landed. So wonderful to see my first Cambridgeshire cranes and to see/hear them hanging around on Burwell Fen. Hopefully a future breeding ground for them.

Hearing their eerie bugling calls echo across the fen had alerted me to their presence, bringing back memories of previous crane encounters in the Norfolk Broads. It was there, in 1981, that cranes – believed to be migrant birds from mainland Europe – bred in Britain for the first time since at least the seventeenth century. Having faced extinction due to a combination of habitat loss and over-hunting, their return was momentous. Fledging first occurred in the Fens on Lakenheath Fen in 2009. A local population grew slowly, spreading to Cambridgeshire's

Nene Washes. With sufficient food available on farmland through the winter, fenland cranes flock together to feed and roost, rather than risking overseas migration.

Adventurers' Fen: May 2019

When I wrote in my diary that I hoped cranes would breed on the fen in the future, I did not imagine there would be a chick just four months later. With a growing local population and suitable habitat available on the reserve, it was inevitable. A pair had built a nest just 2 miles away, at Kingfishers Bridge, the previous spring. In fact, it was the same pair that went on to nest at Wicken. We know this because local crane enthusiast – and former Lakenheath Fen site manager – Norman Sills studies the Fenland population diligently. He observes and carefully records the subtle features of individual birds. Some have more white on their face and neck, some have more red on their head and some have a notably large or small bustle.[*] Norman has a catalogue of sketches enabling him to keep tabs on the various pairs nesting in the Fens. With information supplied from site managers, landowners and keen birdwatchers, he follows the progress of each pair throughout the breeding season.

Standing more than a metre tall with calls capable of carrying up to 3 miles, cranes become surprisingly secretive creatures when incubating their eggs. Seeking space and solitude, nest sites are typically hidden by tall reeds and surrounded by shallow water to deter predators such as fox and badger. Both parents share incubation duties, swapping over every few hours to give the other a chance to feed. It is one of these inconspicuous changeovers – a crane slipping silently into the reeds – that raises suspicion. But it is a well-placed trail camera, installed by the bird ringers, that reveals the first crane chick hatched on Wicken Fen in centuries. About two days after hatching, parents take their fluffy, orange chicks beyond the nest, feeding them on small spiders and other insects plucked from the tall grass. One feeding foray passes the trail camera, proving the Wicken pair have a youngster.

---

[*] Long wing feathers that fall loosely over the tail of both female and male cranes when their wings are folded.

Cranes with chick, Adventurers' Fen, 11 May 2019. (National Trust/Michael Holdsworth)

It was incredibly exciting to have such a high-profile rare bird return to restored habitat. The event also coincided with the twentieth anniversary of the Wicken Fen Vision. This validated the vision, proving that the restoration and creation of wetland habitat – rewilding – was successful in attracting important wildlife. As much as we wanted to shout about the success, we kept the location secret and resisted sharing the news until the chick had grown stronger. I then found myself on local radio, explaining how the cranes had not been physically reintroduced by us, but had naturally found their own way to Wicken. A wildlife success story.

Success, however, can be defined in different ways. Hatching young is one interpretation. But fledging is the most popular, with young cranes taking flight and going on to further increase the population. A crane chick is not capable of full flight for the first ten to eleven weeks of its life. Although the 2019 Wicken chick started its life promisingly, it didn't quite make it off the ground. Frustratingly, aged just shy of 10 weeks, it met a premature end.

The most likely cause was fox predation. Just like the adult cranes, the fox was presumably feeding young. What a stroke of luck, for the fox, to come across a large bird not quite capable of flying away. This is, of course, the way of the natural world. Saddening for us, for sure. But the Wicken Fen Vision aims to create a sustainable, non-prescriptive future for wildlife. While it would be tempting to put protection measures in place, the aim is for nature to thrive without relying on our intervention. The local crane population was increasing and most of the other successful breeding sites had experienced a couple of years with failed breeding before fledging their first young.

The same crane pair would return to the identical spot in 2020, this time failing at the egg stage. They returned again in 2021, failing close to the hatching stage. Meanwhile, the wider Fens population had grown to thirteen other pairs across seven sites, fledging twelve young. Would our pair return in 2022 after three failed breeding seasons? Yes, they would. Each year, I became more interested, more invested and more nervous. From studying their behaviour, we knew fairly accurately the date incubation began. This enabled us to predict when the eggs should hatch: the middle of April. Feeding behaviour was observed, through a telescope a safe distance away, from late April all through May. However, everything then went quiet. About three weeks short of fledging, it looked like the fox had struck again.

8

Winter Days

**• Hen harriers • Resting Sedge Fen •
A vet visit • A fence fails • Winter wonderland •
Seeking the bittern • Life and times of Tim •**

Wicken Fen: Monday, 21 November 2022

My breath condenses in the cold morning air. I lure Oakley into the car boot with a small chunk of pumpkin. He leaps straight up into his dog bed and settles down for the 22-mile drive to Wicken. The dashboard thermometer reads -2.5°C. A forty-minute frosty drive follows. The gorgeous sunrise provides an exquisite start to the day of a ranger. How long will this serenity endure?

Alas, it ends abruptly when the visitor centre telephone rings. There is a horrific report of a loose dog tearing apart a live deer on Burwell Fen. I leap into the Land Rover, Oakley in the back to set a good example (he only chases balls and sticks). Chances are the dog and its owner will have moved on by the time I arrive at the described location.

All is quiet on Burwell Fen. A search does not, thankfully, throw up any mutilated muntjac or ripped-open roe deer. Hopefully – probably – it outran the dog. I move on to the daily livestock welfare checks, making sure no cattle or horses have been attacked. Every animal is fine, thankfully.

By dusk, the temperature has increased to 9°C as I conduct a special roost count from the visitor centre. I am looking out for Britain's most persecuted bird of prey. A winter visitor to Wicken, it has been nine months since last I laid eyes upon this rare species of hawk. Slightly smaller than our resident marsh harriers, the hen harrier breeds further north, where its survival is threatened on driven grouse moors. Here on the fen, its presence is celebrated, worshipped.

Usually arriving in mid-November, there have not yet been any confirmed sightings this autumn. Scanning distant silhouettes towards Verrall's Fen, I glimpse a flash of white rump, the distinctive feature of a ringtail.* So the first hen harrier of the autumn has put in an appearance, albeit distant, on my first roost count, prompting a rush of excitement, barely believing my luck – quite often the best nature sightings are made outside of formal surveys.

The majestic male hen harriers are my absolute favourite. Pale grey with dark wingtips, they glow ghost-like in the evening light. Hen and marsh harriers both quarter over Sedge Fen, picking their spot to settle down for the night. Naturalists and birders frequently visit nature reserves with particular target species in mind. Wicken's biggest winter attraction has to be the graceful hen harrier. Communal roosting was first recorded here in 1978 and has peaked at eleven birds. This year, we are to have three males and two ringtails spend the winter.

Combinations of weather, time of year, time of day and associated wildlife sightings have the power to transport me back in time. For example, blackbirds singing after the rain on spring evenings are especially evocative, while the right shades of sunset sky can take me to a magnificent moment during my first winter volunteering on the fen.

---

*   Female and immature birds look very similar and so both are referred to as ring-
     tails.

Sedge Fen: Thursday, 26 January 2012

When a hen harrier flies so close that I could whisper and it might hear me, it makes my heart beat faster. I get goose pimples watching the males' silvery plumage, contrasting splendidly with a fiery winter sky. But they can easily be missed. Unlike a Harrier jump jet plane, they are near silent. When flying to roost at dusk, birds want to be as inconspicuous as possible and will not settle near any people who may be loitering on the fen, for fear of being seen. They have to feel hidden before settling down for the night. Choosing the right roosting location is crucial for survival. Dense sedge and reed provide cover while standing water deters potential predators. Watching a harrier fly to roost, one can observe how much their crop protrudes, which indicates how well they have fed. Ideally, they will have a full crop. This muscular pouch is an enlargement of the oesophagus (the tube between the throat and stomach). The crop acts as a storage place for food and is found at the front of their neck, just above the chest.

> There was a tremendous orange sky and three hen harriers flying close to Tower Hide. It was such a wonderful moment to be experiencing such a beautiful sky and such spectacular birds.

On that January evening in 2012, I was showing my Anglesey Abbey housemates around the fen. My aim was to give them a great experience of how special Sedge Fen is. The roosting harriers were a perfect selling point. But the days of being able to watch winter harriers from Tower Hide were to be numbered, for good reason.

The lodeside path was becoming progressively churned up by footfall during the wetter months of the year. Duck boards – made from sections of the old wooden boardwalk after it was replaced with recycled plastic – would protect the soggiest spots along the nature trail. However, by 2018, there was concern not just about poaching of the paths (damage caused to the ground by footfall), but also of soil compaction, indicated by the abundance of silverweed. A trial winter closure, from November to May, did the paths and adjacent verges the world of good. Taking away the pressure of footfall, the peat was no longer being compressed. In response, the summer display of wildflowers was greatly improved.

Consequently, seasonal path closures have continued, to conserve fen flora and peat. Rather than saying paths are 'closed' per se, we explain how we are 'resting the Sedge Fen' (choice of words is important when communicating conservation messages). Funding was secured to create a new circular path into an area of woodland on slightly higher ground, north-east of Sedge Fen. This way, visitors can enjoy an accessible winter walk that does not compromise our vulnerable soils or unique vegetation. Although not strictly on the fen, the woodland walk is an ideal setting for festive sculpture trails and 'wild play' such as den building.

Welcoming people is an important part of conservation, encouraging awareness and appreciation of special places while at the same time preserving and protecting them. The role of a ranger involves managing both habitats and access. At Wicken, part of our habitat management is livestock management.

Burwell Fen: Thursday, 24 November 2022

The alarm goes off at 6.00 a.m. I rise, get ready and head out for the day, just as whooper swans are leaving their overnight roost on the nearby Ouse Washes. I watch them gaining height and dispersing as I drive towards Wicken. Dozens of black-headed gulls fly east. Most other motorists will not be looking up, I suspect, so will not see the hundreds of birds crossing the sky with charm and purpose.

At 8.00 a.m., John, countryside manager Alan and I discuss how best to juggle two work parties, a guided walk and a vet visit. Minutes later, I am cycling hurriedly along the Lodes Way. Flinging my bike at the base of 'Cock-Up' Bridge, I ascend the concrete steps and survey Burwell Fen through binoculars. I count the cattle, silhouetted in the low, golden sun. The horses, conveniently, are in the most easily accessible spot, by the watering hole in the field nearest the bridge.

John radios through to update me that the vet has just arrived at the visitor centre instead of going to Priory Farm. He will have to

Kingfisher on Baker's Fen, 25 February 2019. (Kenny Brooks)

drive another 9 miles. I while away the time on 'Cock-Up' Bridge. There must be fifty collared doves in the nearby hawthorns and willows on Harrison's Farm, their breasts glowing lilac in the morning light. Turning towards the sun, a flash of brightest blue darts along Burwell Lode. It can only be a kingfisher. I reassure myself it is a sign of optimism, that nature understands what must happen on the fen this morning.

The vet arrives, shakes my hand and proceeds to gather the relevant equipment from his van. We walk towards the herd as he talks softly, smiling lightly. His gentle humour puts me at ease as he mentions O'Toole's commentary that 'Murphy was an optimist'.* There is no need to debate what must be done, he understands. We walk carefully towards the suffering mare. The vet puts her to rest with dignity, efficiency and utmost professionalism. In a split second, the mare is at peace.

I never know exactly how I'm going to feel until the moment comes. My initial emotion is a brief panic that I have somehow directed the vet to the wrong horse. But, of course, I have not. This is just the undeniable, uncomfortable reality that I have facilitated the end of an animal's life.

---

*   Murphy's law is an adage stating 'anything that can go wrong will go wrong (and at the worst possible time)'.

We examine her body and know by its condition that this was the only option. But it is still a rotten feeling, witnessing life cease for an animal you have spent a number of years checking on regularly and spending time with. Such is the life of a grazing ranger, you witness the whole spectrum of emotions, from the sadness of death to the joy of new life. I hear Ralph's words in my head, 'you have livestock, you have dead-stock'.

Burwell Fen: Sunday, 27 November 2022

After animals suffering, our second-greatest concern is animals escaping. Especially on a weekend when there is just one ranger on duty. The best weekends are drama free, consisting of a morning checking the livestock without the need to hurry, followed by an afternoon catching up on odd jobs, getting to those rarely visited corners of the reserve, chatting to visitors and maybe even having a chance to catch up with the duty manager or visitor centre staff.

Just as I am about to head off and check on the animals, Kerry in the visitor centre passes me the phone. A far-from-friendly voice tells me there is a fence down and cattle out over on Hurdle Hall Fen. The cows in question are not ours, they belong to a tenant grazier. Between loading the Land Rover with fencing tools, wire and armfuls of fence posts, I call the farmer and arrange to meet him in twenty minutes. The Land Rover rattles along the A1123. To be truly honest, I feel one part anxious, about the unknown level of potential chaos that lays ahead, and two parts plain grumpy. Nobody really wants to spend their Sunday morning chasing loose cattle and repairing fences on a back foot.

A few minutes later, I reach High Town Drove. There is a truck coming towards me so I pull into a passing place and wait. The speedy driver fails to raise an appreciative hand as he passes, tearing through a sizeable puddle. A wave of water crashes onto my windscreen like an insult. I mutter expletives under my breath, then instinctively apologise to Oakley for my language.

Reaching Hurdle Hall, I find the farmer in good spirits. He and his son have already coaxed the lone loose cow back into the field. After an hour or so of knocking in fence posts and stapling wire, I am on my way back along High Town Drove. I gaze enviously at the brand-new super-duper deer fence surrounding Burwell Solar Farm. Smiling to myself, I count eight roe deer that have somehow managed to end up inside the area they were supposed to be fenced out of.

Burwell Fen: Thursday, 15 December 2022

My morning commute takes me south-eastwards along the A1123 between Stretham and Wicken. I cross the Great Ouse and then the Cambridge–Ely railway line. The road drops slightly and bends before crossing the Cam. My Volkswagen Polo usually records a slight decrease in temperature between the two rivers, especially when the valley is carpeted in low mist. Today, the temperature reduces considerably between the level crossing and the Cam. As the road rises over the bridge, my car reads −11°C. The clock reads 8.58 a.m., permanently in British Summertime. I arrive at Wicken a couple of minutes late for work, lock the car and head out into the wintry outdoors, down Lode Lane onto the frosty, sparkly fen. It has been dull and grey for several days, but today the sky has at last turned blue.

After a quick cup of tea with the team, I cycle out to check on the livestock. Bike tyres crack loudly through the thinnest iced puddles, but merely slide over most. I am almost suitably dressed for the weather, but two pairs of gloves are not quite enough to stop my hands from turning painfully numb as they grip the handlebars. Riding one-handed, I tuck one hand inside my coat pocket, then swap hands to warm the other, constantly wiggling fingers to increase blood flow.

A thin layer of powdery snow lies on the ground like white sand. Twiggy tree branches are encrusted in hoar frost, forming perfect crystalline features. Although relatively thin, there is enough snow to dampen the acoustics, creating a soft, still atmosphere. It is almost silent. Every way I look, I see snow and frost glistening in the sunshine. The light gives the impression of water, as if the ice is melting slightly. But it isn't, it is merely reflecting the sun. The temperature is still well below freezing.

As if this magical experience isn't special enough, I am about to be rewarded with a sighting of my favourite reed-dwelling creature. Suddenly, I become half-aware of a bird ahead. Barely glimpsing enough detail for my brain to process, I imagine it could be a bittern, simply because such a sought-after species would match the mood of the morning. Dismissing my fantasy, I fix my gaze on the bird as it comes into view from behind a willow. Blow me if it isn't a bittern, glowing gold. It flies over the track in front of me and loops around from my twelve o'clock all of the way to six o'clock. Turning on my axis to savour its every flap, I lap up the delicious spectacle. It drops into the reeds along Reach Lode, disappearing from view. I remember to breathe again, my cake of a day having been well and truly topped with the most glorious icing. This is, in fact, only my second ever bittern sighting on the reserve. The first was a decade ago.

Tower Hide: Sunday, 19 February 2012

How to see a bittern (in winter). Step one. Head to a place, probably a nature reserve, with suitable reedy habitat and where, ideally, there have been regular recent sightings in a specific location. In February 2012, while working in the visitor centre and volunteering on the fen, I heard news of a bittern being seen daily from the old Tower Hide.

Step two. Find a vantage point, preferably a hide, and wait. On a Sunday afternoon, I set off for Tower Hide, determined not to leave until I have set eyes on my holy grail. Patience is key. So is staying alert, it can be all too easy to drift off into a daydream, for me, at least. I must be ready to pick up on a distant flash of movement and set binoculars on it in a split second.

Having heard that numerous sightings had been made from this spot, the odds were surely stacked in my favour. Even so, there were no guarantees. After just half an hour, I spot a streaked, buffy bird flying over the mere. Excitedly, I follow it with my binoculars for barely five seconds before it drops out of sight, not to be seen again that day.

I was not disappointed that it was only a brief glimpse. The rush of pleasure I experienced from seeing it was enough to feel satisfied. I could cycle home smiling, replaying the moment repeatedly in my mind.

Burwell Fen: Saturday, 17 December 2022

Wicken's winter wonderland persists. Defrosting is forecast for tomorrow, along with heavy rain. The crisp, solid ground will revert to a clingy, thick consistency that sticks to your boots. Melting of the ditch, drain, dyke and pond water will be a blessing for our livestock. Some of the ice is so thick you can walk on water. Indeed, on the nearby Cam Washes at Upware, people have been having fun on the ice, with fen skating possible for the first time since 2018's 'Beast from the East' anticyclone.

Out on Burwell Fen, I worriedly spot a horse in a ditch, presumably having broken through the ice. I can identify her straight away because she is our only black horse, Shrek.* Seeing her struggling to get out, a plan instantly starts formulating in my head, casting my mind back almost three years to when Ada got stuck. I will need rope, shackles, a dry suit, an assistant and an off-road vehicle. Remaining calm and measured, I cycle briskly back to base, radioing duty manager Alan for assistance in getting kit and caboodle together. Approaching the tractor shed, who should I spot but Carol, walking her puppy, Bran. From a distance – coronavirus having finally found its way to her cottage – she asks if everything is all right. I swear she has a sixth sense whenever a horse or cow is in trouble. Reluctant to burden her, I concisely announce, 'Shrek is in a ditch.' She offers a few words of wisdom before Alan and I head off in the Land Rover.

On arrival, Shrek is back on dry land with the herd. Fortunately, for both her and us, she has managed to get herself out before becoming too cold or tired. She already seems to have dried off quite nicely and is behaving normally. We will keep a close eye on her but, thankfully, all seems to be well. Cases of horses stuck in ditches are infrequent. The most memorable case occurred ten winters before on a particularly bracing February morning.

---

*   So named because, as a foal, she apparently looked like Donkey from the animated film *Shrek* about a green ogre. 'Donkey' was deemed too confusing a name for a horse, so she was named after the ogre.

Verrall's Fen: Saturday, 11 February 2012

From September 2011 for seven magnificent months, I was incredibly lucky to live in National Trust volunteer accommodation at Anglesey Abbey. Home was in the Jacobean-style house, built on the site of an early twelfth-century Augustinian monastery. Housemates Gemma, Anwen, Emily and I were free to walk around the gardens after the public had gone home. We would also drink a fair amount of red wine and whisky in the kitchen or with locals at the nearby Lode Social Club. These were very happy days. One of the highlights was cycling between the Abbey and the fen, in all weathers:

> Frost on top of the snow made for a perfect sparkling morning, with trees looking brilliant along the Lodes Way. Sadly, my camera battery ran out at White Fen. Should probably also mention how cold it was. It was evidently significantly below freezing and my eyelashes had frosted up as well as parts of my coat and hat. Paula said I looked like an Arctic explorer upon arrival.

According to the reserve's weather station, temperatures fell below freezing the previous afternoon, reaching a low of -14.6°C at 5 a.m. The warmest it got that Saturday was -1.6°C at midday. I spend much of the day in the office working on an interpretation project. Carole and Hugh – who were inspired to volunteer after attending one of Carol's guided walks – set off for Verrall's Fen to check on the Koniks. It is a day they will never forget. Not just because of the cold (Hugh had previously spent time working in Antarctica), but what they find when they arrive on Verrall's around 11.30 a.m..

On the coldest day of the year, poor Tim, a gelding, has slipped into a drain. With staff back-up, dry suits and a tractor, he is hauled onto dry land within little over an hour of being found. Part of the steep-sided ditch edge has to be dug out to aid the rescue. Volunteer Carole watches him head straight to the nearest willow and begin munching intently. Willow bark contains salicin, a chemical with similar properties to aspirin. Tim must know that the willow will provide pain relief.

Over their years checking the herds, Carole and Hugh have concluded that the animals on Verrall's have everything they need, botanically, and the knowledge to find it. In winter, the Koniks root around in wet areas for rhizomes. During spring – which always arrives a little later on Verrall's than the rest of the fen – they nibble on fresh hawthorn leaves. Carol once noticed a steer, Trevelyan, with an upset stomach, gorging himself on hawthorn berries. Bursting with antioxidants, these haws had clearly been sought out, knowing they were what he needed at that moment.

Next morning, Carol heads out to Verrall's Fen. She takes a stick to smash ice with, creating several spots where the horses can drink. This will hopefully eliminate the risk of any more dunking incidents. She is relieved to find Tim looking 'all okay' as recorded in the grazing diary. The 18-year-old gelding is healthy, strong and resilient, with well over a decade ahead of him.

Tim four weeks before his 30th birthday, Verrall's Fen, 22 March 2023. (Mike Selby)

During a meeting with our regional marketing colleagues, early in 2023, we chat through possible press release topics for the year ahead. The thirtieth birthday of our oldest 'original' horse is met with enthusiasm and a shared hope that he continues to stay strong in the lead-up to his birthday.

Two weeks before Tim's birthday, his best friend, Randy, displays a sudden loss in condition. Randy – who had one of his eyes removed many years ago but adapted well to monocular life – was euthanised in his 25th year. Tim, however, makes it to 30. While our regional colleagues share the story on social media, Wicken Fen staff celebrate with chocolate cake. We couldn't let this landmark pass without acknowledging it in some way … and what better than cake?

9

Signs of Spring

• **World Wetlands Day** • **Larks ascending** •
Preparing for spring • **An awesome owl encounter** •
Rambling • **Out in the tractor** • **Snowballs** •
A stork drops in • **Handling horses** •
Spring flowers and migrant birds •

Adventurers' Fen: Thursday, 2 February 2023

Twenty minutes after sunrise, a few dozen whooper swans fly over Lode Lane, hooping as their onomatopoeic name suggests. A typical winter scene in the Fens. Two hours later, I lead a World Wetlands Day walk, pausing near Norman's Bridge to chat a while. 'If Candlemas Day be fair and bright, winter will have another fight,' goes the old English rhyme.

In the fair, bright, almost spring-like conditions, great tits are loudly calling 'teacher, teacher' like squeaky bicycle wheels. On to Baker's Fen, where wigeon, teal, shoveler and mallard are robbed of their colours by the bright sun's glare. Three quarters of the way along Moore's Drove, I gather the group again for the next instalment of my planned commentary. While answering a question, two large, graceful birds catch my eye. In a split second, my brain provides their name, followed immediately with words accompanied by a skyward-pointing finger. 'Two cranes!'

I relax for two reasons. A clear sighting of a special bird has made the walk. The group will go home happy. Also, I am relieved to finally see our pair of cranes back at Wicken for the first time this year. I imagine a new rhyme about cranes on Candlemas promising breeding success, but dare not tempt fate.

Birds bring such joy in winter, especially their song. In a hurried check of the livestock, before my guided walk, I had been serenaded by skylarks ascending above Guinea Hall, slowing a while to savour their song. For me, the only sound that beats Vaughan Williams' masterpiece 'The Lark Ascending' is the lark itself. It is the height above the field that makes their call so beautiful and romantic (if it was too near your ear, I am sure it would sound shouty and aggressive).

Fen View: Friday, 3 February 2023

The needle falls into the groove. A comforting crackle comes through the speakers, 'The Lark Ascending'. Sweet strings fill our lounge, accompanied by golden rays of setting sun through the west-facing window. The nation's favourite piece of classical music for twelve years running.[*] I am sure it is one of Oakley's favourites too, played to him since he was a wee pup.

The sun sinks beneath the horizon, leaving lilac clouds alone in the sepia sky. I flip the record over and gaze across the fields. The opening melody of 'In the Fen Country' seems to evoke many people's perceptions of bleak East Anglian winters. A pair of whooper swans fly right over the house, on their way to roost on the nearby washes. The music matches my melancholic mood, realising these wonderful winter swans will soon be departing for Iceland, leaving me behind. Yet, the sweeping orchestral textures are also idyllic, guiding my thoughts to spring.

Wicken's winter tones seem to last most of the year, but always turn to fresh green eventually. Each year, my ranger colleagues and I compete

---

[*]   Nine weeks later, it drops to number two in the Classic FM Hall of Fame 2023, the world's biggest poll of classical music tastes, ousted by Rachmaninov's 'Piano Concerto No. 2' 150 years after the composer's birth.

to spot the first vernal blooms. Cultivated snowdrops and aconites by Lode Lane don't count. Colt's-foot is usually the first wildflower to be observed. It is named after the hoof-shaped leaves that appear after its yellow flowers emerge in March. February, for me, will feature many a sighting of actual colts' feet.

Adventurers' Fen: Saturday, 4 February 2023

An overcast, perfectly calm morning. Guinea Hall Fen is quiet, except for the sound of distant traffic. There is not a soul in sight. The usual dog walkers haven't yet left their homes. The Koniks also appear to be having a slow start to their Saturday. Yawning, scratching against fence posts, lazing rather than grazing. Slowly waking up after a doze, a yearling colt stretches his back legs one by one as if performing ballet, just like Oakley does. The laughing 'yaffle' of a distant green woodpecker carries on the still air. A hare runs through the grass.

Approaching the spot where a skylark sang two days ago, suspense mounts. He does not disappoint, reminding me of a line I wrote when I was 19: 'Solitary in the sky, beating wings and rising high'. The less musical 'seep-seep' calls of meadow pipits come from nearer the ground. Eight twittering linnets emerge from a hawthorn bush and disappear into the grass, not far from the two cows and five steers. All are sat resting, apart from Max, the youngest. He is busily grazing on the riverbank, his thick black forelock covers his eyes, but he knows I am there. So does the riverside heron, stretching its wings and leaping into flight before I get anywhere near it.

A silent crow flies low to the ground by the horse-licked farm ruins. Five times smaller than the crow, a wren trills noisily from the base of a hawthorn. Some of the horses have trotted over, crossing paths with a magpie. One for sorrow. I scan across the fen, looking for another. Two for joy. There is a clatter as eighteen wood pigeons fly clumsily from the elders. Then I hear it, coming from across the water on St Edmund's Fen. The sound I have been craving. Ah, behold the resonant drumming of a great spotted woodpecker. Such a perfect sound, so satisfying to hear and my first of the year. An early sign that spring is coming.

'This is the willow where the treecreeper was reported,' says local wild-life photographer, Richard. I study the trunk and soon spot a small brown bird working its way up the tree, using its stiff tail as an extra limb. 'There it is.' Not a bird seen regularly on the fen, although a pair nested in a dead trunk by Norman's Bridge a few years ago, found by cuckoo guru Nick Davies. Tucked under the peeling bark of a dead willow, the nest was right by the main path, but most passers-by were completely oblivious to it. Ideal for the treecreepers, undisturbed by the passing people whose presence helped deter any nearby woodpeckers that might be tempted to predate the nest.

We head towards the reedbed. Passing the bird ringers' shed, we cross the soft ground, parting stems to slip into the forest of reeds that stand taller than our heads. I lead the way along the narrow, winding track that I created a couple of weeks ago, brushing against reed leaves with every step. 'I thought you said it was only twenty metres.'

Our destination was probably nearer 100m. You can easily lose sense of distance and direction when surrounded by reeds. We reach a clearing in the middle of the reedbed, 5m by 8m in size. Inspired by Lakenheath Fen, with their three pairs of cranes and numerous fledged young, I cleared this small, secluded spot in the hope it may attract nesting cranes in the spring. The habitat is ideal, as is the lack of distur-bance. But we don't know whether the water depth – which cranes are very particular about – will become too high. Water from Wicken Lode is fed into the reedbed throughout February and March to benefit nest-ing bitterns and marsh harriers. We do not enter the reedbed during spring, to avoid disturbing these rare and sensitive birds. So we do not know exactly how deep it gets, just that it dries out by August.

Richard carefully attaches one of his trail cameras to a bamboo cane pushed into the soft, black soil. The water was switched on two days ago, but has not yet reached this far into the reedbed. There was no need to have worn welly boots, although it's always best to, just in case. Mine have a gaping hole in them anyway. After scaling a pile of vegetation to deter any foxes from the crane clearing, the path leads us

Resident little owl, Priory Farm, 30 May 2019. (Kenny Brooks)

back towards civilisation. We can't help but fantasise about the camera capturing bearded tits, water rails, harriers, bitterns or the ultimate, crane chicks. But both of us are fully prepared that the camera may not record any of these sought-after species.* Just like the visiting group of photographers who haven't yet been lucky enough to glimpse a marsh harrier. The more reliable little owl of Priory Farm awaits them, at least.

In the centre of a small field between Harrison's Drove and the Priory Farm barns stands a modest pile of logs. Viewable in aerial photographs, it has been there for a number of years. More often than not, a little owl can be seen perched on it, sometimes two. Their mottled grey-brown and white plumage blends perfectly with their woody surroundings. The field provides a plentiful supply of beetles, worms and small mammals to sustain them year round. At a little over 20cm tall, they can be difficult to spot. But regular birders and photographers know to look out for them. The Priory Farm wood pile is often a stop-off point on my guided walks. Although not native to Britain – introduced to England in the 1870s – they are much loved, just like the country's four native owl species, all of which have been recorded on the reserve. My personal favourite owl is the least often encountered.

---

*   Alas, the trail camera captures no such species (and is very hard to relocate after a season of reed growth!).

Sedge Fen: Wednesday, 5 December 2018

From cycling beside a hunting barn owl to watching a snoozing immature tawny in a tree, I have been spoiled with winter owl sightings in
East Anglia. These include, of course, the short-eared owl bonanza on
Burwell Fen in 2011. But the long-eared owl is notoriously elusive and
therefore the most rewarding if encountered. So my sole fenland long-
eared owl sighting was a special moment and definitely diary-worthy:

> What an amazing moment this afternoon. Three long-eared owls!
> One flew towards me, just a few metres away. I stared into its orange
> eyes for a split second before it turned away towards Wicken Lode.
> The closest I have ever been to one of my favourite birds.

Fellow ranger Luke and I had stumbled upon a trio of resting owls in
a quiet corner of the fen. Had they stayed still, we wouldn't have seen
them sat silently in the scrub. But the sound of nearby machinery had
disturbed them. Needless to say, we hastily vacated their patch and
ceased any further practical work on that part of the fen for the remain-
der of the winter. I knew, the moment I made eye contact with the owl,
this special moment would stay with me forever.

Another of my most unforgettable days on the fen also featured an
owl sighting. But it wasn't so much the birds that made the day so special, but the birdwatching and relaxed rambling.

Adventurers' Fen: Friday, 7 January 2022

A beautiful morning on the fen with blue skies and hardly a breath of
wind. Deliberately early for my appointment, I embark on a short walk.
In just a few minutes, a short-eared owl, well-marked male marsh
harrier and soaring red kite all put in appearances. I will them to hang
around so my special guest can see them.

Just before 10.30 a.m., a red Land Rover Discovery approaches the car park by Harrison's Drove. The driver and I instantly recognise each other, even though we have never met. Clare Balding winds down her window. I hear my voice coming from her speakers, she is listening to the *Let's Talk Conservation* podcast in preparation for our ramble* together.

Rather than the obvious choice of Sedge Fen, I thought a wander around Burwell and Adventurers' Fens would provide the chance to chat about the Vision, hopefully seeing the Koniks and Highlands. Today, however, the herds of both species happen to be in the furthest corners, well away from the footpaths. I hope that starting our walk at 'Cock-Up' Bridge hasn't set the tone for our walk! All we see is a lone black bull, Duncan, briefly. The short-eared owl, red kite and male marsh harrier are long gone. Clare thinks she has spotted a rare bird, but it turns out to be a crow.

Although wildlife and livestock may be shy today, it is still a wonderful walk. From the start, everything is easy-going. Clare explains that we will just have a pleasant amble and relaxed chat, with sound recordist Maggie following. Conversation flows. Priory Farm provides that much-needed little owl to liven us up and then, over on Baker's Fen, the magic happens. John had suggested turning the water on, a conveniently audible story for radio, linking nicely to the show-stealing wigeon. There they are, whistling away, glowing in the winter sun, inspiring lyrical musings to close the episode, naturally, unscripted. What a lovely way to spend a Friday.

As well as spending time with interesting and lovely people, if I am truly honest, some almost equally special days on the fen have been spent on my own. Well, not completely alone, but in the company of the cattle and horses.

---

* Recording an episode of the long-running BBC Radio Four *Ramblings* series.

Recording *Ramblings* with Clare Balding, Burwell Fen, 7 January 2022. (Maggie Ayre)
Listen online at: www.bbc.co.uk/programmes/m0014pgh

Burwell Fen: Sunday, 5 February 2023

I cycle along the Lodes Way in glorious morning sunshine. Locking my bike to the fence by a cattle grid, I stride through the rough grass towards the resting Koniks, partly hidden in scrub. Every few steps along the way, snipe burst up from out of the grass a few metres ahead, zigzagging into the sky while making their ripping call. A covey of grey partridges also explode from the nearby grass, nine birds fly off haphazardly in various directions, seemingly as startled by my presence as I am by their sudden, panicked eruption.

Splodge is one of the darker horses and has black splodges on each shoulder, hence his descriptive name. Like the Koniks, donkeys have a long, dark stripe that runs down their spine to their tail. Most donkeys have a stripe across their body at the shoulder, known as a 'donkey cross'.* A small number of Koniks display this coat pattern, such as Splodge. I watch him munching on spiky twigs, switching briefly to grass before going back to blackthorn. Not one of the biggest males, Splodge has still managed to hold on to his four mares for a few years now. He regularly rounds them up, keeping his harem close together to avoid other males trying to steal any of them.

Tam's group, by contrast, contains three mares and three other males. He reminds me of a surfer dude, slim and muscular. A long strand of mane, on his offside, is matted together resembling a dreadlock. As if high on whacky baccy, he is chilled out, too laid back to mind another male mounting one of his mares yesterday. Hanty still seems infatuated with the same mare this morning, sticking close by her side. But there will be no babies on Burwell Fen (all males having been vasectomised, or gelded).

Tomorrow, instead of passing my time with livestock and wildlife, I will spend the majority of the day inside the cab of a tractor occupied with the more practical side of conservation.

Bottisham Fen: Monday, 6 February 2023

The windows of the Kubota M9540 tractor are frosted over. I climb inside, slot the key into the ignition and turn the temperature dial to max, slowly filling the cab with warm air. After the windows have cleared, I reverse up to the Spearhead mower and hitch up. John helps me attach the power take-off drive shaft and I begin my 13-mile journey through thick fog. Top speed is 23.3mph. Although you can't go that fast along Great Drove without the mower smashing onto the tarmac as the tractor traverses the deeper dips.

After an hour of travel, I arrive at the furthest part of the property. My task is to mow a strip of grass around the perimeter of a formerly agricultural field, ready for a hedgerow to be planted the following week.

---

* The donkey cross is believed, much like the 'zebra' striping on the Koniks' legs, to have played a role in camouflaging. There are also many religious fables for its existence.

This involves carefully positioning the tractor's mirrors to face the rear of the mower, which protrudes slightly further than the thick wheels. I need to cut up to the fence, but not hit it. After lightly clipping a couple of posts, I get a good line and stick to it. Eyes fixed on the wing mirror. Hands glued to the steering wheel, constantly readjusting it.

Beyond my focused gaze, the mist is dispersing rapidly. A shard of light steals my attention. Out of the greyness, it illuminates a patch of vivid green, like a Pierre de Clausade painting. In less than three hours, the temperature has risen from -2 to nearly 10°C. Winter to spring. Having completed my mowing – and thankfully not clipped any further fence posts – I travel to nearby White Fen. Bouncing over the bumpy road, I reflect on Februaries past. For twelve or fifteen years, I remember the month having this unnatural habitat of changing seasons in the course of a day. Giving hibernating insects and small mammals a premature sense of spring, only for frost to bite back, wilting shoots, damaging delicate blooms and killing insects cold.

I feel warm sun on the back of my neck as I mow alongside the cycle track, preventing the verge from encroaching on the path. Later in the year, a few pyramidal orchids will pop up along here. We adopted a 'No Mow May' and 'Too Soon June'* approach a few years ago, to avoid beheading these attractive flower-heads. A hornet appears inside the tractor cab, its low buzz startling me. Another premature sign of spring. But the colours outside are still undeniably wintry, and the air doesn't yet smell vernal. It will be cold outside tonight when I put Oakley in his kennel at 10 p.m. And it will be March before any spring flowers are spotted.

---

*   Unfortunately, long grass may support hedgehogs in May, only for them to be killed when that grass is mown or strimmed in June. It is very important that long grass is checked carefully before it is cut and the best way is to clear it bit by bit, not all at once, giving wildlife a chance to escape.

Adventurers' Fen: Saturday, 4 March 2023

A swirling storm of starlings merges briefly with a flock of fieldfares. The latter are most likely passing through on their way to their breeding grounds in northern Europe. In a quiet corner of the fen, ruled by reeds, I spot two slender necks sticking out from the straw-coloured grass in the far distance. Black and white with a little red on their head, I know not only who this pair are, but what they are up to. Quietly proud to have spotted them from afar, I leave the two cranes well alone so they can peacefully ponder this year's precise nesting location.

The other sign of spring on my search list is colt's-foot. Finally spotting a yellow flower beside the cycle path, I lean forward to investigate. Its glossy, heart-shaped leaves give it away as, not colt's-foot – I will have to wait nine more days – but another harbinger of spring, lesser celandine, a member of the buttercup family. This native plant will provide pollen for emerging insects, not that there are many out today. There is a bitter coldness in the air. Even so, I feel a strong sense that some of the Koniks are but days away from foaling – another symptom of my excited springtime suspense.

With my morning check of the breeding herd of horses on Adventurers' Fen complete and all animals OK, I head on to Burwell Fen to look at the breeding cattle herd.

Burwell Fen: Saturday, 4 March 2023

My four-legged assistant ranger and I travel along Newnham Drove in the Land Rover. Oakley's black fur is rivalled by the splendid heads of male reed buntings in breeding finery, flitting over farmland and shouting 'si-u'. On the ground, four stock doves peck at the freshly ploughed peaty soil. Unlike the more common wood pigeon, they have no white on their necks, but bands of bottle-green iridescence.

I pull up at the end of the drove to lift the bollard and unlock the gate. A few cows are gathered in the corner of the first field. One of them is Apple, her rear indicating she is close to calving, although not yet imminent. I ponder whether she will give birth to her calf before the first mare has her foal. Either way, they will beat the wild roe deer – of which there are several dozen spread across wider Burwell Fen – it will be May when they have their kids.

The Reach Lode side of the fen is wonderfully wet with abstracted lode water, which is just as well as there has been barely a drop of rain since December. A coil of twenty-two wigeon fly overhead. They won't be around much longer, soon heading north. There are no signs of any spring migrants yet, but I see my first shelduck pair of the year. Following the water's edge, a flock of meadow pipits drop into the grass. Beyond, more wigeon are floating calmly, interspersed with the occasional mallard, gadwall and shoveler. I love the chunky, spatulate bills of the latter, which they use to feed on the surface.

One of the waterside willows provides a perching place for a cormorant, motionless, drying its outstretched wings. Back over on the Burwell Lode side, away from the cool water, things are hotting up with the horses. Gulliver is feeling amorous and mounts the youngest mare vehemently. But she is having none of it, her kicking back legs clearly signalling her disapproval.

In the middle of the fen, the leaves, stalks and young buds of daffodils have started emerging. The bulbs date back over two decades, to when the land was farmed. It will be a few more weeks before the yellow trumpets emerge. Poisonous to our livestock, they know not to forage on Fen *Narcissi*. Although they are not a native fenland flower, they are not spreading or doing any harm, so we leave them be. Some of the bulbs have doubtlessly rotted in the winter water that fills parts of the fen. Those that are shooting up will still have to face a covering of early March snowfall.

Guinea Hall Fen: Thursday, 9 March 2023

Snow, which fell overnight, has been trampled over by 280 Konik hooves, becoming compacted and warmed under the contours of their soles. The resulting hoof-shaped snowballs lie scattered across the fen. Koniks are hardy souls with hardy soles. They very rarely suffer from bruising or abscesses, despite treading on the fen's varied terrain year round. These days, snow is seldom heavy or long-lasting on the fen anyhow. Today, it has soon turned to rain.

For the first time this year, I am wet through. Squeezing my hands into a double layer of gloves has not prevented my fingers from going numb. But I am cheerful because the persistent rain is exactly what the fen needs ahead of spring. The more that falls, the longer it is likely to linger on, providing important habitat for waterbirds as well as keeping carbon locked in the damp peat. Over the coming weeks, growing vegetation will suck up more and more moisture, providing valuable cover for breeding birds.

Burwell Fen: Thursday, 16 March 2023

With the Spring Equinox approaching, I am yearning to hear my first returning chiffchaff on the fen. Like with wildflowers, Wicken rangers compete in a race to spot the first arriving migrant birds and emerging butterflies. Usually brimstones are recorded in February, but the only butterflies I have seen so far are small tortoiseshells and peacocks hibernating inside the Fen Cottage on Lode Lane. Bought by the National Trust in 1974, it was restored at the end of the following decade using traditional methods and local materials, furnished as it

Fen Cottage in the snow, Lode Lane, 4 December 2020. (Ajay Tegala)

White Stork over Burwell Fen, 16 March 2023. (Oliver Bruce)

might have been in the 1930s, with no modern heating or lighting (and virtually no plastic). With its warming fireplace, the cottage is a place I enjoy popping into on cool days. Similarly, it is a great place to cool down on scorching summer afternoons.

I lose the race to find the first colt's-foot in flower by just one day. When I proudly tell Carol I have found the first, she replies that she had seen some the day before. This brings back memories of late warden Ralph, who was notorious for spotting seasonal species earlier than anybody else. I am determined to be the one who hears the first chiff-chaff calling out its name. But the only two-note bird calls this morning are to be great tits.

Beneath serenading skylarks, the vegetation on Guinea Hall Fen is being heavily grazed. Parts of it are almost like a lawn, highlighting how justified we were to move nine more Koniks out of the breeding herd at the end of February. If we were to do nothing, we would have over 100 in the herd within two years and probably lose all suitable skylark nesting habitat.

A few of the remaining seventy horses in the breeding herd are starting to look skinny. When the sugar-rich spring grass starts to grow, their condition will improve. This is absolutely natural and the same for most wild mammals. Meanwhile, I must rush over the lode to Burwell Fen and assist with the vasectomisation of the three stallions moved there a fortnight ago.

Cycling along the grassy track from the lode-bank to the middle of Burwell Fen, a large white bird catches my eye. My first thought is that it must be a domestic goose. With binoculars around my neck, predominantly for spotting distant livestock, I focus in on the intriguing bird and instantly spot a large amount of black on its wings. Then I notice its bright red, long legs and bill. 'Bl**dy hell, it's a stork,' are my exact words (I have seen them in Portugal, but never on home turf). We watch it for half an hour while it stands relatively still a good 100m away from us, seemingly unbothered by nearby Koniks and roe deer. Speculating whether it is a vagrant from Europe or an escapee, I check for leg rings. None are visible, although it is very distant so a dark-coloured ring could easily be missed.*

Naturally, conversation turns to the Knepp Estate in Sussex, where white storks have been introduced. In a nest at the top of an oak tree, May 2020 saw the first stork chicks hatch in the country since the fifteenth century. The last record had been on the roof of St Giles' Cathedral, Edinburgh, in 1416, although this has been debated. I wonder whether there will be storks breeding in the Fens in a decade or two, just as the crane has made a comeback after being extinct for several centuries.

Carol joins in the admiration of this surprise visitor. But I am sure the main question in her mind is, 'when will it fly away?' We need to access the field with vehicles and vets imminently, but do not want to disturb this metre-tall feathered guest. It decides to takes off of its own accord just before the vet shows up. Arriving at the same time, John and Hugh spot the tall bird in flight, initially assuming it is a crane. Just as cranes are a symbol of good fortune in Japan, storks are a sign of good luck in Europe. Prudish Victorian parents would tell their children that storks delivered babies. Ironically, today's vet visit is to prevent babies.

---

* A white stork turns up on the nearby Cam Washes a few days later, a dark grey ring is spotted on its upper right leg, having been ringed in the Netherlands as a nestling in June 2020. It shows up over the fen a few more times over the spring, once even landing on the roof of Tower Hide.

It takes over five hours to vasectomise three stallions. The spermatic cords are particularly hard for the vet to access. Georgie does her best, working carefully and coolly in the middle of a fen, rather than an equine operating theatre. Five-year-old Fleming (named after Sir Alexander, the scientist who famously discovered penicillin) is the most difficult because of notably short tubes to his testicles. This adds to our suspicions that he has a heritable condition known as cryptorchidism, which means 'hidden testes'.

Suspicion arose when we heard from another conservation charity that a mare we sold to them had produced a foal with the condition. Carol worked out that the sire was either Fleming or Koi. This is why Fleming's group was moved to the non-breeding herd. We debated whether to move Koi as well, not knowing which of the two had sired the colt with the retained testicle. Being one of the three stallions imported from the Netherlands to add the genetic diversity of the population, we were reluctant to risk removing Koi from the breeding herd without knowing for sure if he had cryptorchidism. Its probable presence in Fleming was reassurance that we had removed the right stallion and not wasted the considerable investment made in importing Koi five years ago.

Interestingly, both of the group's yearlings were also difficult to operate on, suggesting they were sons of Fleming and had inherited his condition. Choosing who to remove from the herd may seem like playing God. But, in a natural setting, herds would roam over far greater areas, splitting into separate herds then meeting and sharing diverse genes years later (and natural predators would reduce population size). We have to import fresh genes periodically to reduce the chances of inbreeding.

Most of Britain's Koniks are non-breeding. This is why breeding stallions were imported from the Netherlands. So, when we were contacted about the possibility of rehoming two stallions from the Welsh uplands, which were not closely related to ours, we accepted. Although we were trying to reduce breeding numbers and didn't really need fresh genes for a couple more years, accepting these stallions made financial sense – far less expensive than importing animals from mainland Europe a couple of years down the line.

Our favoured horse transporters, Mel and Maggie, enthusiastically accepted the job of collecting the two Welsh stallions. We covered the cost for them to spend the night before in Mid Wales. That Thursday morning in mid-February, they drive the transporter along narrow, winding and very steep back roads. Assuming the Koniks will be corralled ready for loading, they are slightly concerned to spot them on a hilltop several metres above them. Fortunately, Mel and Maggie are experienced horse handlers and have become familiar with semi-wild Koniks thanks to several experiences at Wicken and in the Norfolk Broads. The clock is ticking and rain is bucketing but they hold their nerve and manage to get the pair loaded, against the odds. Once moving in the right direction, a tickle with a French broom is Mel's signature technique. It pays off and they make it to Lode Lane around 2 p.m.

Luck is definitely on our side as the trailer-to-trailer transfer goes smoothly, with a little more help from the trusty French broom. We wave goodbye to Mel and Maggie, still wet from the Welsh rain, and take the Land Rover down Toyse Lane, along Factory Road and up Harrison's Drove on to Lapwing. After a long day of travel to a completely new landscape, this is the ideal place to release our two new horses. Here the grazing is good, compared to the rocky Welsh uplands. In fact, we will have to keep an eye to make sure the change in diet to richer vegetation does not upset their stomachs. They will be left on Lapwing for a month or two while they acclimatise to their new surroundings, before gradually introducing them to the herd to go forth and spread their genes – although it will take them a few months to grow in confidence.

Parked up on Lapwing, the back of our trailer is lowered. Hooves clang on the metal ramp as the two stallions accelerate into the open field. It must look incredibly flat to them. Their new field-mates are five Highland cattle who are more interested in the hay on the trailer ramp than the two stallions that came out of it.

After spending much of the day sat in the back of the Hilux, Oakley has a chance to stretch his legs. Carol stays a while to keep an eye on Fleming and the two yearlings as they come round after their operations. I cycle along the Lodes Way, the hound bounding along beside me. Dozens of noisy black-headed gulls are gathering on Baker's Fen, attracted by the standing water. Some of them are in breeding plumage, their winter white heads having turned rich chocolate brown, a sure sign of spring.

Wicken Poor's Fen: Monday, 20 March 2023

It is the Spring Equinox and I want one thing: to hear my first migrant bird of the year. Looking back at last year's diary, it was around this date that I heard my first chiffchaff. They are on my mind, I am craving their call. At the rangers' docky hut in the morning, I share my wish with the volunteers. Tony nonchalantly mentions that he heard several yesterday while walking to check the livestock on Verrall's Fen. There has obviously been an arrival since Friday when I was last at work. This news makes me eager and excited.

Embarking on a relatively menial task, five of us walk beside the lode, wheelbarrow in tow. My ears are tuning in to every note of birdsong they can detect. It doesn't take long before I hear a delightful 'chiff-chaff, chiff-chaff, chiff-chaff' coming from Poor's Fen. A smile spreads across my face, sustained by another chiffchaff a few metres further on and then a third. It is lovely to have them back, enhancing the soundtrack of the fen.

I find pleasure in all seasons, but there has been a prolonged anticipation for spring. It doesn't arrive in a single moment, but gradually creeps in, like paint from a brush into a jar of water. There is great joy to be found observing seasonal signs, species by species. This week will bring long-awaited brimstone butterflies and a displaying snipe above the visitor centre.

The chiffchaffs have whetted my appetite, fantasising about all the other birds on their way north, soon to grace the fen with their presence and songs. But I never forget our resident species. Song thrushes and blackbirds in full song are among my favourite sounds in all the world. Blackbird song from a hedge along Lode Lane is just as addictive as the chiffchaff, I greedily lap up my fix. But, unlike guzzling coffee, being around birds has lasting mental health benefits. A 2022 study by the Institute of Psychiatry, Psychology and Neuroscience at King's College London proved that seeing and hearing birds improves mental well-being. And a 2019 single by the RSPB – two and a half minutes of birdsong, titled 'Let Nature Sing' – made the top twenty in the official singles chart. All twenty-four of the bird species featured on the track have been seen on Wicken Fen. Now there's a strong contender for the ultimate Desert Island Disc.

10

Blue Skies, Birdsong, Blooms and Booms

• Booming bitterns • First foal of spring • *Wild Isles* • Calf banding • Toby and other friendly bulls • Brimstones and blossom • Easter egg hunt • 120th birthday • A shock in the car park • Dawn chorus • Bittern watch • A lone nightingale •

Adventurers' Fen: Friday, 24 March 2023

With days finally longer than nights, optimism is in the air. Carried on the early morning breeze, a low-pitched boom travels from deep in the reedbed. A smile spreads across my face in the knowledge that we have a territorial bittern on the fen. The river water we have been diverting intermittently into the reeds has created the suitable breeding conditions for this elusive bird. Its scientific name, *Botaurus stellaris*, means 'starry bull', the stars are on its breast and the bull comes from its bill. Rather than singing, like most fen birds, the males fill their enlarged oesophagus with air and expel it as a loud boom, which sounds similar to a bull, or someone blowing into a glass bottle. It is, in fact, the loudest sound made by any British bird, capable of reaching 100 decibels.

During the following few weeks, a team of enthusiastic volunteers will help monitor booming activity in the hope we may have multiple males, a few females and, with a good dose of luck, eventually a new generation of starry bulls.

Following Harrison's Drove to its south-easterly end, I steer left onto Priory Drove. The Koniks are visible just beyond the Guinea Hall ruin, so I lock my bike to the fence by the cattle grid and stride across the field to check on the herd. Between passing clouds, there are brief bursts of bright sunshine and flashes of blue sky. And spirits are about to be lifted further still.

The herd is unsettled, not majorly, but a few stallions are coming into conflict, moving mares around in the process. Meg is among them and she turns out to be the source of the unrest. Just a few hours ago, she gave birth to the first foal of the spring. The filly is steady on its long legs, its pale grey coat drying in the sun. She stays almost glued to mother Meg's side, wearing an innocent expression exaggerated by long eye-lashes. Her dorsal stripe is thick and prominent, her ears pointy, her narrow face sweet. It sounds obvious to say a newborn foal looks like a miniature horse, albeit slightly lankier, but that is the overwhelming impression. Although relatively small, I always think newborn foals are a fair size when you try to picture them tucked up in the womb. A few other mares have similar-sized foals inside them. Daphne must surely be next to give birth, she is looking very heavy (and was the first mare to foal for the previous two years).

I take a snap of the foal and send it to our volunteers. With the 'Grasslands' episode of *Wild Isles* airing in two days, the National Trust's regional marketing team are preparing a press release about our Koniks, which feature in the prime-time David Attenborough documentary. The timing of our first foal is perfect and will appear in local newspapers the following week.

For a significant proportion of British television viewers, their primary experience of the natural world comes via Sunday evening documentaries. As time has gone on, the aim of these series has right-fully tipped towards education as much as entertainment, especially in light of increasing desperation relating to the biodiversity crises.

With National Trust properties featuring in a number of the *Wild Isles* episodes, there is a prime opportunity to promote conservation and campaign for urgent action. This involves launching Save Our Wild Isles in partnership with the RSPB and World Wide Fund for Nature (WWF), a call to action for people to take positive steps and make a difference for wildlife, from community projects to lobbying government.

The Trust also commissions an online mini-series, *The Wild Life*, showcasing the important work done behind the scenes on top nature reserves. The episodes featuring remote coastal sites (the Farne Islands, Northumberland and Blakeney Point, Norfolk) highlight the need to give nature space, whereas, on Wicken Fen, access, engagement and inclusiveness can be promoted thanks to the boardwalk and our education programme. Our episode gives me the chance to spend a day with paralympian Ade Adepitan. I see the reserve through the eyes of a wheelchair user and feel pleased at how accessible the fen is.

With a desire to show the fen off in all its glory, the pressure is on. Happily, the February day is mild and the orange sunset turns out to be an absolute stunner. In the boardwalk hide for our final sequence, the script involves watching marsh harriers fly to roost. The back-up

The first foal of spring, Guinea Hall Fen, 24 March 2023. (Ajay Tegala)

plan of inter-cutting archive footage is not necessary as a beautifully marked male drops onto the fen before us (but they decide to cut out the moment when I excitedly blurt out 'bl**dy hell, two cranes' as a pair fly across the horizon, silhouetted against the glowing sun).

Burwell Fen: Thursday, 30 March 2023

Following the *Wild Isles* hype, the eyes of the public may be on the horses, but ranger eyes are on our most pregnant cow, Apple. Six days after the first foal, the year's first calf follows. It seems like a significant number of our calves are born on weekends, when just one ranger is on duty. On two occasions, I have been duty ranger and borrowed Mike from the visitor centre to assist with ear-tagging (including Carlie-Belle's second calf, Cordelia). Having formerly worked as both a pilot and a nurse, Mike is a calming influence.

Apple's calf arrives conveniently on a Thursday morning, with all four rangers on duty. Reported as a bull by volunteer checker Judy, three of us head to the eastern part of Burwell Fen to do what must be done.

The red calf is indeed a bull and he is already up walking. We coax mother and son into the easternmost field of the fen, shutting the gate to keep the rest of the herd out of our way. I am designated driver, following Apple and calf along the edge of the field. The aim is to keep them moving until the calf becomes tired and lags behind his mother just long enough to drive the Land Rover between them. Holding nerves, eventually we corner the calf by the gate. I shuffle back and forth, creating a triangle out of the Land Rover and the corner of the fence line, thus blocking Apple's access to her calf. He is subsequently ear-tagged on the ground while I reward mother with a large pile of feed. Having had six previous calves, it is almost as if she knows the drill.

Apple's attention diverted successfully from calf to food, I join in the testicle-guddling stage of the operation. Once we are all confident that both 'broad beans' can be felt inside the 'felt purse', I put a latex band onto the applicator and hand it over. We debate whether the band has been fitted just a bit too high. Too low could leave part of the testes attached and thus not be a successful castration, but too high could sever more spermatic cord than necessary and introduce the possibility of infection. So a second band is fitted, a fraction lower. The higher band is then snipped, using a pair of sharp scissors borrowed from the first aid kit. Mission accomplished, we wash hands thoroughly then relax and enjoy a rare chat about our lives outside of work, before heading back to base and registering the birth.

The last calf tagging on the ground I had been involved in took place four years earlier, when Poppy calved in a wet part of the fen, not easily accessible by vehicle. Strangely, she did not seem hugely bonded to her newborn bull calf. So much so, that I was able to fit his ear tags on the ground without her objecting. It was a little nerve-wracking, I confess, without a vehicle to protect me. In hindsight, Poppy's behaviour was a red flag. Her maternal instincts had failed to kick in. Having kept an eye on her and the calf since his birth, it quickly became evident that she had abandoned him (although, luckily for the calf, it would seem she did at least manage to give him his nutrient-rich first colostrum).

With speed now of the essence, the dun calf was relocated to the hospital paddocks for hand-rearing. With his sweet face, he soon stole the hearts of passing visitors and the nearby residents of Lode Lane, especially when bounding across the field at bottle-feeding time. His original name, Moth, did not really seem to fit his personality, so he was renamed Toby.

Toby became the talk of the fen, all staff taking a keen interest in his progress as he slowly put on weight. After ten days, Raven and her similar-aged young calf, Duncan, were brought to join him in the paddock. This gave him the chance to socialise with other cattle. He developed a sneaky technique of suckling from Raven. If she saw him approaching, Raven would push Toby away, wanting to save her milk for her own calf. But Toby learned to approach from behind and not be spotted by her.

After four months in the paddock, the trio were transported back to Burwell and reintegrated themselves with the herd. Toby remained approachable and still liked a tickle under his chin. Another

Bottle-feeding Toby, Lode Lane, 12 April 2019. (National Trust Images/Mike Selby)

hand-reared bull, Stan, also enjoyed a good scratch (just like his mother Wendy had done). Stan was orphaned at just 3 weeks old. Interestingly, neither he nor Toby became high-ranking bulls, spending much of their time on the periphery of the herd. This prompted me to explore what the impact of hand-rearing has on Highland cattle in a rewilding context.

In the absence of a mother's milk, bottle feeding provides calves with the nourishment needed to grow and develop. Three bull calves have been hand-reared at Wicken in eighteen years. All were bottle-fed for up to eight months before being returned to the herd, whereas male calves raised by their mothers tend to naturally wean at ten to twelve months, at about the time the mother produces her next calf, receiving food for longer. As much as strength and size may have a bearing on status in the herd, there is another factor. All herds have a scent, which is recognised and recognisable. It is a large part of how cattle tell members of their own herd from strangers. Hand-reared cattle will have a different scent, putting them on a back foot when they reintegrate. I remember how, for many months, the four Belles would generally be separate from the main herd, still regarded as strangers and not yet accepted.

When hand-rearing males at Wicken, as hard as it is to resist thinking of them like pets, it is important to minimise human influence and maximise contact with other cattle, ensuring they develop appropriate bovine behaviour and do not over-attach to humans. However, as wild as we try to keep the Wicken cattle, we do still have to treat them like domestic stock at times, to fulfil legal obligations. This includes rounding up the herd intermittently to test for bovine tuberculosis.[*] In these situations, having amenable bulls makes handling easier. But, I wonder, does increased amenability in bulls conversely reduce their chances of becoming high-ranking males with mating rights in a free-roaming herd?

Listing all of the 'friendly' bulls she has known, Carol notes that only two out of nine were hand-reared. However, seven of them never made it further than 'middle-ranking' bulls. Interestingly, the exceptions were the herd's first two top bulls. Coming from a domestic background, Ewan was exceptionally friendly. Being the first male to arrive on the fen, he occupied the top bull position by default, without any challengers for half a decade until Edmund overthrew him. From a different male genetic line, Edmund had a much more muscular build than Ewan (described by Carol as 'stacked, absolutely ripped around the chest and neck'). All of the subsequent more successful males have tended more towards Edmund's shape than Ewan's, including the less-friendly Thompson, who became the herd's third top bull. Genetics evidently play a big part.

---

*   An infectious disease in cattle. All keepers of cattle, buffalo and bison in
      Britain are legally required to test their animals as part of a regime reflecting
      regional risk.

Sedge Fen: Monday, 3 April 2023

Overnight frost melts in spring sunshine. Against a beautiful blue sky, two swallows grace the telegraph wires outside the tractor shed. Their cheerful chirping will soon fill the tractor shed as they nest inside it once again. Already, a robin is incubating four eggs in the shed, having nested in a curl of lifting strops hanging on the wall. She will go on to fledge her brood and lay a second clutch in the same nest. A pied wagtail pair will build their nest on the 9540 tractor parked in the yard, prohibiting its use until the fledglings vacate.

Across Sedge Fen and beyond, there seem to be chiffchaffs everywhere. While repairing gates with the Monday volunteer party, I finally see my first brimstone butterflies of the year. Sunlit, their vivid yellow wings are a welcome sight.

Blossomtime has arrived. The delicate white flowers of blackthorn abound across the landscape. But it is the subtle beauty of the willow blossom that brings me the most joy this year. I had been waiting for blackthorn, for brimstones, chiffchaffs and swallows, but I had forgotten the fluffy willow flowers with their delicate yellow dusting. Occasional wafts of floral fragrance reach my nostrils. Winter has a limited scent palette of sawn wood, rank soil and occasional smoke blown from chimneys in the village. Now, pleasant smells are drifting across the fen and will eventually include the two most fragrant flowers, water mint and meadowsweet. Although the latter – historically used to sweeten mead – will not be smelt until after the summer solstice.

Wicken Fen: Thursday, 6 April 2023

Today is a vet day. The subtle scents of spring flowers will be masked by horse poo. We are moving eight yearling fillies out of the breeding herd to reduce its size and slow its growth. Four are going onto Burwell Fen, to join Fleming and friends. The other four are going to the paddock, to be sold on to a private conservation trust in May. Organised at relatively short notice, Carol has been busy preparing. From looking at herd genetics – ensuring valuable lines are not lost – to listing all the tools and equipment we will need to assemble for the day to run smoothly. She has still found time to prepare her annual tractor shed Easter egg hunt, hiding thirty-eight sweet treats in imaginative locations. Every year there is a buzz of excitement as staff and volunteers compete to find hidden chocolate in tractor wheels, on shelves, under tarpaulins and inside grain bins. I luck out with a Lindt bunny hidden in the grazing bay, then leave the rest for the volunteers.

Easter is one of my favourite times of year, the countryside full of promise. But May has been my favourite month since my teen years in rural South Lincolnshire.

Deeping Fen: Tuesday, 1 May 2007

May marks not only the crescendo of birdsong, but also verge verdancy. As a wealth of warblers arrive from Africa throughout April, a plethora of plants emerge from fenland soil. But king of spring has to be the month of May:

> I could see the trees and fields were somehow fuller than yesterday. The greenery was greener, the sky was bluer, there was more cow parsley and the oilseed rape was yellower.

Wicken Fen: Wednesday, 1–Thursday, 2 May 2019

The date 1 May is, of course, when the National Trust acquired its first land on Wicken Fen. Some 120 years later, we indulge in anniversary celebrations. The year 2019 also marks two decades of the Wicken Fen Vision project:

> Vivid dreams involving Wicken Fen, which today celebrates 120 years of National Trust ownership. We celebrated with a terrific cake and the BBC morning weather was presented live from the windpump by Carol Kirkwood.

It is always nice to celebrate milestones and anniversaries. This one provides the opportunity to relaunch and promote the Vision, sharing our work and ambitions with a wider audience. The daughter of a Fenland carrot farmer, general manager Sarah is perfectly placed to liaise with neighbouring farmers. I lead seven guided walks over three days, justifying my high intake of cake and leftover Powter's ham from a special stakeholders' docky. But, rangering during the 120th anniversary week is not all about food and guided walks. Our varied role is highlighted when it becomes apparent there are untoward activities taking place in the car park on 2 May:

> I noticed a car on its own in the back of the car park. Normally I would not have paid any attention. However, it was clear what was going on … I knocked on the window and requested that they kindly move on!

Adventurers' Fen: Monday, 1–Tuesday, 2 May 2023

News comes through of three swifts high over Lode Lane. I had planned to spend the afternoon in the office, but what was I thinking? I need to be outside with the birds. Last night I had been giving a talk encouraging people to enjoy the excitement of spring migration, now I should follow my own advice and admire these wondrous winged travellers. The sun has not been shy this bank holiday weekend. It has enticed several St Mark's flies into the air, their long legs dangling. These shiny, black flies are so named because they emerge around St Mark's Day, 25 April. As well as pollinating fruit trees, the flies provide perfect sustenance for freshly arrived hobbies, their favoured food of dragonflies not yet having emerged.

Cycling on the uneven bank beside Wicken Lode, I excitedly spot two hobbies. These small falcons are slightly slimmer and more streamlined than kestrels. I admire their aerobatic flight. Their black eye masks contrast with white cheeks and necks. Best of all, beneath the belly, I glimpse their rufous trousers. Most years, a pair breed in a line of old willows on nearby Adventurers' Fen with stock doves for nesting neighbours.

Hobby hunting a mayfly over the fen, 16 May 2023. (Simon Stirrup)

Within view of said mature willows, I throw down my bike and reach for my binoculars. A long-tailed, hawk-like bird grabs on to a high branch and announces itself. 'Cuck-oo, cuck-oo.' I heard my first cuckoo at dawn on St Mark's Eve, almost certainly the same bird. This is the first time I have set eyes upon him. Beneath the tree, I spot a pair of grey, leggy birds almost hidden by the tall grass, cattail, rush and reed. Cranes.

Despite standing 4ft tall, these elegant creatures are barely visible in their favoured habitat. I watch them, heads down, moving from side to side as they stride carefully among the vegetation. They are distant, but I am sure they are plucking spiders and flies from the grass. This excites me, combined with the fact this is the first time in a month that I have seen both cranes together. Throughout April, we spotted lone birds flying between their nesting and feeding grounds, taking turns to incubate their eggs. This change in behaviour almost certainly means their egg, or eggs, have hatched.

Twenty-four hours later, I return with my telescope, finding them a good 150m further east. Both birds stay close to each other, moving together. I will them to wander into a patch of shorter vegetation. Only then will I be able to confirm their parenthood, although I could put money on it.

After half an hour, one of the adults strays into a shorter patch of grass. My heart stops. For the following few seconds, time slows down, until a tiny orange delight prompts my heart rate to increase. A second chick appears and I shout out softly in pure joy. Two chicks are better than one, twice as likely to survive. My thoughts turn quickly to chick survival, taking the edge off the elation. It will be ten or eleven long weeks before they are capable of flight. They must dodge danger for more than two months before being able to fly. In four years, no Wicken crane chick has quite made it to its eleventh week.

Cycling back to base, I spot recently emerged hemp-agrimony stems. Their species name, *cannabinum*, relates to the resemblance their leaves have to cannabis, although the plant is not actually related to hemp. By the time their frothy pink-and-white flower buds emerge – which earn it the name 'raspberries and cream' – our crane chicks could be capable of flight ... if they can make it that far. The following weeks will be a suspense-filled time rooting for these chicks. But May and June will also be a most delightful time bursting with beautiful birdsong, especially at dawn.

Adventurers' Fen: Sunday, 1 May 2022

The alarm goes off at 3.15 a.m. It is International Dawn Chorus Day. An hour later, I am stood outside the visitor centre to welcome early walkers gathering for a special tour. Torchlight illuminates surnames on the sign-in sheet, morning sun not yet having emerged in the eastern sky. Once all eighteen attendees have assembled, bird expert Andy and I begin our dawn chorus walk. Although there is no need to actually walk anywhere yet. We stand and listen, taking in the rich soundscape, identifying birdsong species by species. Two grasshopper warblers are reeling within earshot, insect-like song explains their name. Some of our group believe it is actually the call of a grasshopper they are hearing, impressed a bird is capable of producing such a sound. Our management of the fen creates the breeding habitat favoured by this delightful warbler, with a mixture of scrub, grass, reedy edges and scattered bushes. However, across the wider countryside, the species has suffered steep declines in population. So too have nightingales, and this is the third year they have failed to return to the fen. There is a theory that the abundance of muntjac deer have browsed away the nightingales' favoured habitat.

Night is not yet over. The resonant hoot of a tawny owl carries from the trees on St Edmund's Fen as if handing the baton over to the cuckoo. It is not long before we hear a reed warbler, the fellow African migrant[*] whose nests the cuckoo cunningly lays its eggs in, masters of egg mimicry. We walk alongside the reed-fringed edge of Wicken Lode, where Professor Nick Davies has carefully studied cuckoo eggs in reed warbler nests over multiple decades, furthering our understanding of this fas-

---

[*]   Reed warblers spend winter in West Africa, whereas cuckoos over-winter further south in the Congo (as revealed by satellite tracking research undertaken by the British Trust for Ornithology).

Newly hatched cuckoo chick, blind and naked, ejects a reed warbler's egg from beneath the brooding female, Burwell Lode, 2 June 2014. (James McCallum)

cinating ornithological wonder. Nick's brilliant book, *Cuckoo – Cheating by Nature*, weaves together science and poetry to tell the story of a truly remarkable bird. He shares his sheer astonishment of seeing a reed warbler feed a cuckoo chick in its nest, which the warbler believes is its own offspring despite being an incredible five times the warbler's size and weight – the cuckoo chick having instinctively ejected the reed warbler's own eggs from of the nest soon after hatching.

Reed warblers often nest near sedge warblers, sharing a very similar favoured nesting habitat. The calls of the two birds are also similar, although the sedge is slightly more erratic and said to have more of an 'electric buzz'. Both warblers are often termed 'little brown jobs'. The reed warbler is indeed all-brown, but the sedge has a white supercilium (feathers above the eyes). One by one, Andy keeps a count of the various warblers he deciphers from this wall of sound. It is striking how much louder the birdsong is at this time of day, unspoiled by competing noises. I detect the distant boom of a bittern in the reedbed a mile away.

We total ten warblers in the course of our dawn ramble around Adventurers' Fen. Explosions of loud Cetti's warbler song are frequent from reedy ditch edges. The chiffchaff is the most persistent caller on our amble, contrasting with the more melodious song of the willow warbler. Blackcap is added to the list fairly early on and eventually we hear both common and lesser whitethroat. Finally, a garden warbler completes the decagon of warblers.

Our walk ends back at Lode Lane with swifts screeching in the sky, one of the last spring migrants to arrive from Africa. Swifts are also one of the first to leave again, beaten only by the cuckoo who return south rather than fulfilling the parental duty of feeding their young. Food is now on our minds as we head to the cafe, where Trina has been busily making coffee and cooking breakfast. A bacon sandwich tastes its best at the end of a dawn chorus walk. And the dawn chorus is a true natural wonder, worth waking up early for at least once a year.

Adventurers' Fen: Thursday, 11 May 2023

It is shortly after 5 a.m. Team bittern walk along Harrison's Drove as the orange glow of the rising sun starts to break through the cloud. Two of the team peel off and wade through the tall vegetation on Little Drove, the grass and nettles have grown considerably since our last survey a fortnight ago. The rest of us scramble up the lode-bank to our position. I can hear male cuckoos in stereo, one is on Verrall's Fen, the other somewhere towards the mere, calling almost in unison. One is slightly higher pitched and calls half a second after the other. But the show is stolen by a very loud sedge warbler, perched at the top of a buckthorn on the opposite side of the lode. He seems determined not to be upstaged by anything, almost drowning out the booms coming from the other side of the reedbed.

After an hour stood listening, I begin walking to the opposite side of the fen. My tattered shoes have allowed last night's rain to transfer from the grass to my absorbent cotton socks. Precisely 1 mile later, I reach Pout Hall Corner, named after the nineteenth-century building that stood at the junction of Reach and Burwell Lodes. Charles Lucas recorded that a 'little old woman who once lived at Pout Hall used to ferry herself over from one bank of the lode to the other in her washtub, using the linen prop'. It is at the site of this long-ago comic scene that I join the final member of the bittern survey team.

We compare notes, catch a glimpse of a cuckoo and comment on the common terns above the triangular pond across the lode from us. Terns have nested on a floating shingle island here for several years. I first saw the pair three days ago, one with a fish in its bill, completing my mental checklist of all the expected African migrants. It has been half an hour since the bittern last boomed. Unbeknownst to us, it crept into a ditch in search of food. Disturbed by a pair of greylag geese, the large male rises above the reeds, flies 150m, disappears and proceeds to boom from the same spot he was heard earlier. We do not yet know if he is part of a pair or just a lone individual.

My day is made three times over. First, with only my third ever bittern sighting on the fen. Secondly, I catch a glimpse of the two crane chicks, still alive and well so far. And then, a productive bit of twitching completes the trilogy of avian delights. The terms twitcher and birdwatcher often get confused. Birdwatching is the practice of observing birds in their natural surroundings as a hobby. Twitching, however, involves travelling long distances to see rare birds so they can be ticked off a list. So, really, casually swinging by the edge of Verrall's Fen to investigate a reported bird sighting is not full-on twitching. As both a bird lover and Wicken ranger, I would find it hard not to get excited by the report of a nightingale, following a four-year absence from the fen.

Interestingly, the nightingale is reported – by the county bird recorder – in the same spot historically favoured by the species, a scrubby patch beside the lode. As soon as I arrive, I hear the loud trills and indicative churring. Such a rich and complex song. There is a beautiful recording in the British Library of a nightingale singing at Wicken, with cuckoos calling in the background. I could listen to it on loop for hours. But to hear it 'live', I feel like jumping for joy, even if I only have a few minutes to experience it before rushing to my next job. A delay in the transportation of four yearling fillies means they are worryingly close to overgrazing the holding paddock. So Carol and I must spend the afternoon shifting hurdles to give them access to a bit of adjacent grazing without leaving any possible escape routes that could be exploited by mischievous youngsters.

11

Green to Gold

• **Dragonflies** • **Orchids** • **Cuckoo** •
Breeding bittern behaviour • **Pout Hall Corner** •
Bats in the cafe • **Summertime** •
Nocturnal insects • **The fen nettle** •
A missing bull • **Cranes fail again** •
The 'ugly cygnet' • **The joy of raking** •
The wheatear heralds autumn •

Spring to Summer ... Odonata and Orchids

As spring progresses, the hobbies' diet shifts from St Mark's flies to mayflies and then to dragonflies and damselflies. The latter two insects are collectively known as Odonata, which means 'toothed jaws'. The first odonates usually appear on the wing in the second half of May, as the almond-like sexy smells of hawthorn blossom are succeeded by the sweet and spicy scent of elderflower. Dragonflies are descended from griffinflies, which lived in carboniferous forests 300 million years ago, before the dinosaurs. Some griffinflies had 70cm wingspans.

Wicken Fen is one of the best sites in the country to see dragonflies and damselflies, with twenty-nine species recorded. Five species have been extinct since the early twentieth century. The decline in peat digging led to the loss of acid pools and with them acid-loving species.

But five new species have also arrived on the site since the earlier losses. These include the emperor dragonfly, which was first recorded in summer 1988 by head warden Tim Bennett. With larvae 0.5cm long and a wingspan of 10.5cm, the emperor is Britain's largest dragonfly. Its colonisation of Wicken Fen fits with the northward spread of the species, an indicator of climate change.

All British Odonata rely on permanent water, which is why Wicken is an ideal place for them. Sheltered, sunny spots are perfect places for adults to warm their wings. Clean water containing aquatic plants is prime for egg laying and emergence. Some nymphs (larvae) live as long as five years underwater. Adult dragonflies generally live for between one and eight weeks. The adults are able to alter flight speed and direction rapidly to avoid being predated and are even capable of flying backwards. Dragonflies generally hold their wings open while at rest, in contrast to the smaller damselflies that tend to close their wings along their abdomen when resting.

Dragonflies are nature's most successful stalker, catching their prey 95 per cent of the time. Prey items largely consist of small insects, including mosquitoes. It is not speed or surprise tactics that make dragonflies so prosperous, but skills in maths and physics. When hunting, they keep the targeted insect in sight, adjust their flight and predict how their prey will move, enabling them to make their catch with precision. American research used slow-motion filming to reveal the clever techniques that make them twice as successful as great white sharks at catching prey. It is their visual sharpness, clever calculation and speedy reflexes that make dragonflies such lucrative predators.

My favourite odonate has to be the banded demoiselle, after first admiring them fluttering their beautiful wings above the River Nene west of Peterborough. The four dark spots on the males' wings dance in perfect symmetry. I once found a wing near Guinea Hall, presumably plucked by a hobby before devouring the body.

The transition of spring into summer is subtle and open to debate. While arriving migrant birds announce springtime, summer is surely signalled by the flowers on Sedge Fen. On 1 June each year, the summer nature trail opens for four special months. Before the vegetation becomes too scorched by the sun, Sedge Fen looks its absolute best with a very fine floral display.

During the closing days of May, the almost luminous yellow flowers of flag iris emerge, their outer petals drooping like a fleur-de-lis. The rhizomes had many uses in folkloric medicine, including a treatment for toothache, until they were found to cause severe gastric disturbances and so its use died out, understandably. At Wicken, irises are a precursor to a special group of plants. The name orchid comes from the ancient Greek for testicle, relating to the shape of their roots. Due to recent bandings, I have literally touched more bull testicles than I have seen wild orchids so far this year! Very much hoping to change this, I set off in search of summer flowers on my way to check the livestock on Verrall's Fen over the Whitsun weekend.

Verrall's Fen: Saturday, 27 May 2023

It is 21°C in the afternoon sunshine as I stride beside Wicken Lode. All day, black-headed gulls have been flying up and down the waterway. I watch to see if they are hunting fish, or more likely flies, but I keep getting distracted by signs of summer. The fresh leaves of oak and ash are a shade of green only seen at this time of year.

Away from the bustling boardwalk and laden Lodes Way, it is calm and quiet on Verrall's Fen. I haven't been out to Verrall's since late February and its whole atmosphere has vastly changed. There is that warm stillness you sometimes get on summertide afternoons. The fen's three oldest cows sit beneath the dead oak with its illusion of shade. I hear the comic 'ye-ah' call of a distant Mediterranean gull, by no means a common part of the Wicken soundscape. Underfoot, there must be water mint if my nostrils don't lie. Tomorrow, I will find the reddish-purple haze of an abundance of water mint stems on Burwell Fen. On Verrall's today, there are just a few small leaves, which I bend down to crush between my fingers. As I do so, my attention is stolen by another plant, an early marsh orchid with its cluster of exquisite pale pink flowers. In the autumn, new ranger Joe reignites my interest in the less showy plants, too.

This quiet corner of the reserve has one more treat for my eyes as I rush back towards the visitor centre. Perched on a stem is a four-spotted chaser. The iridescent, bronze dragonfly shimmers in the sun. I watch it for a short while before hurrying to respond to a radio call from duty manager Sally. A worried visitor has rung the centre, concerned that one of the ponies was in serious trouble because it was lying down and barely moving. I hurry over to 'Cock-Up' Bridge, where the visitor had called from. The horse in question, thankfully, is in fact merely resting.

Although calls like this are often false alarms, we greatly value the care and concern people have for our livestock. Not just because it is lovely that the public feel invested in the area, but also because there are occasions when a visitor reports a genuine emergency.

I head home a little later than intended but chipper, having had a glorious day on the sunny fen. Halfway home, I see what looks like thick smoke above the roadside trees. A closer look reveals it is not smoke, but midges. I have seen 'tornado' swarms of non-biting flies a few times over the years. But these midges are the most impressive. Tornadoes are created when millions of midges hatch in synchronicity because the weather is just right for them. Termed 'lekking', the males gather to attract females. I think to myself what an easy meal these swirling clouds of chironomids could make for swallows, swifts and bats.

Sedge Fen: Friday, 2 June 2023

While the swallow chicks in our tractor shed are fed on flies caught by their parents in flight, crane chicks are fed on insects plucked from the grass. The young are now around five weeks old, their heads standing about as high as their parents' wings. They are now starting to look like miniature cranes, rather than orange chickens. I try to spot them every day, just to reassure myself they are still there. My plans to check on them this afternoon are changed when duty manager Isabel asks if I fancy walking the nature trail, which opened yesterday. How can I refuse? I haven't walked it since last autumn. Striding out, we discuss how particularly brilliant the hawthorn blossom has been this spring and also how attractive the guelder-rose flowers are. On the northern edge of the trail, we find an abundance of ragged robin with its reddish-pink, long and thin petals. This damp-loving species is, according to the Victorian language of flowers, a symbol of ardour and wit.

The more we look, the more orchids we spot, including southern marsh, which has richer purple flowers than the early marsh, although both species are variable. They can also hybridise with each other, making identification even more challenging. But the hardest member of the family to find is the easily overlooked common twayblade, with its leaf-coloured flowers that can total up to 100 on a single stem. There is a spot on the western edge of Sedge Fen where they have been histori-cally recorded, however we do not spot them today. A strong desire to move on is brought about by the stench of a dead roe deer in the dyke beside us. Our walk concludes with a broad-bodied chaser, distinguish-able from the similar black-tailed skimmer by its wider abdomen.

Isabel is keen for new visitor centre staff to get around the nature trail, nurturing their appreciation. Three weeks later, I walk the 2-mile loop with Toby,[*] who seems more interested in seeing the dead roe deer he has heard about than the plants. But the impressive display of orchids does not fail to impress. As for the bloated deer carcass, thank-fully the smell has subsided and no unsuspecting visitors were alarmed by it spontaneously exploding.

Sedge Fen: Thursday, 8 June 2023

Other than orchids and Odonata, cuckoos are what Wicken is most famous for in June, ahead of the adult birds beginning their return migration. Isabel has organised a special walk with Nick Davies for

---

[*] Not to be confused with the bull of the same name!

visitor-facing staff and volunteers, so they can learn a few facts about this fascinating bird with which to wow walkers, cyclists and boat trip customers. Bike and boat assistant Sally clutches her copy of Nick's book and clings to his every word. I tag along for the charm of listening to him, having somehow always missed out in previous years.

As well as helping monitor the crane chicks, Nick has been watching reed warblers along Wicken Lode. He parts the reeds carefully with a treasured stick – given to him by late warden Ralph Sargeant – and invites the group of twelve to step forward, one by one. Taking turns, we peer into a nest and see the fluffy warbler chicks within. The parent bird utters single notes of alarm call telling the chicks to keep still. 'Isn't nature amazing,' exclaims Julie, 'shame it cocked up with humans big time!' There is more to be amazed by when she learns how cuckoos cleverly mimic reed warbler eggs.

It is almost an hour into the walk before we hear the 'cuck-oo' call of a male coming from the opposite side of the lode. Nick brings his left fist up to his mouth and blows between the thumb and forefinger, using his right palm to restrict air flow, delivering a perfect 'cuck-oo'. But, this year, his scientific party trick fails for the first time, the male bird neglecting to investigate the rival call. Are the birds becoming shyer as well as fewer?

Each spring, it is as much a relief as a joy to hear the first cuckoo, fearing that one year they might not come back to the fen. In 2012, no chicks were raised at Wicken, for the first time in probably centuries. Thankfully, it hasn't been all downhill ever since. Eleven years on, we have around five males and two females, and one of the latter has been heard making her 'bubbling' call on the edge of St Edmund's Fen. There is hope yet. A cuckoo can lay over twenty eggs in a breeding season.

Pout Hall Corner, Thursday, 22 June 2023

When their chicks hatch, the lives of parent birds expeditiously become dominated by the need to feed their young, with the exception of cuckoos, of course. Birds, from tiny wrens and reed warblers up to tall cranes, catch insects to feed their offspring. For marsh harriers, chicks are fed on the flesh of birds and small mammals. By late June, male marsh harriers may often be seen hunting over farmland to feed their young. For bitterns, it is the female who cares for her nestlings, regurgitating fish and frogs for them. Slightly worryingly, considering Wicken's extensive wetland habitat, I encounter incredibly few frogs on the fen and rarely see frogspawn. So I assume the bittern chicks' diet consists mostly of small fish.

Yes, bittern chicks!* Being in the right place at the right time is significantly easier thanks to knowing roughly where a bittern's nest is, which we do, due to our monitoring. In fact, reported sightings of a female flying over Burwell Lode have been frequent near Pout Hall Corner. So team bittern assemble on the lode-bank for a sunny morning of waiting and watching, camping chairs in tow. We share this quiet corner of the fen with two fishermen. They are friendly and have local knowledge. Fish knowledge. Apparently, the triangular lake in the corner of Pout Hall Fen is full of fry. Perfect prey for the cormorants, nesting common terns and also the bittern, which they claim to have seen flying in and out of the lake over the last week or so.

I am fascinated by the history of Pout Hall. What it must have been like to live there, how it came to be used by smugglers, how it vanished, how the site somehow came to be a small lake. And I am fascinated by the bitterns, their behaviour, their every move, so few of them witnessed. Volunteer and keen birder Keith recounts to me how he recently saw a bittern chasing another at nearby Ouse Fen, and the strange sound made by the female being pursued. We hear an odd gurgling call coming from the other side of the lode, which I assume is a cormorant. But he says it sounds very similar to the strange bittern call he had witnessed, a bit like the bubbling call of a female cuckoo. Could there be a bittern just a few feet away from us? Was it foraging in the spot where the infamous Pout Hall once stood?

After an hour seeing nothing, we go on to observe four flights, two heading into the reedbed and two heading into the triangular lake.

---

*   Bitterns have bred on Adventurers' Fen since 2009 (although not every year), following a seventy-two-year absence.

Bittern. (Ajay Tegala)

One flight goes right over Colin's and Andrew's heads, giving them a cracking view. At that very moment, a dog walker passes them, audio-book blaring out from her phone, oblivious to the bittern mere metres above her immaculately styled hair.

Due to the absence of any deep pools in the reedbed, the deeper water of the lake provides an ideal hunting ground with its healthy supply of small fish. It is exciting and satisfying to not only more than double my Wicken bittern sightings tally, but to gain an insight into this site-specific behaviour – something I had longed to achieve since first volunteering on the fen.

The Docky Hut Cafe: Thursday, 27 June 2019

My first day volunteering with the Wicken wardens, back in July 2005, started at the docky hut. This little staffroom between the tractor shed and workshop had been so-known for years. About a decade later, it was decided that the cafe should be named 'The Docky Hut'. A great name for the cafe (which itself had been a tractor shed originally), albeit a tad confusing for staff to have two different places with the same name. But most of the folks sipping tea in the cafe will probably be as blissfully unaware the fen has two docky huts as they are that dozens of bats may be just a few feet away, inside the wall cavity.

On becoming a (paid) fen ranger, in August 2018, I learned that around 100 soprano pipistrelle bats roosted in the south-west-facing side of the cafe. At just 4cm in length, soprano pipistrelles are one of our smallest – and most common – bat, but still easily capable of eating 3,000 insects in one night. Of the seventeen breeding bat species in Britain, just four have been recorded on Wicken Fen. The following June, I jump at the chance to conduct a roost count, always having been fascinated by bats. More agile fliers than most birds, bats are in fact more closely related to humans.

The summer of 2019 was wonderfully batty, due to a fantastic opportunity to co-present a BBC documentary about British bats. Five days before the Wicken roost count, I had been surveying a Daubenton's bat roost at Linlithgow Palace, and a month later I was helping monitor a greater horseshoe maternity roost in Dorset. All three were magical experiences, but only one involved deck chairs.

Sat comfortably in a deck chair outside the visitor centre, I hold a clicker counter in one hand and a heterodyne bat detector* in the other. At 9.21 p.m., according to my survey form, the first pipistrelle emerges from a tiny hole beneath the cafe gutter. Over the course of the following half an hour, I watch in amazement as a further 127 squeeze out of the hole and fly into the night. I found it hard to believe before seeing it for myself. They flew so fast, most of them leaving in a rapid stream, flinging themselves into the air with speed and agility.

The Joy of July

All months hold memories for me and those of July are particularly joyous, swapping studies for waterside wanderings. At Wicken, white water lilies float on the lodes, their large white flowers opening in the sunshine. They are Britain's largest flower, growing up to 20cm in diameter. The smaller, cupped flowers of yellow water lilies are said to smell like the dregs of wine, giving rise to the alternative name 'brandy bottle'. Another wonderful name for it is spadderdock. Water lilies provide cover for fish and nectar for insects. Less beneficial to invertebrates is greater bladderwort, another floating aquatic plant with yellow flowers. It gets its name from the bladders on its feathery fronds. When a

---

* Device that converts bat calls into sounds that the human ear can hear, used for immediate bat identification in the field.

water flea brushes against the trigger hairs of a bladder, a trap opens and the prey is sucked in. Research undertaken in Wicken's old brick pits has shown that individual plants may catch a quarter of a million tiny prey items each year.

July is not only the month I first volunteered on the fen, but when I began my first paid contract, too, becoming a seasonal cycle hire assistant in 2011. That summer, an Ely-based water sports company were operating stand-up paddleboard safaris along the lode, in partnership with the Trust. As well as helping with the occasional safari, I would often take a paddleboard out after work, sometimes with my fellow cycle hire pals Pete and Becky. After getting my balance, I found it a delightful way to see the fen. Reeds either side, the water like a window onto fish below, dragonflies darting around, water lilies brushing the edge of the board. On warm July days, grass snakes are sometimes seen swimming across the water, head slightly raised, body weaving from side to side for propulsion. Meanwhile, another of the fen's reptiles, the common lizard, may be basking on the boardwalk.

Rangers rarely have a chance to bask in the sunshine, however. Path edges, gateways and corrals require mowing at least fortnightly to prevent access routes becoming engulfed by encroaching vegetation. Much of the fen is left untamed at this time of year, but rights of way and trails must be maintained. Occasionally, I take the 9540 tractor to Tubney Fen and beyond, to mow the bridleways. As pleasant as it is cutting to a soundtrack of Abba hits, I become unsettled when the temperature dial tips closer to 'H' than 'C'. This is due to an overheating incident in 2020, when the water pump failed. Three years on, with radiator coolant filled to the max in the morning, I grow uneasy as the temperature needle approaches the red. In Commercial End, I pull over, lift the bonnet and let the engine cool for half an hour in the summer breeze.

Barely a mile further along the road, in Swaffham Prior, the needle reaches the top of the red. Devil's Dyke car park is a few hundred metres ahead on the right. It becomes my urgent destination. Alas, within sight of the Anglo-Saxon earthwork, the tractor loses power. I manage to steer off the main road onto the verge as it comes to a standstill. I feared this would happen one day, budgets still tight as a result of the pandemic.

It is one of those things beyond control (like a few weeks later, when a stone gets whipped up by the ride-on mower and shatters a nearby van window). Roadside assistance arrives at the stranded tractor within an hour, but it cannot be started. Fortunately, John knows the local farmer, who is kindly able to tow our tractor to his yard. We disconnect the mower and arrangements are made for the tractor to be collected for repair the following day (and I manage to collect Oakley from doggy daycare just before it closes for the night).

Night is a magical time on the fen in summer, often preceded by golden sunsets. With minimal light pollution and the absence of pesticides, Sedge Fen is an ideal place for glow-worms. Adults spend the day burrowed in soil, emerging after dark when the flightless females ascend stems to attract mates with their bioluminescence. In contrast to the beautiful glow of the adult beetles, larvae kill their prey with toxic bites that paralyse then dissolve slugs and snails. While the digestive proteins do their work, glow-worm larvae have been known to ride on snails' backs. Like crane flies and mayflies, the adults lack usable mouth parts. Their 'dates' do not involve dining, just urgent reproduction.

In the nineteenth and early twentieth centuries there would frequently be a hive of activity at dusk, with naturalists hoisting white sheets and illuminating them with gas lamps to attract moths. The light confuses their navigational systems, drawing them to the lit sheets, whereupon specimens would be collected, identified and pinned. A century on and moth trapping continues, using electric ultraviolet lights above box traps, with all insects released upon identification rather than killed. Just over 1,250 different moth species have been recorded on the reserve.

Wicken is home to a small selection of scarce species that moth recorders look forward to encountering during overnight surveys. In Britain, the reed leopard moth is found only in three English counties: Chippenham Fen and Wicken Fen in Cambridgeshire, the Norfolk Broads, and a single site in south-east Dorset. Adults have particularly long abdomens, extending well beyond their wingtips. The growing larvae spend two winters underwater inside reed stems. In the third year, the caterpillars move between reeds above water. The marsh carpet is another nationally rare wetland species, found in just East Anglia and Yorkshire, and its hidden larvae feed on ripening seeds of meadow-rue. Both Chippenham and Wicken Fens also boast the silver barred moth, which flies by day as well as night. Like the marsh carpet, it is attractive and distinctive. The silver barred is also found on peat bogs in south-west Ireland and on two coastal marshes in Kent.

Sedge Fen: Wednesday, 5 July 2023

On an early July evening guided walk around Sedge Fen, I introduce a group of Girl Guides to various flora and fauna. Throughout our hour-and-a-half walk, swallows and house martins circle above constantly, catching an evening feed of flying insects. I tell the group how bladder-wort is carnivorous and that saw-sedge can cut to the bone. But they don't believe me when I show them a nettle that does not sting. At a glance, the fen nettle looks very similar to the common nettle, however it lacks stinging hairs. Fen nettle grows beside the boardwalk, but so too do stinging nettles. So one must be careful, especially when showing groups of schoolchildren, as one former ranger found out to their cost when an unintended stinging incident occurred!

Cambridgeshire: Monday, 10 July 2023

In the muggy evening air, my friend Rick and I jog over the uneven tarmac of a Fenland back road. We chat about our respective days. His was spent at a desk, homeworking. Mine was mainly on Burwell Fen, looking for Bottom. This 3½-year-old black bull had been prov-ing elusive. Last week, tempers were high in the herd, younger males challenging for dominance and managing to overthrow the top bull, Socks. As one of the prime agitators, Bottom gave (and received) his fair share of knocks. Blows to both body and ego required some time out to regroup. It later became apparent that Bottom lived by the maxim, 'He that fights and runs away, may turn and fight another day.' He could hardly be blamed for going into hiding while things settled down. A few weeks later, he would be very much back in the running for top bull.

We try our best to find every animal every day. And we virtually always do, even with the livestock's ability to disappear behind a wisp of reed at a moment's notice. How an 800kg creature can vanish in a flat landscape is one of life's mysteries. I vow not to leave Burwell Fen until I have found our errant bull. The 165 hectares are mostly a sea of reeds and tall grasses, gradually turning from green to gold in the summer sun. It is almost like looking for the proverbial needle in a haystack, even with the Land Rover. A bittern flies over Reach Lode, a fox trots beside Newnham Drove, hundreds of meadow brown butterflies flit between thistles, roe deer stop and stare, but Bottom remains out of sight. Having circled the boundaries of all ten compartments, I park up by 'Cock-Up' Bridge and let Oakley out to stretch his legs in the lightly cooling breeze.

'He must be in the reeds,' I think to myself as I lean on the bridge railings, surveying the fen through binoculars. Almost immediately, I spot a distant black blob emerging from the reedbed and striding into an area of open grass. Now, it could be Duncan, he was in that area half an hour ago. 'It's probably Duncan,' I say to Oakley, loading him back into the Landy and zipping to the other side of the fen. As we draw closer, the wide, almost vertical horns give away his identity. It is Bottom and he is walking much better than last time he was seen (in just a few weeks, he will be a strong contender for top bull). There is a prosperous ending to my search. Although a colleague at Kingston Lacy tells me, 'you need some GPS collars'.

'We have never completely lost an animal,' I say to Rick. He points out that technically we had lost Bottom, albeit for a short while. Approaching the railway, 3 miles into our run and about a mile from the Ouse Washes, we spot five large, majestic birds in the sky, flying towards us. I don't normally like to break the pace, but ask if we can pause a minute to take in the cranes. They fly right over our heads, circling briefly before setting a straight course towards the Old Bedford River.

Seeing cranes so near to home always steals my attention and brings excitement. But today's sighting is bittersweet. The Wicken chicks have not been since the Summer Solstice. So, I wonder whether two of the birds above us could be the Wicken pair, failed breeders for a fifth year (believing a fox has procured a hearty meal). However, there is no evidence to prove this. While, equally, with no sightings of them in the vicinity of the fen, we have no proof the chicks fledged, it is not impossible that the secretive birds surreptitiously left the fen as a flying family and headed further afield. It was once believed that a pair on Lakenheath Fen had failed just when the young should have taken to the wing, only later to be discovered they had sneakily relocated under the radar. Could it be the Wicken crane chicks have fledged after all? We cannot say for certain.

The second half of July sees an upsurge in families visiting the fen, schoolchildren having broken up for their summer holidays. Themed trails and events are put on to entertain, enthuse and educate our summer visitors. But some of our winged summer stayers depart. Return migrations are brought on by gradually decreasing day length. 'Cuck-oo' disappears from the soundscape, followed by the 'shree' of screaming swifts. Africa beckons.

Meanwhile, mute swans lead their cygnets along the dykes and lodes, gliding past lily pads. Summer 2023 sees a curious case of 'ugly cygnets'. Not, in fact, swans raising a duckling, but two goslings. These young greylags end up being cared for by pen and cob, instead of goose and gander. The eggs presumably ended up being incubated by the wrong species. Like the reed warblers that hatch cuckoo chicks, these swans must have hatched goslings and therefore believe they are their offspring. By the end of July, just one gosling remains, which the swan pair protect diligently through August, spending much of their time on Verrall's Fen.

There are about 6 miles of droves on Sedge Fen, including Verrall's Fen. These straight, grassy tracks, 5m to 10m wide, provide both access and unique habitat, the maintenance of which requires at least annual cutting. This was once done with scythes and later with motorised mowers. Clearance of the arisings (cut vegetation) is important for management of the precious fen flora as leaving cut vegetation in situ inhibits plant growth beneath. The Fen Harvester cuts and collects the litter. But, prior to its acquisition, a large number of ranger and volunteer hours would be spent raking in the summer and early autumn. What would sometimes take a couple of months manually can be completed by the harvester in a mere few days.

John recalls how much of a toll raking seemed to take on people, especially when it would be the primary task for entire working days. A wide variety of minor incidents have occurred on the fen over the years, ranging from cuts to almost comical falls in the lode, but the most common injuries by far have been raking-related. So the harvester has made the fen a safer place for the team as well as more efficient. However, as effective as it is, the drove margins just don't seem to be quite as floristically sensational as they were when raking opened up the thatch, creating more of an open seedbed than the harvester is able to.

I well remember a week's late summer volunteering on Sedge Fen in 2008, which was spent mostly raking. Although fairly laborious, it was satisfying work, especially in the evening when you could really relax after a day of physical activity in the fresh air. I was raking alongside two students from the University of Hertfordshire who were a few weeks into their placement year, living in Rose Cottage on Lode Lane. During that week, National Trust director-general Dame Fiona Reynolds visited the fen and we were allowed to meet her. It was clear how appreciative she was of our volunteer support.

For the students, their placement year was to be just as valuable as their degree. Indeed, I was inspired to contact various National Trust nature reserves in search of a similar residential placement. I ended up on the North Norfolk coast the following summer. The volunteer accommodation at Blakeney became a holiday cottage a few years later. Eventually, Wicken's Rose Cottage followed the same

trend, necessitated by post-pandemic financial constraints putting
pressure on the property to generate income.

Approaching Autumn

As summer comes to a close, a favourite Eagles song of mine,
'Waiting in the Weeds', inevitably springs to mind. While it is easy to
feel wistful at this time of year, I always welcome autumn with open
arms and think also of a wonderful line from French philosopher, Albert
Camus: 'Autumn is a second spring when every leaf is a flower.' After the
increasingly hot British summers, autumn is a welcome breath of cool air.
Light morning mist tickles dawn dew. But, before August is out, there is
often fair weather to be savoured. Sat in her garden on the edge of the fen,
Carol tells me this is one of her favourite times of year. On a warm early
evening, I can see why. As much as I love spring, I always feel like it passes
too fast and that I never quite make the most of each moment before it is
gone. By contrast, nature seems to slow down in August, fruits ripen at a
leisurely pace, seemingly inspiring us to slow down a little and relax in
the warmth before temperatures start to fall. Meanwhile, nearby farmers
are kept busy harvesting crops, making hay and baling straw.

While ripe ears of wheat are harvested, the wheatear makes a welcome
return to Burwell Fen. This charming member of the thrush family passes
through in mid-April on migration to its breeding grounds in northern
and western Britain. Four months later, it passes through again on return
migration. I usually spot them standing on posts. The solar farm fence
beside Newnham Drove has become an ideal perching point for them.

I slow the Land Rover down to a gentle stop and reach for my binoculars to admire this beautiful bird. Black cheeks contrast with white
supercilium, as does grey back with pastel peach breast. Most striking
of all is the characteristic black 'T' against its white rump, flashed in
flight as it flits from one fence post to the next, leading me along the
drove. The bird's name does not come from ears of wheat, but from the
Old English 'hwit-ærs' meaning white rump.

Although it is still two weeks until the school summer holidays end,
the wheatear whispers autumn to me and I look forward to all it will

bring. The onion-like scent of freshly harvested leeks floats on the air. Spring blossom has become autumn berries. Hedgerows brim with ripening blackberries, hawthorns and sloes. Apple and plum trees become laden with fruit. I gather a few fruits to make a crumble. In September, we will pluck pears and apples to make more crumbles as well as juice. There is something so satisfying about seasonal foraging, it fastens you to the natural world and feels so wholesome.

Wicken: Tuesday, 2 October 2018

After work, we all went apple picking, arriving at Carol's garden with bags full of fruit. A peeling session precedes juicing in Gez's press. There was a lovely, timeless atmosphere... and lots of delicious fresh apple juice.

Whenever I forage autumnal fruits, I think of the thrushes that fly from Scandinavia to feed on them. In our garden, I planted a rowan tree in the hope that one day a waxwing might feast on its bright red berries. Whilst waxwings are a rare treat, there are birds that migrate to the Fens each autumn without fail, species also adored by Finnish composer Jean Sibelius, who wrote in his diary:

The swans are always in my thoughts and give life its lustre. Nothing in the whole world – neither in art, literature or music – affects me like the cranes and the swans and the wild geese. Their cries and their very being. This is the thread running through my life.[*]

Hearing the Fenland crane population calling in unison in September and the returning whooper swans in October, I will think of Sibelius' words and feel a similar adoration. Spring–summer is so different to autumn–winter that I could never chose between them. One always follows the other. It is the changing seasons that make the British countryside so perfectly wonderful to observe throughout the year and the Fens demonstrate perfectly how much the atmosphere of a place can change in the course of the year.

---

[*]   Source: *Sibelius Volume III: 1914–1957* (2009)

12

Weird Wicken

**A Collection of Eerie, Intriguing and
Unusual Happenings on the Fen**

• Ghost walk • The missing policeman •
The lantern men of Wicken Fen • Fen blows •
Storm Eunice • The drought of 2022 •
Ralph • A cocky bird • A bogie bird •
Swallows and a super blue moon •

Sedge Fen: Saturday, 29 October 2011

It is about to turn 6.30 p.m. Underneath the furthest section of
boardwalk from the visitor centre, I am hiding in vegetation. The
cold, dark night is eerily silent. I am dressed in hessian with chains
around my wrists and my face ghostly white. I smile to myself,
painted face wrinkling, thinking what a truly bizarre moment in my
life this is. The childlike excitement and anticipation builds as I wait
for my first 'customers'.

The previous few hours have seen a transformation of the visitor centre, parts of the fen and many of its staff and volunteers, too. There has been a terrific team effort to make the now locally famous Hallowe'en ghost walk as atmospheric as we possibly can. Mock gravestones have been put in place, haunting props suspended from trees, carved pumpkins have been lit and a smoke machine has been rigged.

The name Wicken – listed as 'Wicha' in the Domesday Book of 1086 and 'Wiken' around 1200 – derives from the Old English 'wicum', which means 'dwellings' or 'trading settlement'. But, tonight, history has been rewritten and the name is spelled 'Wiccan', relating to paganism.

Before the brave, daring families head through the dry ice onto the boardwalk, they are told a story to set the scene. Local legends feature, including Black Shuck, the devil's dog. Shuck, allegedly the inspiration for *The Hound of the Baskervilles*, was first reported in woodland between Peterborough and Stamford in a twelfth-century chronicle about England's history, becoming part of East Anglian folklore. Tonight, Old Shuck roams Wicken Fen in plywood form, an LED playing the part of its piercing red eye.

The far stretch of boardwalk is open and exposed, lulling ghost-walkers into a false sense of security, believing, quite reasonably, that there are no more frights until they reach the trees yonder. Little do they know that I am there, hiding. Waiting until they are within a couple of metres, I rattle my chains, groan and roar, taking people by surprise. A grown man screams and runs away. I feel strangely satisfied with that.

This will be one of the last ghost walks due to a growing number of dropped cameras, wet pants, slips, trips and near misses. I was pleased to have been part of the ghostly glory days. Another of the actors was Mike, from the visitor centre, who felt slightly uncomfortable playing the part of policeman Peak, a real person who went missing on the fen.

Wicken: Friday, 17–Saturday, 18 August 1855

The Red Lion pub, opposite Pond Green, is the setting for a hay sale. In attendance is young Richard Peak, Wicken's second ever police constable. According to his great-granddaughter, long-serving Fen Cottage volunteer Jill Peak, locals drinking in the pub that evening became rowdy and so the landlord asked PC Peak to stay on. Local artist and historian Anthony Day writes that Peak did not leave the Red Lion until around 3.15 a.m. 'in order to restrain the last noisy drinkers'. Setting off on foot across the Fens to Burwell, he was never to be seen again, leaving behind a widow and young son.

There are various versions of what happened. The Police Roll of Honour records that he went missing from his beat in suspicious circumstances and that 'it was suspected he was murdered by a local gang but his body was never found'. According to Day, the body was 'either buried deep below turf pits or cremated in a kiln'. He could, perhaps, have simply fallen into a turf pit or one of the many steep-sided, deep watercourses between Wicken and Burwell. A story that used to be told to children in the village tells how the buttons from his police uniform were found in a brick kiln. Two years after his disappearance, a report appeared in the *Cambridge Independent Press*:

PC Richard Peak in his uniform, 1852. (Peak Family Archive)

A human skeleton has been found under the surface of a field in Wicken Fen, and is supposed to be that of the policeman Peak, who it was thought met his death by the hand of an assassin near this spot ... being in the same direction he must have gone to meet the Burwell policeman, at conference point, on the very night he was missed.

However, there is some doubt as to whether the bones were ever identified for certain. The mystery therefore remains unsolved and the murder theory unproven.

Almost 150 years after her great-grandfather's disappearance, Jill Peak meets a medium in the hope of uncovering the family mystery surrounding her forebear. As they walk along the path beside Monks' Lode, the medium tells Jill that the locals had not intended to take his life, just beat him up and scare him a bit, but they went too far. Stopping partway along the path, he tells her this is where the incident had happened, at an old farm, since destroyed. Consulting a Victorian map reveals they were stood by the site of Ragamore. Indeed, an old path led directly from the village across St Edmund's Fen and over a footbridge to the building. Curiously, the most direct route from the Red Lion to Burwell village would not have passed Ragamore but headed out half a mile to the east.

The medium also tells Jill that PC Peak was not her only relative to lose their life on the fen. A young girl had also died there. This comes as a surprise and she later relays the information to her aunt, who is astounded that the medium could possibly know this. It was true. Jill's grandma's niece, Beatrice Ivy Granfield, lived in Wicken. In 1902, at the age of 3, Beatrice went to play with some friends on the fen. She fell into the lode and became tangled in reeds and other vegetation, which, very sadly, resulted in her drowning.

Not normally a believer in the paranormal, Jill was to experience another moment of astonishment after meeting the medium. He had told her a message, 'look out for the wheel arch'. Having recently scraped her car in Ely, she remarked that the message had come too late. A few days later, Jill went to London. Trying to read a street map while walking, she tripped over, falling to the ground. After standing up and dusting herself off, she noticed her fall had been caused by tripping on a wheel arch lying on the pavement.

The Lantern Men of Wicken Fen

The lantern men of Fenland folklore are another local, nocturnal mystery. Ghostly dancing lights over the fen were believed to be evil spirits, luring their victims to a watery death among the reeds. Dog walkers and fishermen have witnessed this spectral spectacle, often while whistling to themselves, which was said to draw the spirits in. The lantern men could supposedly be evaded by lying face down on the ground and sucking the mud. Not a particularly pleasant prospect and even less so with the knowledge that these strange lights were, in fact, merely the result of a chemical reaction.

Bioluminescence has become extremely rare since most of the fenland has been drained (with the exception of glow-worms on Sedge Fen in June and July). It is occasionally encountered on the coast on warm summer evenings, usually formed by algal blooms of phytoplankton. The lights of the lantern men were in fact the result of gas produced by decaying organic matter on the fen.

Fen Blows

Perhaps the most famous fine particles encountered in the fenland air are those of light peaty soil whipped up by the wind. With few trees to act as windbreaks, strong winds sweeping through the flat landscape can whip up the dry, peaty soil, sometimes creating clouds of dust hundreds of yards wide, blocking the sun. This is known locally as a 'fen blow'. The best description I have found comes from Alan Bloom, relating to a blow on Adventurers' Fen in May 1942:

A chocolate-coloured fog, that's what it resembled, only it wasn't chocolate and it wasn't fog … it was something which neither man nor beast was made to endure.

Working hard to reclaim land for wartime agriculture, the loss of topsoil, sugar beet seedlings and fertiliser was serious, a 14-acre field having been literally swept into the ditch. The cottage at Priory Farm had been spring-cleaned only the day before. It would take days to clear the black coating that now covered everything, fine dust having crept in with ease like smoke through cracks around windows and doors. Mixing the peaty soil with the heavier clay beneath it, known as 'claying', became a common process of mitigation, improving the capacity to retain moisture and nutrients (albeit releasing carbon into the atmosphere).

Fen blows in the twenty-first century are, fortunately, far less frequent or extensive. However, I recall one in April 2019 on Bottisham Fen, recording in my diary how 'the light, peaty soil made it into my eyes and ears'.

Storm Eunice: Friday, 18 February 2022

On Thursday evening, suspense builds. Tomorrow, Cambridgeshire is forecast to experience wind speeds between 40 and 60mph, with gusts as high as 80. Before leaving work, we proactively put signs out across the property stating 'reserve closed due to high wind forecast'. Storm Eunice looks set to rival the great storm of 1987. Due to staff on leave, I will be the only ranger on duty to conduct our daily livestock checks. Contemplating my 22-mile commute along exposed fen roads, some beside steep drains, I grow slightly nervous at the prospect of flying debris and powerful gusts of side wind.

I arrive at Lode Lane an hour early. My plan is to complete the checks and get home safely before wind speeds peak around mid-morning. First, I secure the chicken coop, its roof having blown across the paddock. I conceal a guilty smirk at the idea of that aggressive cockerel getting blown away across the fen and never being seen again. With the roof ratcheted down, I hop into the Hilux and head for the herds.

Conveniently, all the animals are easy enough to find. The breeding Koniks are sheltering by a line of scrub near the maltings. My main concern is the three-day-old colt, our first foal of the year. Extreme changes in weather during a foal's, or calf's, first week can reduce its chances of survival. But the well-established herd are wise. Multiple horses surround the foal, protecting it from the elements. He looks sturdy and stoic. Content, I walk across the field back to the Hilux, now facing the strengthening wind head-on. The few hundred metres are surprisingly tiring, every footstep an effort. I am happy to be back inside the vehicle, pleased to get back to base and relieved when Isabel responsibly rings in advising staff to head home.

A couple of neighbours lose roof tiles and a fair few find garden fence panels blown down. Over the following days, we will chainsaw and clear fallen trees on the fen, around the woodland walk and over at Houghton Mill near Huntingdon. Thankfully, no buildings or stock fences suffer significant damage on our land. But this will not be the only day of the year that Wicken Fen closes due to extreme weather.

Heatwave: Monday, 18–Tuesday, 19 July 2022

Five months, to the day, since Storm Eunice, I find myself checking the cattle and horses in a heatwave. A month of hot, dry weather has already turned most grass across the region from green to straw-coloured. All of the shallower areas of water have long since dried up in the strong sun. The livestock on Verrall's Fen have ditches, dykes and drains to slurp from, on Adventurers' Fen there is New River, but Burwell Fen now has just three borrow pits and one of those has become very shallow. If it doesn't rain soon, we will have to take water troughs out there and devise a way of filling them.

It is my first day back on the fen after a warm week in central France. By midday, it will be hotter here. I am advised to take the air-conditioned Hilux, rather than a bike, due to the lack of shelter. When temperatures exceed 30°C, visitors tend to avoid the fen, with its distinct lack of shade. Trina has decided to close the cafe early as it won't do much business and her staff are already overheating.

Out on the fen, our resilient animals are coping. Some of the cattle are stood in water and a few of the horses have been rolling in cool soil. This is not just a hot summer's day, the record-breaking heatwave is a very serious symptom of human-caused climate change. Many of our native wildlife species simply aren't able to deal with temperatures in the high 30s, not to mention the risk of wildfires, which are now breaking out across the country.

The thick swards of grass, reed, rush and sedge across the fen are like tinder. We have cobbled together and created fire flappers in case any part of the reserve ignites, waiting nervously for conditions to improve. Our other concern is an outbreak of New Forest Eye among the cattle, having experienced this in a prolonged dry spell four summers previously.

As I arrive home in the evening, the digital thermometer in my car reads 39°C. I head to the freezer and take out the pre-emptively chilled old bed sheet. Letting Oakley into the back garden for a few minutes to stretch his legs, I wrap him in the cool, white sheet. He had his daily walk early in the morning, before the tarmac became too hot for his paws. The same drill will be adopted tomorrow, which will be hotter still.

With temperatures set to reach a record-breaking 40°C in Cambridgeshire, it is decided that only one ranger needs to come into work. The corporate work party, who were planning to help pull ragwort, have naturally been called off. It would be foolish to spend even one hour pulling ragwort in this heat, its roots held tightly in the sun-baked soil. I spend the day catching up with computer-based tasks at home; my appropriate 'uniform' consists of just a pair of swimming shorts.

The weather station at the visitor centre records a high of 38.46°C. At 3.30 p.m., Cambridgeshire Fire and Rescue Service are called to a fire on Factory Road. This is one of dozens of wildfires in the county and hundreds across the country. It sweeps along a ditch edge, charring bushes and telegraph poles, but is extinguished before reaching our land. The nervous suspense continues for five more weeks, with the continued dry spell making us nervous that a discarded bottle or cigarette butt – or, heaven forbid, disposable barbecue – could set the fen ablaze. For years, smoking in the summer has been banned on Sedge Fen due to its abundance of dry vegetation.

On 30 July, more than fifty firefighters attend a 'well-developed fire involving around 200 acres of farmland, including bales, hedgerow and crops' on Grunty Fen, working tremendously hard for four hours to make the area safe. Two days later, I am shocked by the sight as I pass the singed expanse on my commute to Wicken.

Rain finally comes on 25 August. The welcome, soothing precipitation falls steadily from 5 a.m. into the early afternoon. I don wellies and dance onto St Edmund's Fen, savouring the sound of raindrops on reeds. The fen is dampened, softened, rehydrated. We are relieved, excited, overjoyed.

Mr Crowley

As Wicken Fen rangers, we regularly come close to half-ton Highlands and sparring stallions, sometimes handling them in tense situations, always aware of the proximity of horns and hooves. In open fields, we scoop up newborn calves from beside their protective mothers, to fit ear tags and perform castrations.

Reading and understanding animal behaviour is a key part of our role, as is being able to communicate clear signs to the livestock at pivotal moments. Confidently holding arms out wide and shouting loudly will prompt running horses to veer around us. The Koniks never intend to harm humans as long as their boundaries are respected, but it pays to keep an eye out for sudden changes in behaviour. The mood of the herd can change in an instant, with resting animals suddenly fighting or running. We have to be one step ahead. This is why we strongly encourage visitors not to linger among the herds or try to hug and pet them.

In the breeding herd of cattle, there is a loose hierarchy of bulls. Up and coming youngsters will push against the established status quo, sometimes resulting in injuries (which usually heal rapidly). Encounters like this between males can domino through the herd, forming a tense and edgy atmosphere.

To avoid potentially triggering a wound-up individual, rangers on daily welfare checks are sensitive and alert to the herd's emotional state, reading their behaviour accurately while projecting calm confidence. This is normally enough to allow us to approach most situations with assurance. However, the animal to provoke the most trepidation, for both John and myself, is neither a big bull nor a sturdy stallion ... but a 4kg chicken.

Unlike our large male herbivores, which do not see human men as competitors for their respective cows or mares, the cockerel in the Fen Cottage garden perceives us as a threat to his three hens. According to *The Happy Chicken Coop* publication, Dorkings are 'known to be calm, friendly and tolerant'. But Crowley definitely is not. As a chick, Carol named him after a *Good Omens** character because she liked the pun. But, given the connection to occultist Aleister Crowley ('the wickedest man in the world'), did this name predestine the bird's character?

There have been poultry beside the cottage since the days of warden Ralph Sargeant. A true Fen character, he kept a large collection of fowl on the edge of the fen and pigeons at his home on Chapel Lane in Wicken village. I remember him telling me, when I began sporting a beard, that I should rub goose poo on my face to help it grow. To this day, I am not sure whether he was joking or not. I chose not to take his advice on that occasion.

When Ralph passed away in 2016, the National Trust inherited his coop and birds. The silver Dorkings now had sentimental value. When I became a fen ranger in August 2018, the two senior chickens in residence at the time were Mrs Bun and Reg, who were sweet and harmless. Both passed away about eighteen months later and were eventually replaced by young Crowley and his trio of hens, restoring the 'Wicken Hen' visitor attraction beside the Fen Cottage.

---

*   English novel and later a fantasy comedy television series.

Caricature of Ralph Sargeant.
(Wicken Fen Archive)

Crowley, Lode Lane, 7 March 2022.
(Ajay Tegala)

While visitors found them charming, I would go slightly weak at the knees whenever it was my turn to collect the eggs and replenish their food and water. No matter how calmly I entered the coop, Crowley would always rear up, flap and jump at me, bearing his sharp spurs and scratching claws, adhering vehemently to the cockerel mantra of 'protect and serve'. Despite being a bird lover, I have always found plucky poultry slightly unnerving and never enjoyed entering their personal space.

Carol offers advice. Much like with the cattle, be assertive. Spread your arms and loom down on him, pretending to be an eagle. If that fails, pick him up. However, my eagle impressions were pretty poor and I had zero desire to attempt grabbing the rogue rooster, even after practising with the hospitable hens. But I was determined not to be beaten by the blooming bird!

Having recently nurtured an interest in crystals, Harry sends me to work with a Shiva Lingam stone, said to have a calming impact on animals. Being of a scientific mind, I would not normally consider such things, but I am willing to give it a try. Sadly, no luck. I casually share this experience with my friend Zoë, who suggests the stone's phallic shape and intensifying energy might have had an exacerbating effect, making him more territorial. Zoë gives my dilemma consideration and comes back with a lengthy email containing a trio of suggestions.

Firstly, instead of associating him with 'Master of Darkness' Aleister Crowley, she suggests the altogether lovelier Gary Crowley.[*] Next, Zoë looks up deities associated with roosters. As she predicted, Mars comes up, with its war-like associations. The following day is Tuesday, the planetary day of Mars. I find myself petitioning to an astrological force. Not something I ever imagined I would do. During the hour of Venus – 'to balance the Mars energy with something more calming, friendly and harmonious' – I light a red candle and pop a handwritten note underneath.

Lastly, Zoë recommends the good old-fashioned method of simple communication. Instead of swearing[**] at him, I kindly, but firmly, explain I am not a threat but a friend. I have not come to compete for the affections of his hens, I have come to bring food and water, to make his life nicer before leaving him in peace, without overstepping any boundaries. I am simply amazed by the result. Through speaking calmly and gently, my body language is relaxed, not tense, which he picks up on. For the first time, I spend a few minutes in the coop without being attacked or chased to the door as I vamoose. What a miraculous result. Kindness prevails. But my favourite bird encounters will always be with those in the wild.

---

[*]   English broadcaster, television presenter and disc jockey.
[**]   One morning, I was literally swearing, oblivious to the fact that general manager Sarah was walking past. She found it rather amusing!

Verrall's Fen: Sunday, 13–Monday, 14 February 2022

Many birders have a bogey bird, that one species they always seem to miss. Mine is the white-tailed eagle. While working on *Winterwatch* at Wild Ken Hill, one is reported at Holkham. On a shared afternoon off, three of us whizz eastwards along the coast in search of it. Our colleague Jack has seen it just an hour before we arrived. I am hopeful that I am finally going to see my feathered will o' the wisp. Alas, it is nowhere in sight and, after a bit of searching, we have to get back to base for my night shift monitoring the remote cameras.

Three weeks later, at 10 p.m., I receive a message from Cambridgeshire's county bird recorder, Jon Heath. A satellite-tagged eagle from the Isle of Wight, the same bird that was at Holkham, has gone to roost on Wicken Fen. He sends me a map showing its exact location, among the carr in the western corner of Verrall's Fen, known to rangers as Compartment 1[***], a corner of the reserve left undisturbed. Next morning, I am actually due to be working very close to this part of the fen with the Monday volunteer party.

Heading out to Verrall's on Monday morning, I have a nagging feeling that I should have come before the crack of dawn. Indeed, I really should have. By the time we arrive on Verrall's, the eagle has already gone. Once again, I am just a little too late. But the fact it chose to roost on the fen raises hope that it could return. Sadly, the eagle does not return to roost on the fen that night, or the next, but I assure myself it is only a matter of time before there will be a second Wicken sighting.

[***] Every ditch, drain, dyke, drove and track has a name and every field has a number.

Super Blue Moon: Wednesday, 30 August 2023

Twelve years have passed and I am returning to the bird ringers' reed-bed shed for my second swallow roost experience.* Just like the last time, the air is damp and slightly cool. Evening sun warms my face as I cycle beside Wicken Lode, heading for Harrison's Drove. Venturing deeper into Adventurers' Fen, I push my bike through the rough grass, feeling nettle stings and the prickles of thistles through thin trousers. A distant water rail lets out its weird, pig-like squeal. Reaching the reedbed, I receive a warm welcome from the five ringers. Neil jovially remarks that my presence must be a 'once in a decade' event, remembering that I worked in cycle hire when I last joined a roost session and commenting on how much time has passed since then.

There is a terrific sense of anticipation as we watch scores of swallows dart across the sky, attracted by the recorded calls playing to lure them in. These birds are not necessarily local breeders, but populations from further north and west, passing through as they begin their autumn migration. They are attracted to the fen by its insects (food) and reedbeds (perfect pre-migration roost sites). Most of the swallows we see are juveniles, hatched earlier this summer, now virtually the same size as the adults, but with shorter tail streamers and paler orange faces. In a moment of excitement, the narrower wings of a swift are spotted above the flock, a notably late record. There is further emotion when a hobby speeds into view, prompting the swallows to beat a hasty retreat.

Has this bird of prey scared off the birds we are hoping to catch? It all goes quiet and several minutes pass without a single swallow sighting. Just as the sun disappears beneath the horizon, they return, this time flying much closer to the ground, avoiding the hobby … but not the mist nets. Twenty minutes after sunset, the ringers carefully extract eighty-two swallows, eight slightly smaller sand martins and a single, smaller-still, reed warbler. The birds are lifted gently from the net pockets and put safely into soft drawstring cotton bags.

---

*   See Chapter 1.

Super blue moon over Adventurers' Fen, 10.43 p.m. on 30 August 2023. (Ajay Tegala)

With all ninety-one birds bagged individually and the nets taken down (so that no further birds are caught), our eyes stray to the horizon. Directly in front of us, partly concealed by buckthorn and willow, the super blue moon adds to the magic of the occasion. A male tawny owl calls out. Inside the shed, it takes the team just shy of two hours to diligently ring, measure and weigh each bird. Once they have had a tiny, metal leg ring fitted and their statistics recorded, the hirundines are put inside cardboard roosting boxes (made by Neil) to safely spend the night. When dawn breaks, they will be released into the safety of daylight, rather than disorientating darkness. I, however, must cycle into the night on a mile-long ride back to Lode Lane.

My night ride is far from disorientating, partly because I know the route like the back of my hand, but mainly thanks to the illumination of August's second full moon. Rays of light bathe the fen's ageless beauty in shades of silver and graphite, resembling a perfect charcoal sketch. What a pleasure and privilege it is to be on the reserve in this rarely witnessed celestial atmosphere. It will be fourteen years until the next super blue moon. Maybe I will attend my third swallow roost before then!

13

Ever Onward

• 'If Wicken Fen was a person ...' •
Reserve reflections • Safeguarding soil •
Herd welfare • The complexities of rewilding •
Access and conservation • Diversity in the
countryside • Hopes and dreams • Happy here •

AN ASSORTMENT OF STAFF and volunteers are gathered in the learning centre for a meeting. The National Trust are running a session on visitor experience, rightly requiring the views and knowledge of people who know the reserve well. We are set the task of imagining 'if Wicken Fen was a person' and describing what they would be like. At first, I inwardly groan and visibly cringe. There are inevitably cheesy answers. But, when somebody describes Sedge Fen as being like someone on life support, I begin to appreciate the value of this exercise. It seems a bit crazy at first, almost uncomfortable, but this analogy actually hits the nail on the head.

When explaining the reserve to someone who has never visited before, this description is a fitting metaphor for the intensive management needed to conserve the incredibly precious fragment of rare fenland. It is not a wilderness in its prime, it is practically in a coma, an arrested state, a period of time that has long since passed. The penny dropped for nature conservation and wildlife advisor Stuart Warrington when he realised that Wicken Fen is a wetland and yet it stands higher than the land around it. 'Imagine a bath sponge on a tray,' he says, 'and trying to keep it totally wet by dripping water onto it.' It could be argued that the fen should be left to scrub up and dry out, to rest in peace. Only that would be like letting a treasured, historic building fall into disrepair. This relic of East Anglia's lost wetland must be protected.

The early twenty-first century has seen financial crisis and austerity, the impacts of a global pandemic and the ongoing biodiversity and climate crises. Increasing temperatures and decreasing water availability pose a huge challenge to Britain's wetland sites. Slightly acidic rain is subtly changing the fen's chemistry and rising sea levels have the potential to flood much of low-lying East Anglia with saltwater.

During the same time period, there has been a notable increase in the number of people visiting Wicken, as reflected in the cafe expansion and multiple car park extensions. In addition to a succession of passionate naturalists who have valued the site continuously since the days of Darwin, people now visit the fen for fresh air, peace and solitude, coming to relax, exercise, socialise and admire the grazing livestock. Car parking and entry fees, along with shop and cafe sales, help to fund conservation of the reserve. For decades, young minds have been inspired by curious creatures encountered during pond-dipping adventures run by the National Trust. Peat is no longer dug, dried and burned, it is protected, rewetted to sequester carbon and mitigate damage done by humankind. But peat is still under pressure in the wider landscape, being a super growing medium, and erosion continues each year when root crops are extracted from the Fenland soil. Every harvest results in the loss of a little more peat until it is completely gone, exposing the clay beneath.

Conceived and launched when the political, agricultural and socioeconomic landscape was very different, the first ten years of the Wicken Fen Vision project saw rapid land acquisition. Especially in the low, wet and hardest-to-farm areas. The decade that followed saw the evolution of Wicken's landscape-scale rewilding project, although land acquisition slowed, due largely to a marked increase in direct government subsidies for farmers. In the third decade of the Vision, with the hottest summers on record, climate change pressures have increased, carbon markets began to develop and soil has become much more valued. Regenerative farming puts greater care into soil conservation, maximising its fertility and reducing release of carbon, benefiting biodiversity in harmony with food production, creating connectivity between wildlife habitats.

There has been a rapid increase in sustainable power generation across East Cambridgeshire. Indeed, large areas of former farmland in Burwell became solar farms. With these fields no longer under the plough, the peat is protected (except for strips removed to create access tracks). It is encouraging to see green energy being produced and soil safeguarded. But it would have been extremely useful and timely if some of this land had become accessible to Wicken Fen's expanding herds of grazing animals. While sheep grazing around solar panels is viable, Koniks would undoubtedly cause damage with their teeth (you only have to look at the National Trust's Land Rover to see what their teeth can do!).

I stand on the concrete at 'Cock-Up' Bridge, leaning on the handrail. Oakley by my side, we gaze out over Burwell Fen. The view is peppered with the red, black and blonde spots of distant Highland cattle. When my colleagues and I carry out the daily welfare checks, we look at each cow and horse individually. This evening, pausing to reflect a while, I see them as one entity, part of the landscape. However, unlike the roe deer or brown hares, these are not strictly wild animals. They are our livestock, our responsibility (arguably, the welfare of all animals – domestic and wild – is the moral responsibility of humankind). And, lately, there has been a lot to consider.

Seventeen years since the first calf and nineteen years since the first foal, over 100 cattle and more than 200 horses have been born on the reserve. Naturally, there have been deaths as well as euthanasia, castrations, vasectomies and as many appropriate horse sales as possible. Looking at the herd of non-breeding Koniks, I feel a nagging unease. These animals certainly have a high quality of life, able to interact with others and behave naturally. But their ability to reproduce has been taken away because the Wicken Fen expansion project has not been able to provide the breeding herd with enough space to grow at their pace.

I cannot help but feel that the lives of the non-breeding horses would have been better – more 'natural' – had they remained part of a breeding herd. Experience has shown that breeding is better for the herd ... and better for the landscape. For over a decade, the National Trust has been hoping for adjacent farmland to become available. A prime area came up for sale in the late 2010s but, for varied reasons, the opportunity was lost.

I contemplate what a fully rewilded, self-sustaining Wicken Fen would look like, with nature taking care of itself. This dreamy goal is a long way off, beyond my lifetime but by no means beyond capability. Recovery of natural processes is more achievable on a bigger scale. Restoration and connectivity require a multi-generational journey of intervention and management. As Rewilding Britain director Alastair Driver identifies, there is a spectrum of rewilding, with regenerative agriculture and small-scale efforts complementing the larger projects. Rewilding in Britain cannot be a simple case of leaving nature completely alone to take its course, it is too depleted and constrained to recover by itself in tiny, isolated pockets. If Wicken Fen expands to the intended 33 square miles, it will still not be big enough to support a top predator to keep grazing herbivore numbers in check. And there will always be animal well-being to consider. In a modern, caring society, animal health will always be a priority.

Contraception is a possible means of slowing the growth of Wicken's Konik herd – during the wait for spreading space to become available – providing it is effective, practical to administer and comfortable for the 'unbroken' animals, without undesirable side effects. Vasectomising the lead males in the herd does not necessarily slow down reproduction because subordinate males will sire foals, their natural instinct to reproduce is innate. Forming separate non-breeding herds is a sticking plaster solution and not necessarily ideal for longer-term animal welfare. Non-breeding mares, in a wild-type setting, typically put on weight, which can make them more susceptible to laminitis (not easily treatable in a free-roaming context).

Harvesting animals for human consumption is a traditional method of population management. Free range cattle are indeed very marketable. Horses, however, are considerably less so (in Britain, at least), despite being a sustainable, environmentally friendly source of food, much like deer. The Wild Pony Meat Company sell taffety* produced to sustain the semi-wild herds of Dartmoor ponies in Devon. For doing so, they have to deal with hate mail and abuse.

The Wicken Fen Vision has always been described as a long-term project with no fixed endpoint being imposed on the evolving landscape. Its aim is to facilitate a robust, flexible and dynamic landscape that is resilient to the pressures of climate change. The 100-plus-year project is very much a journey, as noted by Francine Hughes in her research articles on Wicken's rewilding. While ecological restoration generally involves fixed targets to be achieved by prescribed activities, the goal of the Vision is to create mobile landscape mosaics. Like a river, Wicken's rewilding journey meanders and shifts over time. The challenges and changes faced (some unanticipated) are different courses to chart along the way. As author Isabella Tree states, 'it is the journey, the intention, the striving for an increase in wilderness and natural processes and a progressive release of human management that are important in Britain'.

A quarter of the way into the Wicken Fen Vision, the herds do not have the space they require. But, being far from a finite endpoint, this may yet happen. Until then, adjustments in herd management are required. These may be complicated and costly, requiring support, understanding, creative thinking and sufficient funding. There is no silver bullet.

---

* Pony meat. Similar to venison, it is red meat from animals that have lived low-stress, drug-free lives with diets untainted by chemicals.

Hurdles will continue to be lifted, loaded, ratcheted and shifted. Vets will keep on visiting. Bovine tuberculosis will still need to be tested for. The fallen animals collection service will carry on being called. And there will inevitably be more bureaucracy and backache. Almost ironically, acts of management, taming and control are required in the journey to create a wild ecosystem.

Alongside practical ranger responsibilities on the fen, engaging with people is key. While the number of people coming to Wicken has increased markedly since the twentieth century, there is still a wider audience to reach. Visitors receive a warm welcome at the information centre and an imaginative programme of engaging events and trails are available to families throughout the year ... providing they are able to get to Wicken. The vast majority come by car. Keen cyclists can pedal 7½ miles south from Ely railway station or 14½ miles north from Cambridge. The fen has historically been practically unreachable by bus (unless you arrive from Ely on a Thursday afternoon and stay until the following Thursday morning). Remoteness is an obstacle to a significant proportion of the population, including many people based in inner-city areas. For example, a large number of Londoners have no idea what or where the Fens are.

During my early days as a volunteer, I helped with a school visit to Wicken from London. Most of the group had never been anywhere like rural Cambridgeshire before and were clearly intrigued by it. One child wondered 'where are the shops?' and another asked how we survived here. These youngsters gained a great deal from the opportunity to visit, helping them connect with nature (to use an overused phrase). Nobody should feel that the fen is not for them. Everyone is welcome. A small caveat is that certain areas must be left completely undisturbed for nesting, resting and roosting wildlife. Mindful of this, as the nature reserve grows ever bigger, there may well be a large core area where no humans are allowed to go. However, there will be plenty of high-quality habitats to explore on a wide range of access tracks. I believe strongly that respectful appreciation of nature should be available to all.

Since the days of yore, when the Barnes brothers wardened the reserve, it has been pleasing to see a marked increase in the number of women in ranger roles. The grazing livestock have consistently attracted several women to volunteer. But, for a run of some years, the weekly practical work parties had only one regular female volunteer, Lesley. After a post-pandemic volunteer recruitment drive, she was finally joined by others. Wicken Fen's many volunteers across the various departments contain a huge range of skills and talent ... but, it must be said, a distinct lack of ethnic diversity. This is largely a reflection of the reserve's rural location.

A 2022 survey revealed that, out of 620 National Trust rangers across England, Wales and Northern Ireland, only myself and two others came from ethnic minority backgrounds. I have been in a racial minority since my South Lincolnshire school days and on literally every nature reserve I have visited. In the conservation sector, I have rarely worked alongside people from similar backgrounds to myself. However, I have consistently found that sharing a passion for nature and dedication to teamwork provides a firm foundation for good working relationships. And the range of different people working in conservation and visiting wildlife sites has been expanding slowly, thanks to social media and initiatives such as inclusive walking groups.

After being singled out as Wicken's sole example of diversity at a few of the annual whole-team meetings, it was pleasing when an inclusion session appeared on the agenda and a subsequent 'Everyone Welcome' hub was set up by general manager Emma. Pride flags were flown outside the visitor centre for the first time in celebration of our work to make members of the LGBTQ+ community feel more welcome. Young volunteer nature champions were recruited, aged 14 to 18 (the age group I belonged to when I first volunteered on the fen). I believe that the best way to protect and improve biodiversity is to include as broad a spectrum of perspectives as possible. I absolutely love the magical atmosphere of the fen and its beautiful wildlife ... and I want everyone, regardless of age or background, to be able to experience that magic and share that love.

Looking to my left, I pan across Burwell Fen through binoculars and spot a hunting barn owl. Fine serrations on the edge of its wing feathers, like the teeth of a comb, break up the air, silencing its buoyant flight. Listening for small mammals, sounds are funnelled towards its ears by its heart-shaped face, hidden by feathers. Memories of many bird encounters come flooding to mind. I think of Eric Ennion, who knew and loved this fen before it was drained eight decades ago. Did he ever imagine that the birds he loved would return here in the twenty-first century?

I find myself dreaming of the birds I would love to be breeding on the fen in the twenty-second century. I hope that short-eared owls will start nesting here again, also turtle doves, nightingales, more bitterns and more cranes (and, more to the point, crane chicks finally fledging). Perhaps, thanks to conservation projects elsewhere in the county and country, corncrakes and white storks will go on to inhabit the reserve.

Barn owl over the Fens. (Joss Goodchild)

Maybe there will even be white-tailed eagles nesting in Compartment 1 on Verrall's Fen! Hopefully there will be resident beavers helping keep the fen wet and knocking back scrub. Straying into the realms of complete fantasy, I imagine a green, wetland corridor extending from Cambridgeshire all the way to the Norfolk Broads, enabling the swallowtail butterfly to spread south-westwards and recolonise the Fens.

Drifting back to the present, I feel thankful for how fortunate I am. Of course, there are challenges ahead, battles to be fought and compromises to negotiate, but much has been achieved. Nature has returned to Burwell Fen, rewetted by the National Trust and rewilded by the nuanced behaviour of the livestock that have created a rich mosaic of habitats for a diversity of wild species. And spending time with the herds is fascinating, from the excitement of births to the suspense of watching individuals grow up. I have seen adorable, fluffy calves turn into confident cows and macho bulls. I have formed special, interspecies relationships with stallions and mares. Working with livestock, wildlife and people makes the work of a ranger varied and dynamic. I am often asked to 'describe a typical day on the fen' and I find it surprisingly difficult, seldom giving the same answer twice. It is a job that changes with the seasons ... some elements are fixed, others fluid ... an enchanting mixture of the reliable and the unpredictable ... from the laborious to the life-affirming.

Dyson. (Ajay Tegala)

Oakley has been waiting patiently while I have stood reflecting. He looks up at me, gently signalling his desire to carry on walking. 'OK hound, let's go.' We cross onto the southern bank of Burwell Lode, coddiwompling westwards, ever onward. The tallest tree on the fen stands ahead in the distance like an old friend. A late reed warbler flits from one side of the lode to the other, prompting thoughts of their imminent southward migration. The young, scarcely 3 months old, must now fly some 3,000 miles. I wonder how many Fenland miles I have walked since first stepping on this grassy lodeside bank two decades ago, before I knew the names of the birds I could hear. Since then, I have trodden this path with family, friends, colleagues, conservationists and, of course, my Labrador.

The sinking summer sun bathes Wicken Fen in golden light, the evening air still and quiet. Some of the most spellbinding sunsets I have ever beheld have been here in Cambridgeshire. Mountainous landscapes may be more popular places to head for time in nature, but I firmly believe the Fens are equally beautiful and justly important. On this magnificent, peaceful evening, I have no desire to be anywhere else.

Bibliography

* The six books marked with an asterisk, I recommend wholeheartedly as further reading, for more information on the science (*Wicken Fen*), nature (*Adventurers' Fen*; *Cuckoo*) and history (*The Farm in the Fen*; *The Fenman's World*) of Wicken and archaeology of the East Anglian Fens (*The Fens*).

Albright, J.L.; Arave, C.W. (1997), *The Behaviour of Cattle*, CABI Publishing.

Ausden, M. (2010), *Habitat Management for Conservation – A Handbook of Techniques*, Oxford University Press.

Bloom, A. (1944), *The Farm in the Fen*, Faber and Faber.*

Bloom, A. (1953), *The Fens*, Robert Hale.

Bloom, A. (1958), *The Skaters of the Fens*, W. Heffer and Sons Limited.

Borgstede, M. (2021), 'Evolutionary Dynamics of the Trivers-Willard Effect – A Nonparametric Approach', *Ecology and Evolution* 11(18): 12,676–12,685.

Brown, J.; Kirk-Wade, E. (2021), *Coronavirus – A History of 'Lockdown' Laws in England*, House of Commons Library.

Buscall, D. (2020), *Wild Ken Hill Land Use Model* [online]. Accessed at www.wildkenhill.co.uk/wp-content/uploads/2021/04/Thought-Piece_-Land-Use-Model-2020.pdf

Buxton, J.; Durdin, C. (2011), *The Norfolk Crane's Story*, Wren Publishing.

Davies, N. (2015), *Cuckoo – Cheating by Nature*, Bloomsbury.*

Day, A. (1985), *Turf Village*, Cambridgeshire Libraries and Information Service.

Day, A. (1999), *The Eye of Wicken – Emma Sophia Aspland 1871–1948*, Milton Contact.

Dempster, J.P.; King, M.L.; Lakhani, K.H. (1976), 'The Status of the Swallowtail Butterfly in Britain', *Ecological Entomology* 1: 71–84.

Ennion, E.A.R. (1949), *Adventurers' Fen* [2nd edition], Herbert Jenkins Limited.*

Ennion, E.A.R.; Walthew, B. (2011), *Bird Man's River*, Benton Street Books.

Friday, L. et. al. (1997), *Wicken Fen – The Making of a Nature Reserve*, Harley Books.*

Friday, L.; Harley, B. (2000), *Checklist of the Flora and Fauna of Wicken Fen*, Harley Books.

Gardiner, J.S. (1926–32), *The Natural History of Wicken Fen*, Bowes and Bowes.

Global Peatlands Initiative (2022), *Global Peatlands Assessment: The State of the World's Peatlands*, United Nations Environment Programme.

Gooders, J. (1986), *Field Guide to the Birds of Britain and Ireland*, Kingfisher Books.

Hastie, G. (2010), *Coat Colour Basics of Highland Cattle* [online]. Accessed at www.scottishhighlandcattle.com.au/html/coat_colour_basics.html

Hughes, F.M.R.; Stroh, P.A.; Adams, W.M.; Kirby, K.J.; Mountford, J.O.; Warrington, S. (2011), 'Monitoring and Evaluating Large-Scale, "Open-Ended" Habitat Creation Projects: A Journey Rather Than a Destination', *Journal for Nature Conservation* 19(4): 245–243.

IUCN National Committee United Kingdom (2018), UK Peatlands Strategy, IUCN.

James, M. (2014), *Cambridgeshire Folk Tales*, The History Press.

Knowles, M. (1902), *History of Wicken*, Elliot Stock.

Laidlaw, C.; Tegala, A. et. al. (2011–23), *Wicken Fen Grazing Diaries* [unpublished].

Laidlaw, C. (2018), *The Behaviour of Free-Roaming Herds of Highland Cattle and Konik Polski at Wicken Fen Nature Reserve*, Anglia Ruskin University.

Lucas, C.A.S. (1930), *The Fenman's World – Memories of a Fenland Physician*, Jarrold and Sons Limited.*

MacArthur, R.H.; Wilson, E.O. (1967), *The Theory of Island Biogeography*, Princeton University Press.

Murkin, A. (2003), *The Illustrated Tour of Burwell: Part 3*, Fortspring.

National Trust (1899–2023), *Wicken Fen Property Database*, National Trust.

National Trust (1947), *A Guide to Wicken Fen* [3rd edition], National Trust.

National Trust (2011), *Wicken Fen Vision – The Grazing Programme Explained*, National Trust.

Pryor, F. (2019), *The Fens: Discovering England's Ancient Depths*, Head of Zeus.*

Rewilding Britain (2022), *What is Rewilding?* [online]. Accessed at www.rewildingbritain.org.uk

Richardson, H. (1990), *Burwell – A Stroll Through History*, Black Bear Press.

Rotherham, I.D. (2013), *The Lost Fens – England's Greatest Ecological Disaster*, The History Press.

Rouse, M. (2018), *How to Speak Fen* [revised edition], Ely History Publications.

Sedgwick, I. (2016), *Wicken Fen*, National Trust.

Sills, N. (2019–23), *Cranes at Wicken Fen: 2019–2023* [unpublished].

Tawaststjerna, E.; Layton, R. (2009), *Sibelius Volume III: 1914–1957*, Faber and Faber.

Tegala, A. (2005–23), Private diaries [unpublished].

Tree, I. (2018), *Wilding – The Return of Nature to a British Farm*, Pan Macmillan.

Tree, I.; Burrell, C. (2023), *The Book of Wilding – A Practical Guide to Rewilding, Big and Small*, Bloomsbury.

Wareham, A.F.; Wright, A.P.M. (2002), *A History of the County of Cambridge and the Isle of Ely: Vol. 10 – Cheveley, Flendish, Staine and Staploe Hundreds (North-Eastern Cambridgeshire)*, Victoria County History.

Waterlife Recovery East (2021), *A Mink Free East Anglia – Operational Plan* [online]. Accessed at www.waterliferecoveryeast.org.uk/about-us/#OurCurrentPosition

Wentworth-Day, J. (1970), *History of the Fens* [reprint], S.R. Publishers.

1841 England Census, The National Archives.

1901 England Census, The National Archives.

Appendices

Appendix 1:
Species Recorded
on Wicken Fen

Wicken Fen is the most species-rich site known in Great Britain, with 9,428 species recorded across all taxonomic groups. The total includes at least ten species that were new to science and a further twenty-five firsts for Britain. The oldest records date from the 1820s. A total of 7,390 species are listed in 2000's *Checklist of the Flora and Fauna of Wicken Fen*. Between 2000 and 2023, over 2,000 more species were recorded due to the addition of new land and habitats to Wicken Fen nature reserve and the northward spread of species across Britain with the changing climate. Credit is due to Stuart Warrington for compiling the following table diligently.

Group of species	Number of species
Flowering plants	442
Mosses and liverworts	140
Algae and other microorganisms	351
Fungi	695

Lichens	131
Birds	230
Mammals	34
Reptiles and Amphibians	7
Fish	24
Butterflies	35
Moths	1,253
Beetles	1,775
True flies	2,067
Bees, wasps and sawflies	853
Dragonflies and damselflies	29
Other invertebrates	1,362
Total species recorded	**9,428**

Appendix 2:
Notable Koniks
Mentioned in the Text

Adonis *(p. 66)*	Big Tiny Little *(p. 103)*
Born: 5 July 1998	Born: 31 August 2012
Origin: Netherlands	Mother: Esther
Stunning, chunky stallion that didn't quite deliver the goods his name promised, as he was believed to be sub-fertile.	Named after a 1950s pianist (whose birthday he shared), 'BTL' was a feisty little male with a golden coat and dark muzzle.
Boxer *(p. 90)*	Cetti *(p. 100)*
Born: 6 June 2015	Born: 14 May 2014
Mother: Wren	Mother: Sashka
An amiable male, identifiable by a swan-shaped star between his eyes. He co-tended a harem for multiple years before becoming its sole stallion.	A friendly, fairly chunky mare, identifiable by a white semicolon-shaped marking on her forehead.
Cygnus *(p. 90)*	Dyson *(p. 115; 239)*
Born: 11 May 2019	Born: 29 June 2017
Mother: Napia	Mother: Sprite
Friendly and affectionate with known companions, Cygnus is part of Eric's harem and one of my favourite mares.	A friendly and inquisitive male, who I helped to head-collar train, Dyson is one of my all time favourites.

Eric *(p. 67–69)*	**Gulliver** *(p. 103; 172)*
Born: 10 May 2006	Born: 6 May 2016
Mother: Krieka	Mother: Meg
The first foal born to Adonis' harem, young Eric recovered well from his early ditch swim. A tough cookie, he now looks after one of the largest harems on the fen.	A mid-ranking stallion in his younger years, Gulliver went on to hold his own harem when he successfully attracted five fillies in the non-breeding herd.
Gypsy Spirit *(p. 103)*	**Harry Konik** *(p. 67)*
Born: 13 April 2009	Born: 1 May 2004
Mother: Anita's Gracie	Mother: Oriola
Annoyingly friendly as a foal, Gypsy became largely indifferent to humans once his hormones kicked in at the age of 3 or so.	Harry was the first Konik foal to be born on the fen. Named after Harry Connick Sr, 'The Singing District Attorney'.
Jelly Roll *(p. 110)*	**Koi** *(p. 176)*
Born: 24 March 2020	Born: 8 April 2016
Mother: Maggie	Origin: Netherlands
Named after pianist Jelly Roll Morton after he 'rolled' into a ditch while still wobbly on his feet after birth. Safely rescued by rangers, he was later moved to Dartmoor, at the age of 2.	Unlike the two stallions he arrived with, Koi has not managed to form his own harem, seemingly preferring to badger everyone else and generally be a bit of a disruptive wazzock!
Kors *(p. 66–67)*	**Krieka** *(p. 67–69; 91)*
Born: 11 June 2002	Born: 10 March 2000
Origin: Netherlands	Origin: Netherlands
Brought over as a yearling, Kors was initially a loner. However, Adonis' mares – frustrated by the lack of foals – actively sought Kors out and his first foal, Eric, was born.	Mother of Eric, Krieka is one of the herd's 'maverick mares' who has a habit of moving between various harems without seeming to settle in any of them.

Meg (p. 182–83)	**Nanja** (p. 67–69)
Born: 7 January 2009	Born: 20 July 2000
Mother: Krieka	Origin: Netherlands
Named after the mare in Robert Burns' poem 'Tam o' Shanter', Meg is small with stunning blonde highlights in her mane.	A sweet, finely-built mare with a compact frame and distinctive cheek dimple. She is one of the fen's 'original' mares.
Oriola (p. 68)	**Peat** (p. 100)
Born: 1 June 2001	Born: 1 May 2005
Origin: Netherlands	Mother: Napia
A small and friendly mare with a dark face, she was one of my favourite mares.	The fourth Konik foal born on the fen, Peat was castrated after some bold escapades.
Randy (p. 160)	**Shrek** (p. 157)
Born: 12 May 1998	Born: 23 July 2013
Origin: Norfolk Broads	Mother: Esther
A mid-ranking gelding, Randy's status gradually diminished in part due to age. He later became a constant companion for the elderly Tim.	The second all-black foal born in 2013, Shrek was a gorgeous smoky grey colour at birth with preposterously long, donkey-like ears.
Spod (p. 90)	**Talitha** (p. 91)
Born: 18 July 2010	Born: 31 July 2019
Mother: Nanja	Mother: Felicity
A fine-looking stallion with a golden coat, Spod is a bit of a feckless troublemaker, known for getting into scraps with other stallions.	A small mare, Talitha tarted her way around numerous harems and stallions before settling in a group with multiple younger stallions.

Tam *(p. 169)*	Tim *(p. 158–60)*
Born: 11 January 2009	Born: 20 April 1993
Mother: Kaluna	Origin: Norfolk Broads
Born in January, a fortnight before Burns' Night, Tam is named after the main protagonist in the poem 'Tam o' Shanter'.	One of the 'original' geldings, Tim went on to be a group leader, later moving down the ranks as he aged. Tim reached the age of 30 in 2023.

Appendix 3:
Notable Cattle
Mentioned in the Text

Apple *(p. 184)*	**Binky** *(p. 77–78; 119)*
Born: 14 June 2014	Born: 2 June 2015
Mother: Gale	Mother: Morag II
Colour: Red	Colour: Red with white
A sensible, steady lass, Apple has the classic wide, upswept Highland cow horns. Some of her calves have apple-themed names, such as Strudel.	With his rather unusual, piebald (red and white) colouration, Binky was one of the most distinctive animals on the fen.
Bottom *(p. 93; 208–09)*	**Bramble** *(p. 95)*
Born: 2 December 2019	Born: 18 April 2006
Mother: Anna-Belle	Mother: Malda Rhua II
Colour: Black	Colour: Black
Born in the same year as his elder brother, Prospero, Bottom managed to outrank him in the competition for top bull position.	Daughter of original bull, Ewan. Bramble was chosen as a companion for bull calf Stan after he became orphaned.

Canute *(p. 121)*	**Comfrey** *(p. 83–84)*
Born: 7 September 2021	Born: 6 April 2006
Mother: Carlie-Belle	Mother: Griannach
Colour: Red	Colour: Blonde
Castrated within a week of birth, Canute was the first calf I had the experience of 'banding'.	The fifth Highland calf to be born on the fen, Comfrey and her mother were very strongly bonded companions.
Cordelia *(p. 184)*	**Duncan** *(p. 167; 185; 209)*
Born: 9 November 2019	Born: 9 April 2019
Mother: Carlie-Belle	Mother: Raven
Colour: Black	Colour: Black
Known to the rangers as simply 'Dee', in 2022 she gave birth to the 100th calf tagged on the fen.	My favourite black bull, Duncan was a companion to abandoned calf, Toby, in their early days.
Edmund *(p. 187)*	**Ewan** *(p. 70; 187)*
Born: 14 April 2006	Born: 31 March 2003
Mother: Malda Rhua I	Origin: Oban, Scotland
Colour: Red	Colour: Dun
Impressively muscular, Edmund succeeded Ewan as top bull. Friendly despite his status, he and Carol maintained strong bonds of mutual respect, working together to bring in the herd one notably icy winter!	The very first bull in the Wicken Fold, arriving on the fen in 2005 from the west coast of Scotland, Ewan was a good-tempered, cracking bull that sired some super calves. He is very much missed.
Gale *(p. 98–100)*	**Munin** *(p. 81)*
Born: 11 March 2008	Born: 4 April 2018
Mother: Cannach III	Mother: Raven
Colour: Red	Colour: Blonde
Gale spent the first months of her life in a field with a wild fruit tree, and developed a love for apples.	Blonde 'Moo-nin' was one of the lower-ranking bulls, possibly linked to his suspiciously small testicles!

Prospero *(p. 93–94)*	Stan *(p. 186)*
Born: 1 January 2019	Born: 17 December 2014
Mother: Anna-Belle	Mother: Wendy
Colour: Red	Colour: Black
Despite his name, Prospero does not quite possess the required confidence to make a top-ranking bull ... but will always be one of my favourites.	Orphaned at three weeks, Carol developed a great affection for Stan while hand-rearing him, becoming one of her favourite bulls.
Strudel *(p. 79; 120)*	**Thompson** *(p. 187)*
Born: 12 April 2017	Born: 29 April 2008
Mother: Apple	Mother: Morag II
Colour: Blonde	Colour: Dun
Inquisitive and curious as a youngster, adolescence saw Strudel turn into a stroppy, difficult bull, leading to his removal from the breeding herd.	Thompson took over the top bull position from Edmund. He held the spot for just shy of half a decade before being challenged by younger bulls.
Toby *(p. 185–86)*	**Wendy** *(p. 70)*
Born: 29 March 2019	Born: 21 March 2001
Mother: Poppy	Origin: Mull, Scotland
Colour: Dun	Colour: Black
A dun-coloured bull, Toby was abandoned as a calf. Hand-reared by Carol and Gez, I helped with bottle-feeding, developing a strong bond.	Hand-reared as an orphan on Mull, Wendy was an engaging cow with bags of character. One of Carol's all time favourites, Wendy is remembered with much warmth and affection.

Appendix 4:
List of Ajay Tegala's
Media Appearances

Ajay has appeared (*or been credited) on the following national television programmes:

2012   *The Great British Story*: 'The Taming of Cambridgeshire' (BBC 1).
           Countryfile (Series 24): 'Summer Special' (BBC 1).
           Autumnwatch (Series 7): 'Episode #4' (BBC 2).

2014   *Walking Through History* (Series 1): 'North Norfolk' (Channel 4).
           Homes by the Sea (Series 1): 'Norfolk' (Channel 4).

2015   *Winterwatch* (Series 3): 'Episode #1' and 'Episode #2' (BBC 2).

2016   *Springwatch: Unsprung* [live] (Series 8): 'Episode #7' (BBC 2).
           Coast (Series 11): 'East Anglia' (BBC 2).

2017   *Secrets of the National Trust* (Series 1): 'Episode #2' (Channel 5).
           Curious Creatures (Series 1): 'Episode #7' (BBC 2).

2018   *Celebrity Eggheads* (Series 8): 'The Theory of Nothing' (BBC 2).

2020   *Inside the Bat Cave* (BBC Two).

2021   *Our Wild Adventures* (Series 1) – [*Production Team] (BBC 2).
           Springwatch (Series 17) – [*Production Team] (BBC 2).
           Springwatch (Series 17): 'Episode #10' (BBC 2).

2022   *Winterwatch* (Series 10) – [*Production Team] (BBC 2).
           ITV Evening News: 27 May 2022 (ITV 1).
           Channel 4 Evening News: 1 June 2022 (Channel 4).
           Teeny Tiny Creatures (Series 3): 'Crane Flies' (CBeebies).

2023   *Wild Isles*: 'Grasslands' – [*Thanks] (BBC 1).
           Channel 4 Evening News: 27 April 2023 (Channel 4).
           ITV Evening News: 24 November 2023 (ITV 1).

Ajay has contributed to the following nature podcasts:

2020	*Get Birding* (Series 1): 'Episode #5'.
	Let's Talk Conservation: 'History of UK Conservation'.
2021	*Get Birding* (Series 2): 'Episode #5'.
2022	*In Conservation With*: 'Confessions of a Nature Ranger'.
	Into the Wild: 'UK Bats and Life as a Ranger'.
2023	*Planty Planty Zoo Zoo*: 'Planty Planty Interview-View #1'.

The destination for history
www.thehistorypress.co.uk